HODDER SCIENCE

28

Pupil's Book

Second Edition

B

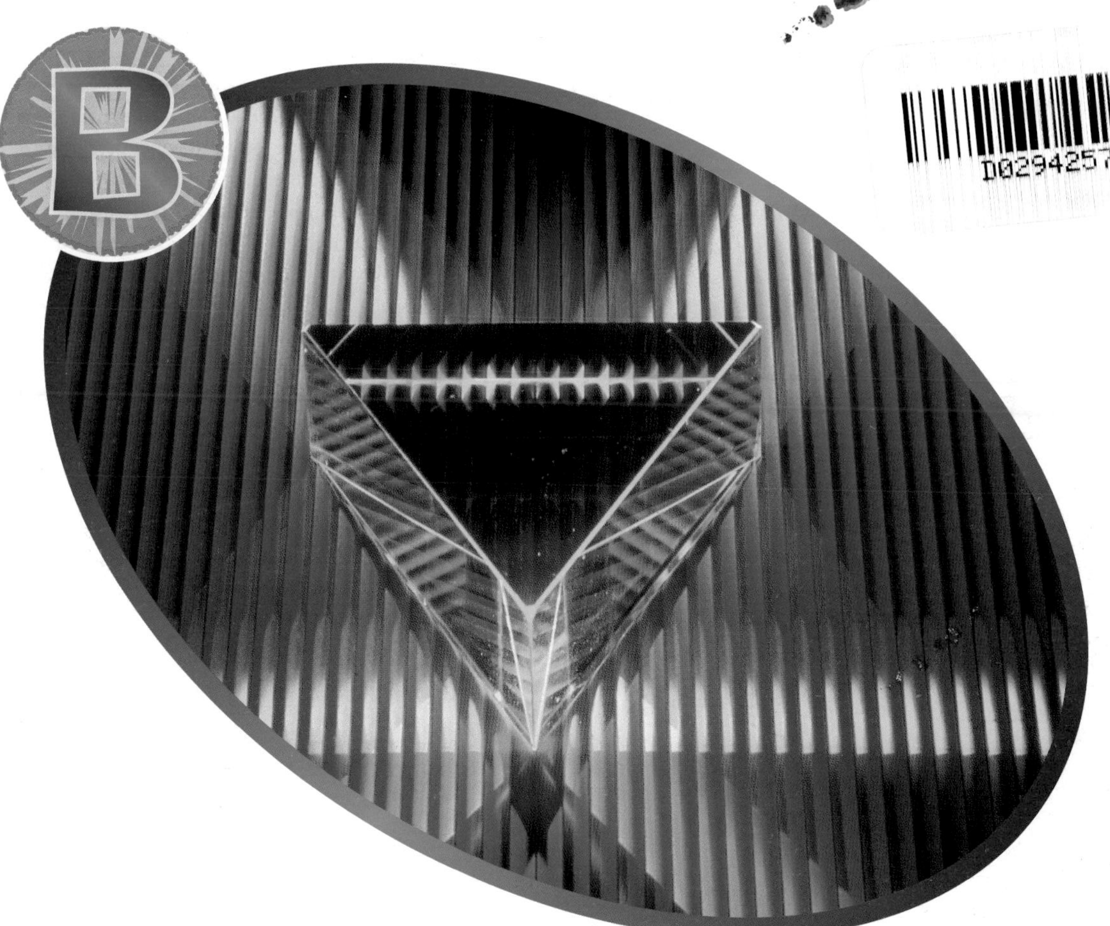

Nigel Heslop
David Brodie
James Williams

Hodder Murray
A MEMBER OF THE HODDER HEADLINE GROUP

The Publishers would like to thank the following for permission to reproduce copyright material:

Photo acknowledgements

Action Plus (40 top); Alamy Images (89 right)/Jeff Morgan (48 right); Andrew Lambert (17, 21 all, 56 right, 57 bottom, 64, 92 top, third and fourth from top, bottom and third and fourth from bottom, 106 bottom, 109); Associated Press (54 top left, 102 top right, 114); British Antarctic Survey/Peter Bucktrout (32 both); British Army (117 right); Bruce Coleman Ltd (117 top left and bottom left, 119); Empics (4 left, 39 right both)/ Tony O'Brien (62 top left); Getty Images (62 middle right); GSF Picture Library (95 right, 128 bottom left and bottom right, 134 both); Hodder & Stoughton (54 middle right); ISG Thermal Systems Ltd. (35); John Dempsie (85); Life File Picture Library (2 top and bottom, 3 top two, 4 top right, 18 top left, bottom left, top right, right second from top, right second from bottom, 20 left, 28 both, 40 bottom, 54 bottom right, 58, 78 bottom left, 90 all, 91 top left and right, 95 left, 97 both, 102 top left and bottom left, 106 top, 108 right, 128 top right, 135); Mary Evans Picture Library (16 top, 79 middle right); Natural History Museum (129 bottom); Omicron (14); Oxford Scientific Films (116); Peter Arnold Inc/Matt Meadows (77); Redferns (143, 144 both); Rex/Martin Lee (62 bottom left)/Sam Morgan Moore (89 left); The Ronald Grant Archive (110 left, 111 left); Science Photo Library (10, 84 all, 88 bottom, 91 bottom, 129 top, 137, 146 top right)/ Biophoto Associates (3 second from bottom and bottom, 67 right)/ Phil Jude (6 right)/ Paul Shambroom (16 bottom)/ Alfred Pasieka (18 bottom right)/ Martin Bond (18 left second from top)/ David Parker (18 left second from bottom, 110 right)/ Tek Image (20, top right); Charles D Winters (23, 92 second from top)/ Geoff Tompkinson (25 left)/ Clive Freeman/Biosym Technologies (25 right)/ Mauna Loa Observatory (31)/ Bruce Iverson (34)/ Maximilian Stock Limited (37)/ John Bavosi (42 left)/ BSIP Laurent (42 right)/ John Radcliffe Hospital (44)/ Adam Hart-Davis (46)/ Damien Lovegrove (48 left)/ Chris Priest (67 left)/ Biomedical Imaging Unit, Southampton General Hospital (75)/ Eye of Science (76 top left)/ Dr Linda Stannard (76 right)/ Juergen Berger (76 bottom left)/ Rosenfeld Images Ltd (78 top left)/ Dr P Marazzi (78 right)/ St Mary's Hospital Medical School (79 bottom)/ Sinclair Stammers (92 second from bottom)/ Robert Knowles (96)/ Tony Craddock (98)/ Adam Jones (100 left)/ Simon Fraser (100 right)/ George Post (102 bottom right)/ Brad Lewis (105 right)/ Adrian Thomas (111 right)/ Stephen & Donna O'Meara (125)/ BSIP KOKEL (146 top right)/ BSIP SR LR (147 top)/ Alexander Tsiaras (148)/ Merlin Tuttle – Bat Conservation International (150); Still Pictures (124); The Wellcome Trust (146 top left, 147 bottom)/ Mark Lythgoe & Chloe Hutton (112)

Every effort has been made to trace all copyright holders, but if any have been inadvertently overlooked the Publishers will be pleased to make the necessary arrangements at the first opportunity.

Orders: please contact Bookpoint Ltd, 130 Milton Park, Abingdon, Oxon OX14 4SB. Telephone: (44) 01235 827720. Fax: (44) 01235 400454. Lines are open from 9.00–6.00, Monday to Saturday, with a 24 hour message answering service. Visit our website at www.hodderheadline.co.uk.

First published in 2000
This edition published in 2005 by
Hodder Murray, an imprint of Hodder Education,
a member of the Hodder Headline Group
338 Euston Road
London NW1 3BH

Impression number 10 9 8 7 6 5 4 3 2 1
Year 2010 2009 2008 2007 2006 2005

Cover photo Science Photo Library
Typeset in Garamond 11.5pt by Fakenham Photosetting Limited, Fakenham, Norfolk
Printed in Italy

A catalogue record for this title is available from the British Library

ISBN-10: 0 340 88679 X
ISBN-13: 978 0 340 88679 3

Contents

Dedications

To my family, especially Will, for their inspiration and their perspiration.

Nigel Heslop

To my wife Joan, for her patience, understanding and practical advice, and to Laura and Sarah Grant for their expert advice in choosing the photographs.

James Williams

To Tom, Eleanor and Claire, not so much for being supportive as for being.

David Brodie

Picture this . . .

This section is to help you work out 'not understanding'.

Start off by reading this:

Everybody was there at junior school sports day. Luis, Maria, Vince and Serena had been friends since they all arrived in Britain with their parents, looking for a safe community to live in.

They lined up for the 60 metres sack race with two boys from another class. Maria had 'grown up' earlier than the others. She was much bigger and taller than her friends – her long legs seemed twice as long as theirs. She was bigger and stronger when they played games and they knew she would win for sure.

Miss Jack was the starter official. She was new to the school this year. They thought she looked cool with her bleached, braided hair and white Nike tracksuit. They concentrated on listening to her instruction.

The whistle blew and they were off. Some scuttled along and some hopped. The scuttlers put their feet in the corners of the sacks and ran. The hoppers pulled the sack up tight to their waist and hopped. Maria was a hopper, and a good one. By half-way she was well in front of the others, but then there was a crack and Maria fell to the ground with a scream.

The others were past her in no time and heard her whimper. At that moment the three friends turned, like synchronised swimmers, forgot the race and went back to comfort their friend.

Did you see the pictures in your head?

- School sports day
- Maria bigger and stronger than the others
- Miss Jack, the cool young teacher

And did the race play like a video in your head?

When you SEE THE PICTURES IN YOUR HEAD it means you understand what you are reading.

When you read or have something explained in science, try to make the pictures of what is happening appear in your head.

At first, perhaps it's just still pictures, of each stage in a description. You might see still pictures of Maria, the race, and Miss Jack. Then, if you concentrate hard, you can 'animate' the picture to make them play like a video. This is what UNDERSTANDING is like.

Task

Draw six boxes like this on your page. Look at each box in turn and imagine still pictures of the stages of making a cup of coffee for mum.

For example:

Coffee jar, milk and sugar	Kettle boiling	Spoon of coffee and sugar into cup
Add boiling water from kettle	Add milk	Stir and give to mum

Now imagine these still pictures and animate them to make them play together like a video. Can you see the whole process?

Working with words

Words usually have one meaning, but a word can have more than one meaning. This makes life a little bit complicated. So how are words constructed and can we work out what words mean in science?

Words are constructed like this:

Words always have a root. This is the main part of the word. We can add to the root to change the word. The bits that we add are either prefixes (added in front of the word) or suffixes (added to the end of the word).

If we take the word 'carnivore' apart we can look at the root and see what's been added.

The root of this word is 'carni': it means flesh or meat.

The suffix '-vore' means feeding.

When we add the two together we get the word 'carnivore' which means meat eater or meat feeder. The word Bronchitis is made up in the same way. The root of the word is 'bronch' meaning windpipe and the suffix 'itis' simply means inflamed or diseased. So 'bronchitis' means that your windpipe is inflamed – something that gives you a cough!

Task

See how many meanings, of the words below, you can work out from the table of roots, prefixes and suffixes shown.

- lithosphere
- metamorphic
- oxygen
- dioxide
- geothermal
- photograph

Root	Meaning
lith-	rock
morph-	to change
graph-	drawing/writing
ign(eous)	from the fire

Prefix	Meaning
mono-	one
di-	two
sulph-	containing sulphur
ox(y)-	containing oxygen

Suffix	Meaning
-ide	simple compound from . . .
-ate	compound with oxygen from . . .
-sphere	globe/ball

Prefix	Multiple		Example
giga-	1 000 000 000	billions	gigajoule
mega-	1 000 000	millions	megahertz
kilo-	1000	thousands	kilometre
milli-	$\frac{1}{1000}$	thousandths	milligram
micro-	$\frac{1}{1\,000\,000}$	millionths	micro
nano-	$\frac{1}{1\,000\,000\,000}$	billionths	nanosecond

Food and digestion

Opener
Growing smaller

What you eat can affect how you grow. A large number of Americans may be suffering from eating too much fast food.

Year	British	American
1775	1.67 m	1.73 m
1975	1.70 m	1.75 m
2004	1.75 m	1.73 m

Height comparisons for British and American people

As more food became available and our diet got better we grew taller. In 1775 the average British man was 1.67 m. Today, the average British man is 1.75 m. Americans are getting shorter. In 1775, when the American Revolution took place, the average American man was 1.73 m. In 1975 they had grown to 1.75 m, but by 2004 they had shrunk back to 1.73 m.

Look at what scientists think could be causing this decrease in average height:

Questions

1. Put the causes in the order that you think has the most effect on height down to the least. Give a reason for each choice.
2. Compare your reasons to those of your neighbour and come up with an agreed order.
3. Work out the average height of the pupils in your class, or on your table.
4. Which factor that affects our height is the most difficult to change?

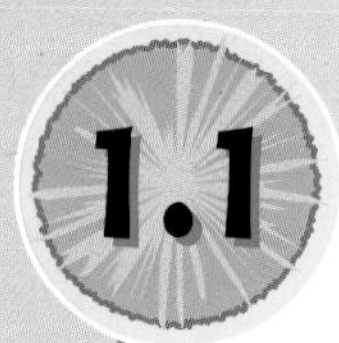

You are what you eat!

We need to eat a balanced diet to stay healthy. A balanced diet is made up of seven different food types.

In order to grow, remain healthy and have energy, we need food. The food we eat is broken down in our **digestive system** and transported around the body by the bloodstream. The chemicals that make up our food can be grouped into seven types. Each of the seven types is needed to keep us healthy. A **balanced diet** contains the right amount of all seven types.

The table on this page and the next tells you about the different food types.

Stop and think!

What have you eaten today? Which food types have you had and how much of each type? The nutrition panels on the packaging give you a lot of information.

Questions

1 Which are the two food types that give us 90% of the energy we need?

2 Where might we get the other 10% of our energy needs from?

3 What do we mean when we say that to be healthy we must eat a balanced diet?

4 Make up a diet sheet for yourself or a friend for a week. It should provide a balanced diet without being boring. (You can include some 'junk' food provided it is not too much and not too often!)

5 Many foods we buy have extra chemicals added (usually shown as a letter E followed by a number on the label, e.g. E211, E122). Why might these have been added?

6 Babies need milk to provide them with their balanced diet. Make a list of the things that milk contains. Which mineral do babies store in their liver that is not provided in milk?

Food type	Common foods	Why we need them
Carbohydrates (chemicals made from carbon, hydrogen and oxygen)	Bread, potatoes, rice, pasta, jam, sweets, fruit	These are energy-giving foods. Up to 50% of all the energy you need will come from carbohydrates.
Proteins	Meat, fish, eggs, cheese, milk, bread	For growth and to repair damaged tissue. Muscles are mainly made up of protein. Some proteins can be used to give us energy.

Figure 1
Carbohydrate-rich foods

Figure 2
Protein-rich foods

Fats	Butter, cream, oils, meat, cheese, margarine	Up to 40% of the energy you need will come from fats. The body stores energy in the form of fat.
Figure 3 Fat-rich foods		
Minerals	Cheese, milk (calcium)	Good for bones and teeth. A lack of calcium can lead to rickets (see Figure 6).
	Liver, eggs, bread (iron)	Essential for making the chemical that transports oxygen around the body, haemoglobin (this also makes our blood red in colour).
Figure 4 Foods rich in minerals		
	Salt (sodium)	Low sodium is one possible cause of cramp in the muscles.
Vitamins	A – liver, butter, green vegetables	Essential for good eyesight, especially in the dark!
	B1 – bread, milk, potatoes, meat, yeast	
	B2 – cheese, milk, liver, eggs	Mouth sores and dry skin are common if we lack B2.
	B12 – meat, milk, yeast	A lack of B12 can lead to anaemia (a reduced number of red blood cells).
	C – oranges, lemons, fruits, green vegetables, tomatoes	A lack of vitamin C can cause scurvy (bleeding gums and internal bleeding).
	Figure 5 One symptom of scurvy is swollen, bleeding gums.	
	D – eggs, margarine, cod liver oil	Essential for healthy bones. A lack of vitamin D can lead to a disease called rickets (the bones are soft and can be bent out of shape as you grow!).
	Figure 6 Rickets affects the bones of growing children.	
Roughage (also known as fibre)	Vegetables, bread, cereals	Insoluble fibre increases the bulk of food and helps to keep the intestines working properly as the muscles in the intestines squeeze the fibre through.
Water	Many drinks, juices, milk and foods contain water.	Two-thirds of your body mass is water. An adult needs to drink about 2.5 litres of water each day. Without any water, a human being will die very quickly.

Diets

Magazines and newspapers are full of diets and ways to lose weight. Many different types of 'diet plan' exist. They range from sensible balanced diets that encourage people to exercise, to dangerous crash diets where a person only eats one type of food for an extended period of time, such as a pasta diet or a fruit-only diet.

Figure 1 Exercise is a good way of losing weight and staying healthy.

Figure 2 Children come in lots of different shapes and sizes.

Most people think that the easiest way to lose weight is to go on a diet. This is not always so. Scientists have shown that nine times out of ten, weight taken off during dieting is put back on at a later date.

Do children need to diet?

Lots of young people, girls and boys, go on a diet at some time. Very often dieting is not necessary.

If you look at Figure 2 you will see many different shapes and sizes. Until your late teens, your body is still growing and the speed at which you grow can make you appear to be overweight when you are not. Very few children are overweight to such a degree that they need to diet. If you are very overweight, or obese, it can affect your health.

Read the following report about children in Hong Kong.

Child obesity in Hong Kong

Children in Hong Kong are being warned of a growing serious health risk – obesity. In a single generation, Hong Kong children have moved from healthy traditional diets to living on fast food and high fat snacks.

During break time, secondary school students crowd round food stalls, buying fried chicken wings, crisps and other fatty snacks.

Children are taller and fatter than they used to be, but their cholesterol levels are amongst the highest in the world and obesity is being seen as the top health risk.

Plump children

Dr Henrietta Ip, of the Hong Kong Child Health Foundation, says parents like their children to be plump.

'They don't see it as a problem. That is more worrying,' she said. 'Traditionally, little fat babies are loved and thought to be healthy.

continued next page

Parents are very proud that their children are a bit podgy.

'Because they are fat when they are little, they grow up into little fat kindergarten children, become fat primary school children and this goes on. In fact, the parents may be quite fat.'

Busy fast food restaurants are part of the problem. With both parents often working full-time, the traditional Chinese diet with several shared dishes is being swapped for convenience foods.

As well as eating junk snacks, many children do not get regular exercise. Hong Kong is one of the most overcrowded cities in the world and playing fields are in short supply.

Dr Ip says most children spend their free time indoors.

'They adopt the lifestyle of their parents. They sit in front of the television or computer, they have transport to go from home to school and school back home,' she says.

'All the high rise flats have fantastic fast lifts so they don't have to walk upstairs or downstairs. It's unheard of to walk.'

Medals for fitness

The authorities have launched a special awards scheme to try to persuade children to get fit. Children train at school for regular tests in running, sit-ups and other exercises, winning medals if they pass.

Teacher Carmen Li has made the scheme compulsory for all her pupils, but even so, about a third of the children are still fat.

'They cannot control themselves. Hong Kong students have an abundance of snacks to buy everywhere," she says.

'They will eat all the time. Some of them will eat during their lessons.'

One of Ms Li's star pupils is Geoffrey. He eats sensibly, loves sport and already has a silver medal in the awards scheme. But many of his friends would rather sit down than join him on the sports field.

'Some like playing basketball or football but I know some of them don't like to play. They just like to play computer games at home or read books,' says Geoffrey.

It's very difficult for the fat boys or fat girls to do exercise. 'They think that it's very difficult and very uncomfortable to sweat,' said Ms Li.

But getting fit could prove an issue of life and death. The western diet is bringing western-style disease. Heart attacks are now affecting those in their thirties and forties, something almost unheard of in the past.

For the fat children now refusing to play outside, heart disease could come even earlier.

Questions

1 What does the term 'obese' mean?

2 What similarities are there between the diet of children in Hong Kong and your diet?

3 Imagine you have a pen friend in Hong Kong who is obese. Write them a letter explaining how they should look after themselves to avoid health problems.

4 Construct a survey to find out the eating and exercise habits of your classmates. Try to include the following items in your questionnaire:

- how fit they think they are;
- how often they exercise;
- what sort of exercise they do;
- how regularly they have meals;
- what sorts of food they eat;
- how much of each type of food they eat.

Stop and think!

Teenage magazines often show pictures of very thin models and young men with a 'six pack' stomach. Why might this promote unhealthy eating habits?

Remember

- Being a little overweight is not the same as being obese (very fat).
- The only successful way to lose weight is to be careful what you eat and take regular exercise.
- Crash diets do not work!
- In your teens your body is undergoing a lot of changes.

In one end, out the other

It can take up to 24 hours for the food you eat to pass completely through your body. On its journey it is broken down. Useful chemicals are absorbed into our blood and moved around the body. Anything that we eat that our body doesn't immediately need is either stored or, if that is not possible, excreted as waste. Figure 1 shows you what the human digestive system is like.

Once food and drink is popped into the mouth, the process of digestion gets started.

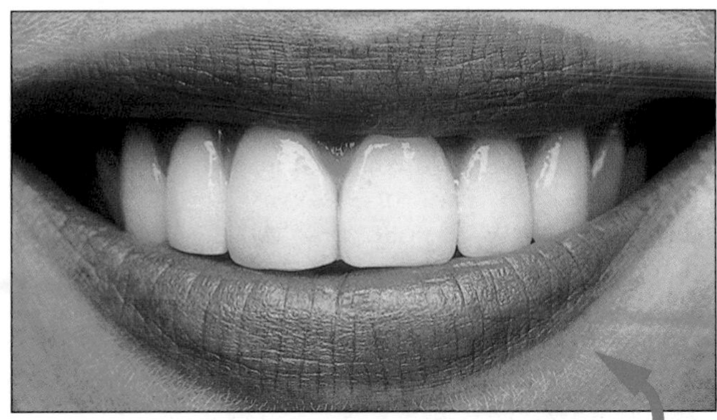

Figure 2 The teeth and saliva in the mouth begin the process of digestion.

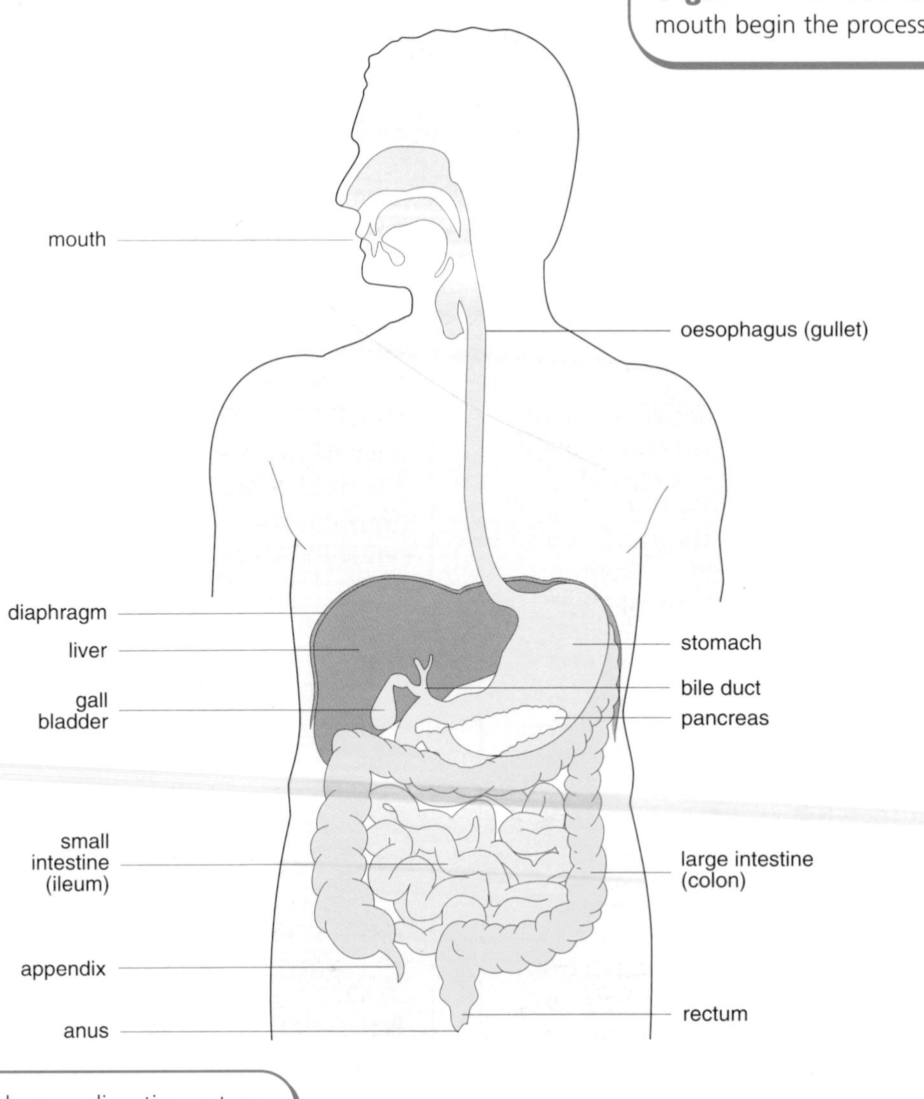

Figure 1 The human digestive system

Stage 1

The first thing we do is break up food by chewing it. We use our teeth to cut, slice and grind the food. We also add saliva to the food and this begins to break down any **starch** and convert it to sugar.

Stage 2

We swallow our food after the tongue has rolled it into a ball, called a food **bolus**, and it passes down the **oesophagus**. This is a tube of muscle and it squeezes the food down into the stomach. It is also known as the **gullet**.

Stage 3

In the stomach, the food and drink mixes with **gastric juice**. This juice contains **hydrochloric acid** that helps to break down the food. There is also another chemical called **pepsin** in the stomach. This is an **enzyme** that will break down any protein into simpler chemicals that can be absorbed into the blood (you'll learn more about these chemicals on the next page). When all the food has been turned into a liquid, we call it **chyme**. This liquid is squirted from the stomach into the **small intestine**.

Stage 4

In the first part of the **ileum** or small intestine, the **liver** adds **bile** – a chemical that neutralises the acid and stops the fats clumping together. Bile also adds old, broken down red blood cells to the contents of our small intestine and this gives our waste an interesting brown colour . . . yuck! More enzymes are added by the **pancreas** to break down what is left of the protein, the carbohydrates and the fats. As the liquid moves through the small intestine, yet more enzymes are added and the broken down food is absorbed into the bloodstream. The small intestine of a normal adult is nearly 7 m long, so it's a long journey.

Stage 5

By the time the liquid reaches the **colon** or **large intestine** (called 'large' because it's wider than the small intestine not longer!) all the useful parts of the food have been absorbed into the bloodstream and all that's left is waste, fibre and water. As water is very precious, the large intestine absorbs this back into the bloodstream so that all that's left is nearly solid waste. This we get rid of at regular intervals through the **rectum** and out through the **anus**.

Questions

1. Your body can store fat quite easily, but it cannot store vitamins. What happens if you take in more vitamins than your body can use?
2. What happens if you eat more fat than you can use?
3. If you chew a piece of bread for a long time, why do you think it begins to taste sweet?
4. Describe what happens to a chip when you eat it and as it passes through your digestive system. (You could make this into a cartoon strip if you wanted to.)
5. It can take up to 24 hours to fully digest a meal. Why do you think it takes this long and what advantage is there in taking so long to digest food?

Stop and think!

Next time you eat a burger – meat or vegetarian – and some fries, think about what happens to it as it travels along your digestive system. How is it broken up, which bits are the useful ones, what will end up as waste? Are you eating too much of any one food group?

Remember

Digestion starts in the mouth and carries on in the stomach, but most digestion takes place in the small intestine. Useful chemicals from our food are absorbed into our bloodstream and transported around the body. Waste from our food has any useful water taken from it and is then pushed out of our body through the rectum. Digestion can take up to 24 hours to complete.

1.4 Breaking up is hard to do

The food that we eat may taste nice, look nice and smell nice, but we have to break it down in order for it to be of any use to us. When we eat something, chemicals in our stomach and small intestine break up large molecules into smaller ones that we can deal with more easily.

If you remember from pages 2–3, there are seven different food types, and a balanced diet means we eat enough, but not too much, of each type.

Carbohydrates

The name **carbohydrates** simply means that molecules in this group contain carbon, hydrogen and oxygen. Carbohydrates can be split into two groups, **starches** and **sugars**. Starch is a very large molecule. In fact starch is made up of lots of glucose molecules all joined together in a long, mostly branching, chain like the one in Figure 1. There are lots of different types of sugars. One of the most useful to us is **glucose**. This is the type of sugar that gives us energy. (A quick tip: chemicals whose name ends in **-ose**, e.g. gluc**ose**, sucr**ose**, fruct**ose** and lact**ose**, are all different types of sugar.) Sucrose is the sugar that we sprinkle into our tea or onto our food, glucose is used in some fizzy drinks, fructose is the sugar that makes fruits taste sweet and lactose is found in milk.

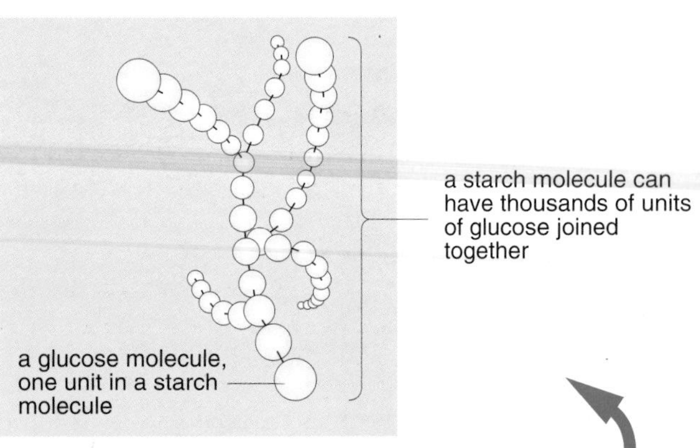

Figure 1 A long branching molecule of starch. Each unit in the chain is a molecule of glucose.

Proteins

Proteins are large molecules that can form chains. Protein chains are often folded. They are also made of units joined together. The units are called **amino acids**.

Figure 2 A protein molecule is a long chain that can be folded up.

Fats

Fats are also large molecules that are made up of two parts:

- fatty acids, which make up most of a fat molecule;
- glycerol, which is similar to glucose.

We use fats to give us energy when we run out of glucose. When this happens, it's the glycerol we use.

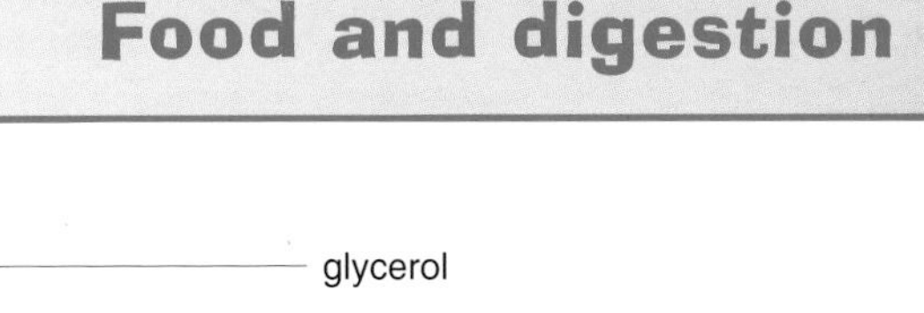

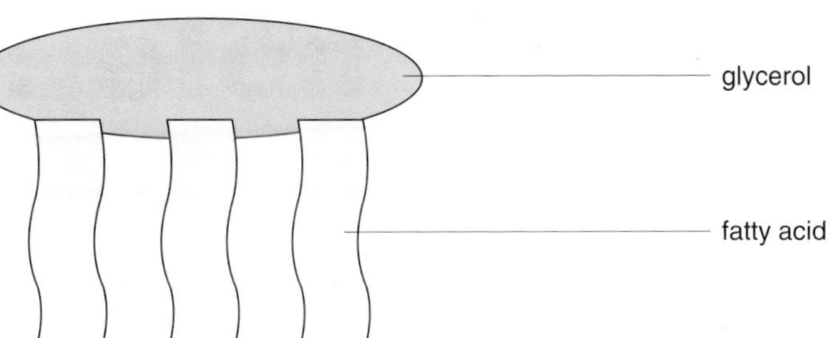

Figure 3 A fat molecule, made up of a glycerol molecule with three fatty acid 'tails'

Vitamins and minerals

Vitamins and **minerals** are very small molecules compared to the others we have talked about. They pass quite easily through the wall of the small intestine into our bloodstream without having to be broken down first.

Enzymes

In order for all these molecules to be useful to us, we need to transport them around the body to places where we need them, for example glucose needs to get into our muscle cells to give us energy. What our digestive system has to do is break down the large molecules so that they can pass through the cells in the wall of our small intestine and to release those bits of the molecule that are useful to us. To do this we have special types of proteins called **enzymes**. Enzymes are mixed in with our food during digestion. Different types of enzymes act on different types of foods and they break them down into their units. The enzymes themselves are not changed or broken down, so can be used more than once to do the same job.

Enzymes have many other uses. 'Biological' washing powder contains enzymes. These enzymes must be similar to the enzymes in your digestive system, because they break down materials like tomato sauce, egg yolk or fatty substances that make our clothes dirty.

Enzymes only work at low temperatures. They are complex particles that become 'unravelled' and stop working when they get too hot.

Questions

1. In what types of food and drink might you find the following types of sugars:
   a) fructose
   b) glucose
   c) sucrose
   d) lactose?
2. When starch is dissolved in water, the liquid looks cloudy. Why might this be? (*Hint*: think of the size of the molecule!)
3. Saliva in the mouth and hydrochloric acid in the stomach can break up starch. Bread and pasta are rich in starch. Where are these foods mainly digested?
4. Describe (with diagrams if it helps you) what happens to a starch molecule after it enters your mouth and before it is used in a muscle cell to release energy.
5. What is an enzyme?
6. What sort of shape do you think an enzyme may have? (*Hint*: think about what an enzyme is and look for a clue on the opposite page!)

Remember

Chemicals that end in **-ose** are different types of sugars. (You could keep a list at the back of your book of all the different types of sugars you come across.)

Many of the food types have large molecules that need to be broken down by **enzymes** before our body can use them.

Enzymes are special proteins that help to break down different types of foods. They will have a shape that is similar to the protein molecule shown on page 8.

There's a hole in my stomach Dr Beaumont!

The process of digestion in the stomach was discovered after a shooting accident!

Read the following incredible account of how Dr William Beaumont discovered the process of digestion in the stomach, then answer the questions.

On 6 June 1822, on Mackinac Island, Michigan, a French–Canadian fur trader named Alexis St Martin (1794–1880) was accidentally shot. It left a hole 'more than the size of the palm of a man's hand' and exposed the inside of his stomach. Dr William Beaumont (1785–1853), a US Army surgeon, treated the wound, but couldn't get the hole in St Martin's stomach to close over. For a while, the hole had to be covered to prevent food and drink from coming out. As he was no longer able to work as a fur trader, Dr Beaumont employed St Martin as a handyman.

Figure 1 Dr William Beaumont, who discovered how we digest food in our stomach

On 1 August 1825, Dr Beaumont began his experiments on St Martin, becoming the first person to see human digestion as it happens in the stomach. Beaumont tied pieces of food – pork, beef, bread and cabbage – to the end of a silk string and dangled the food through the hole into St Martin's stomach. Beaumont would pull the string one, two and three hours later to examine the appearance of the food (the silk was not affected by the gastric juice). Five hours after he first put the food into St Martin's stomach, Beaumont removed it because St Martin began to suffer from indigestion. The next day, St Martin still had indigestion which Beaumont treated.

On 7 August 1825, Beaumont asked St Martin not to eat for 17 hours, and then took the temperature of his stomach. It was 38°C. He took some gastric juice from St Martin's stomach, then placed it in a test tube with some corned beef to observe the rate of digestion. He also put another piece of meat, of the same size, into St Martin's stomach. The stomach digested the meat in two hours while the test tube of gastric juice took 10 hours to complete digestion. Beaumont tried different foods in St Martin's stomach and carried on experimenting on and off for the next few years. The foods he used included raw oysters, sausage, mutton and 'boiled salted fat pork'.

In April 1833, Beaumont went to New York and began work on publishing his observations in a book, *Experiments and Observations on the Gastric Juice and the Physiology of Digestion*. In May 1833, St Martin left for Canada due to the death of one of his children, and the two never met again.

Alexis St Martin lived for 58 years after his accident.

Digestion is the breaking down of food into smaller, simpler substances so it can be absorbed by the bloodstream. Dr Beaumont proved that part of this process happens in the stomach. The transfer of the simpler substances to the bloodstream takes place in the small intestine.

Gastric juice in the stomach is very acidic. This helps the enzymes to break the food down into smaller molecules. Gastric juice contains a lot of hydrochloric acid, just like the substance you use in the laboratory. The stomach has to have a special lining to withstand attack from the acid.

If you are sick you can taste the sour acid from your stomach. People who are sick a lot or deliberately make themselves sick a lot find that the stomach acid eventually damages their teeth.

Digestive enzymes work best at body temperature, which is 37°C. They still work at lower temperatures, but they work more slowly.

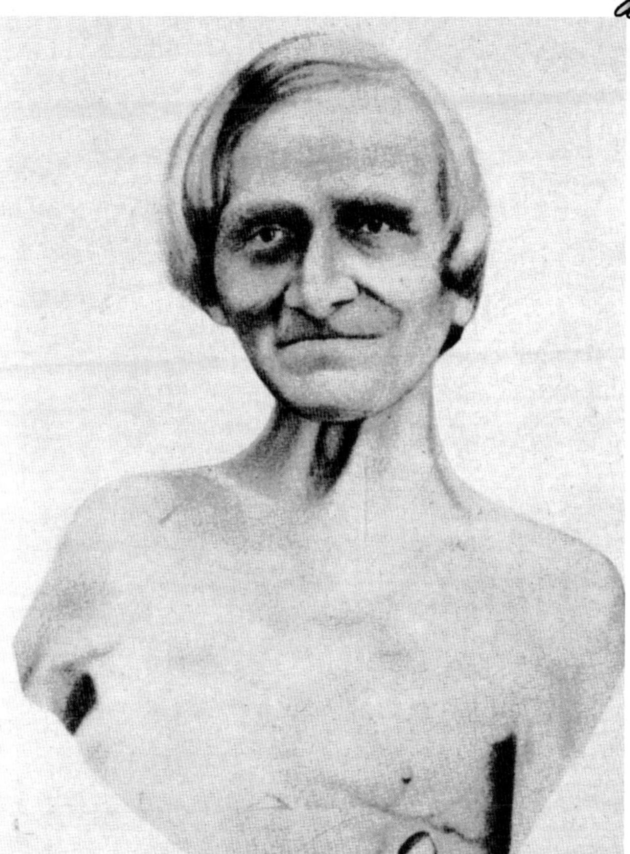

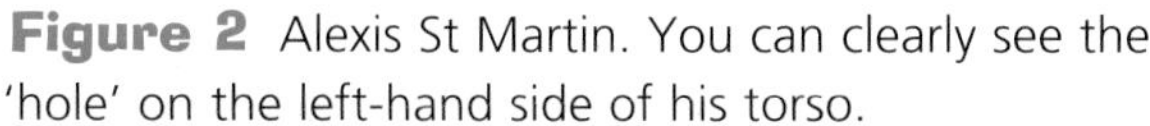

Figure 2 Alexis St Martin. You can clearly see the 'hole' on the left-hand side of his torso.

Questions

1 Why might Dr Beaumont have tied silk to the meat and not cotton?

2 Dr Beaumont looked at digestion in St Martin's stomach. Which parts of the digestion process were missing?

3 Write out a simple method for Dr Beaumont's first experiments on St Martin. What was he doing that made his experiment a fair test?

a) What variables was he trying to control in his first experiment?

b) What variable(s) couldn't he control?

4 What were the main types of food tested by Dr Beaumont?

5 How might he have tested other food types and what results might he have got?

6 Why did the corned beef take longer to break down in the test tube than in St Martin's stomach?

Remember

Match the words below to the gaps in the sentences.

food gastric small intestine stomach types

Digestion mostly happens in the ___1___. Digestion is the breaking down of food into simpler substances that can be absorbed by the blood. The ___2___ is broken down by the ___3___ juices.

Most ___4___ of food are broken down in the stomach. The simpler substances produced by digestion then move into the ___5___ from where they pass into the bloodstream.

Closer

Are you a super-taster?

What we taste in food varies from person to person. On the surface of the tongue we have thousands of taste buds, specialised cells which allow us to taste our food.

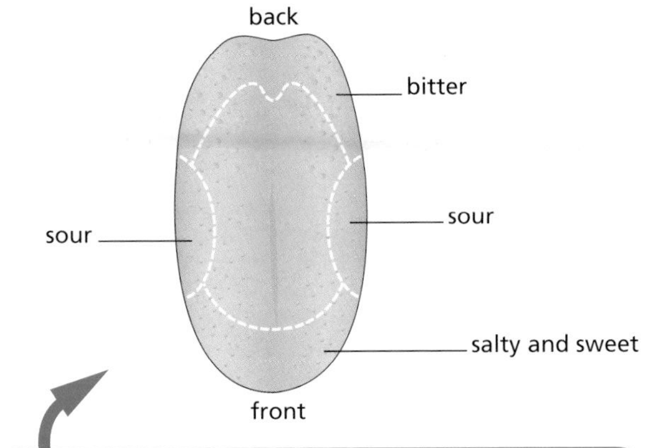

The taste areas of the tongue

About 25% of the population are non-tasters who find it difficult to taste bitter things. 25% are super-tasters who find bitter things horrible to eat. About 50% of the population are somewhere in between, normal tasters. More women are super-tasters than men. Super-tasters have more taste buds per square centimetre than normal tasters.

Take this test to see if you are a super-taster. Do you agree or disagree with each statement?

The more statements you agree with the more likely you are to be a super-taster.

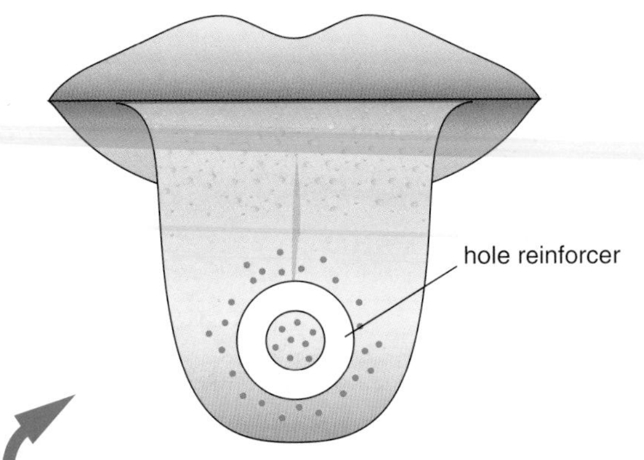

The end of a tongue with a hole reinforcer placed on the surface

1. I do not like most vegetables, especially Brussels sprouts and cabbage.
2. I prefer plain cooked food with no sauces and spices at all.
3. I do not like very spicy foods with lots of different tastes.
4. I prefer to have sauces on the side so that I can taste the main food before adding the sauce.
5. Food cooked in restaurants is never quite the way I like it.
6. I don't like very fatty or salty foods.

You may be able to try the following test in school or at home:

- Using a cotton bud, spread a small amount of food colouring on the tip of your tongue (blue or green is good). Put a hole reinforcer on your tongue and see how many pink taste buds are inside the hole.
- Look in a mirror and compare your tongue to the ones in the diagram.
- Once you have finished, dispose of your reinforcer and cotton bud carefully in the bin.

Questions

1. Why are women more likely to be super-tasters (think about them protecting their young)?
2. Super-tasters are less likely to have serious heart problems. Why could this be?
3. Work out how many people in your class are likely to be non-tasters, normal tasters and super-tasters.
4. Suggest some jobs that super-tasters could be good at.

Building blocks

Opener
Element superheroes

Atoms are the building bricks for substances. They are the basic tiny particles of matter that cannot be changed in chemical reactions. Some substances have only one type of atom in them. These substances are called **elements**. Elements can have special properties.

Activity

Some more elements want to become superheroes. They think they have super properties. Make a superhero poster for an element. Either choose from this short list or make up one of your own:

- Phosphorus – Greedy for oxygen, burns fiercely.
- Copper – Conducts electricity well, kills mould.
- Radon – Heavy poisonous gas, leaks from the ground to predict earthquakes.
- Lead – Used in batteries and as radiation shields, but it is a poison.

2.1 Tiny atoms

The smallest particle of matter that you can have is an atom.

Everything can be made into smaller and smaller bits until you get down to things called **atoms**. Atoms are the smallest particles that exist on their own in the world around us.

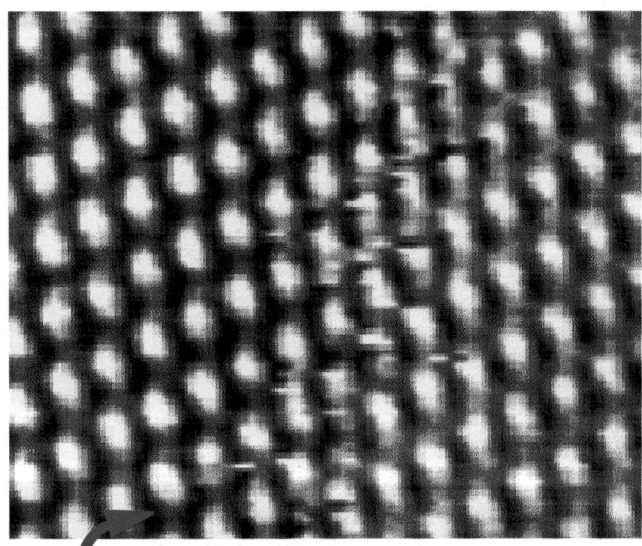

Figure 1 Viewed under an extremely powerful microscope, atoms are a bit like fuzzy round balls. These are gold atoms magnified 20 million times.

Elements, mixtures and compounds

Mixtures are things that can be separated into different pure substances. For example, salt water is a mixture. Pure substances are a much harder idea to understand.

Pure substances are those where all the particles are exactly the same. They can be divided into two types:

1 **Elements** are pure substances where all the atoms are the same type;

2 **Compounds** are pure substances where different atoms join together to make the same type of particle. These particles made from groups of atoms are called **molecules**.

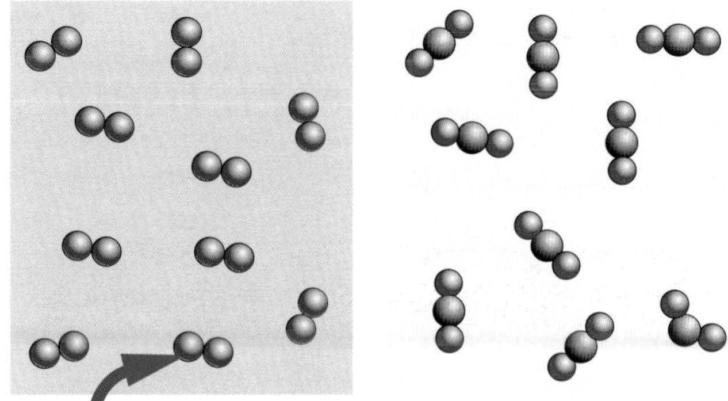

Figure 2 Oxygen (left) is an element. It contains only oxygen atoms, but the atoms 'go round in pairs' to make oxygen molecules. Carbon dioxide (right) contains carbon atoms and oxygen atoms so it is a compound. All carbon dioxide molecules contain one carbon atom joined to two oxygen atoms.

- Argon is an element in the air, but argon atoms go round in ones.
- Nitrogen is an element in the air, but nitrogen atoms go round in twos like in oxygen.
- Ozone is also made of the element oxygen. But in ozone, the oxygen atoms go round in threes to make a different type of molecule. You may have heard of ozone – it absorbs harmful ultra-violet light in the upper atmosphere.

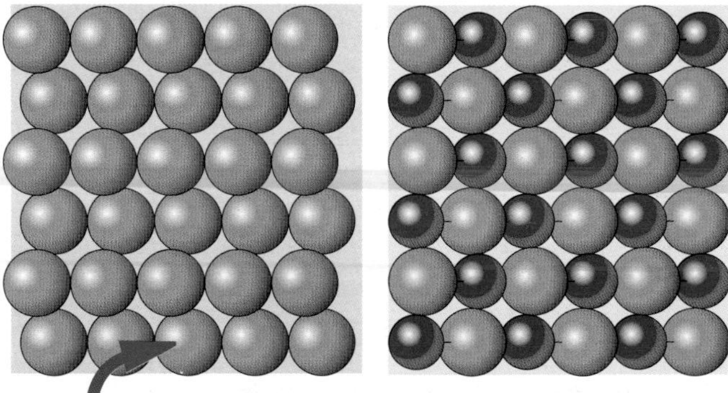

Figure 3 Copper (left) is an element. The copper atoms are in a regular pattern because it is a solid. Copper oxide (right) is a compound. There is one oxygen atom for every copper atom.

Questions

1 Explain each of these terms:
a) atom
b) element
c) compound
d) molecule

2 Look at the Periodic Table on page 151. Fill in a table with the headings shown below. Make it as long as possible.

Elements I have heard of	What I know about them

3 Water molecules have two hydrogen atoms and one oxygen atom. Draw a particle picture of water vapour.

4 Draw a particle picture of ozone molecules.

5 Draw a big particle picture of air. Air contains oxygen molecules, nitrogen molecules, argon atoms and carbon dioxide molecules.

6 Look at the particle pictures below.

(i)

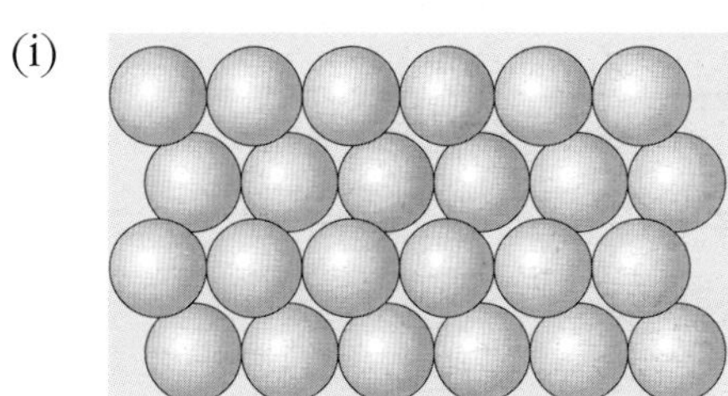

(ii)

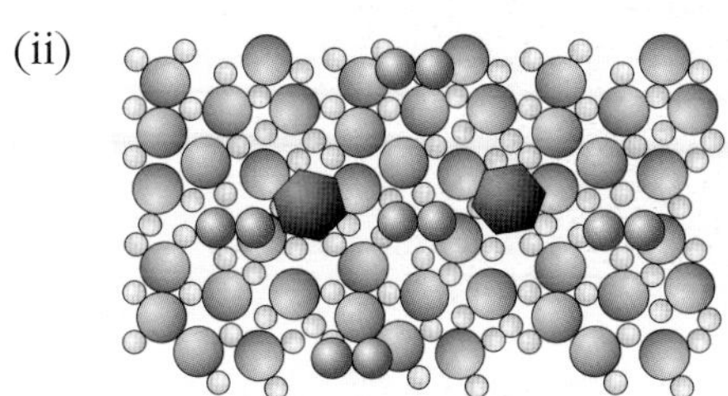

(iii)

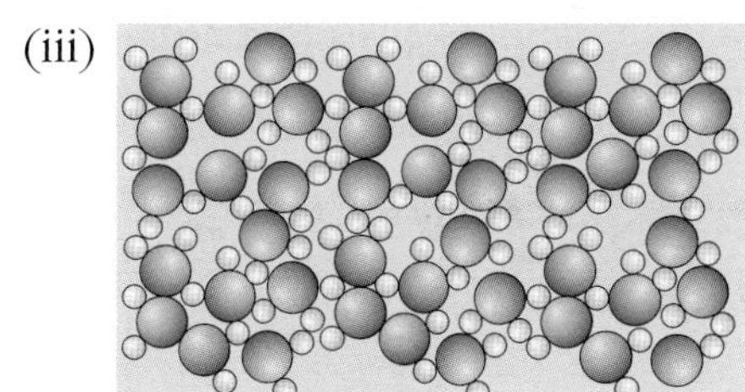

(iv) (v)

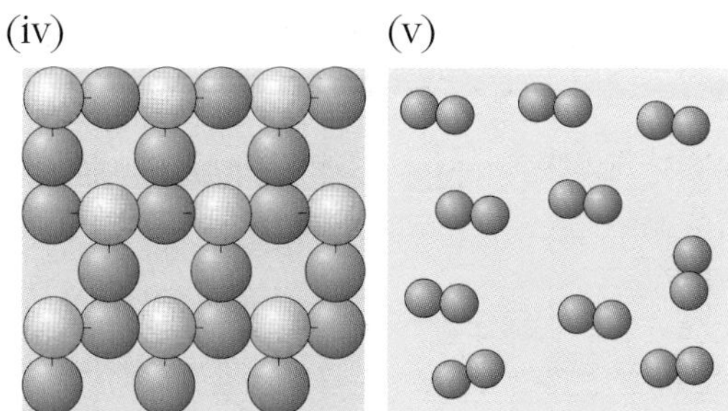

a) For each, say if it is solid, liquid or gas.

b) For each, say if it shows an element, compound or mixture.

If your head was the size of the Earth ...

- an atom would be the size of a pea;
- a water molecule would be the size of a small grape;
- a sugar molecule would be the size of a music cassette;
- a fat molecule would be the size of a ring binder;
- a plastic molecule would be the length of a car;
- a cell in your body would be the size of a shopping centre;
- one hair on your head would be five kilometres in thickness.

Remember

Find the missing word by solving the clues. The first letter of each answer forms a word that tells what atoms never do.

A pure substance – but not an element. (8 letters)
Joins with oxygen to make water. (8 letters)
The smallest particle that can exist on its own. (4 letters)
The gas that makes up most of the air. (8 letters)
A state of matter that can squash. (3 letters)
A substance made of lots of the same atom. (7 letters)

2.2 A list of elements

The Periodic Table is a useful list of the elements. Each element has an international symbol as well as a name.

The **Periodic Table** is a list of all the elements we know (look at the full Periodic Table on page 151). It is a list in order of atomic number, and groups similar elements together.

There are just over 100 elements, but only 90 of these are found naturally in the Earth's crust.

Just the first 20 elements are shown here with their symbols. The number above the symbol is called the **atomic number**, the number below the symbol is called the **mass number**.

Atoms

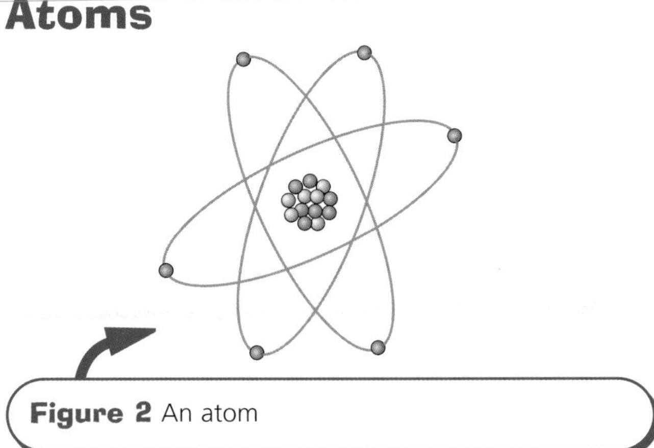

Figure 2 An atom

Atoms are very small. So small that it is hard to imagine them. One hundred million atoms in a line would fit into 1 cm. Atoms are made of smaller particles called **protons, neutrons** and **electrons**. The outer part is made up of electrons. Atoms are fuzzy at the edges; they tend to stick together by sharing their electrons.

Figure 1 The first part of the Periodic Table

1 **H** Hydrogen 1			
3 **Li** Lithium 7	4 **Be** Beryllium 9	5 **B** Boron 10	6 **C** Carbon 12
11 **Na** Sodium 23	12 **Mg** Magnesium 24	13 **Al** Aluminium 27	14 **Si** Silicon 28
19 **K** Potassium 39	20 **Ca** Calcium 40		

Lithium carbonate is used to absorb carbon dioxide gas on the Space Shuttle.

Beryllium is found in the gemstone blue beryl.

Hydrogen gas was used to make the Hindenberg airship lighter than air. It burns very fiercely.

Carbon as charcoal is used to help purify water.

Sodium vapour is used in yellow street lights.

Boron is used for the control rods in nuclear reactors.

Silicon is a grey solid. Combined with a few atoms of another element, it is the material for computer memory circuits.

Potassium chloride is used in low salt diets.

Marble is a very hard form of calcium carbonate.

Magnesium is a very light metal. It is used to make pencil sharpeners and racing car wheels.

Kitchen foil is made from aluminium.

Questions

1 Draw a line 1 cm long. Label it 'one hundred million atoms'.

2 Which elements shown in the Periodic Table are gases?

3 Which elements are metals?

4 Are any of the metals gases?

5 Which two elements react to make water?

6 Which gas is used to fill light bulbs? Explain why.

7 Which element is used in computer memory?

8 Which two gases have been used in airships? Explain why.

9 Draw a picture in full colour of what you think an atom would look like if you were just as tiny as it.

10 What is the name of the element with the same atomic number as your age?

Remember

Put these words and numbers in the right places.

90 1 100 000 000 6 3 8 Periodic Table

Atoms are made up of ___1___ types of smaller particles called protons, neutrons and electrons. There are ___2___ atoms in a line 1 cm long. Only ___3___ elements are found naturally. These are listed in the ___4___. Hydrogen is number ___5___ in order of mass, carbon is number ___6___. There are ___7___ elements on the second row of the table.

Key

1 ← atomic number
H ← symbol
Hydrogen ← name
1 ← mass number

his gas is not very active. It is used to fill crisp packets.

Pure oxygen is used to help people with breathing difficulties.

Fluorine is used to etch glass with security codes.

Modern airships are filled with safer helium gas.

			2 **He** Helium 4
7 **N** Nitrogen 14	8 **O** Oxygen 16	9 **F** Fluorine 19	10 **Ne** Neon 20
15 **P** Phosphorus 31	16 **S** Sulphur 32	17 **Cl** Chlorine 35	18 **Ar** Argon 40

Neon discharge tubes are bright red lights.

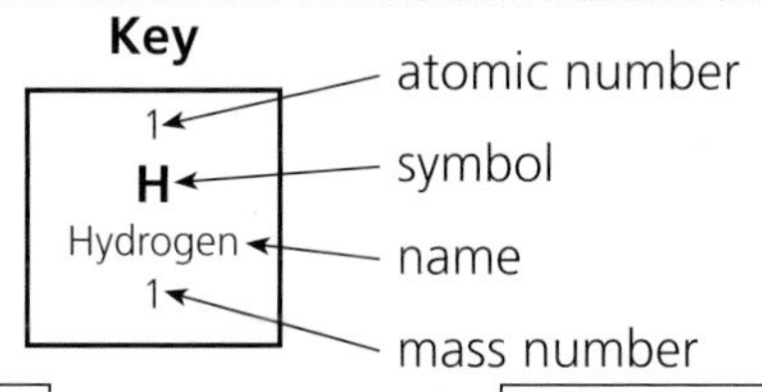

Phosphorus burns ery fiercely. It was used in bombs.

Sulphur is added to rubber to make it hard.

A compound of chlorine is put into swimming pools to kill germs. It has a distinctive smell.

Argon is used to fill light bulbs. It is an inert gas.

2.3 Multi metal

Metals are very useful materials. They are the only solid materials that transfer energy easily by conduction.

There are many different metals. We use metals to do lots of different jobs that can't be done any other way.

Metals are usually shiny, bendy and go 'ting' when they are tapped. We look for these properties when deciding whether or not objects are metal. But:

- the surface of all metals (except gold) goes dull after a while;

Figure 1 Gold is used for jewellery because it stays shiny.

Figure 2 Iron is used for bridges because it is very strong.

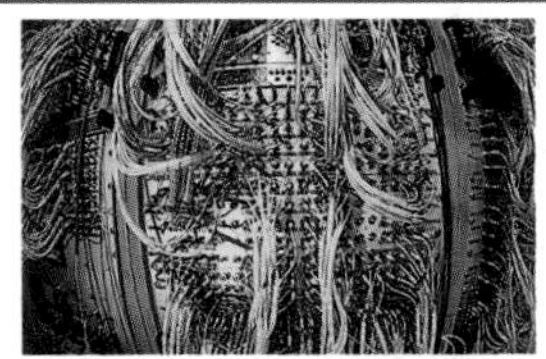

Figure 3 Copper is used for electric cables because it conducts electricity well and is flexible.

Figure 4 Brass is used for electric plugs and switches because it conducts electricity well and is hard.

Figure 5 Stainless steel is used for saucepans. It is strong even when thin and conducts heat well.

Figure 6 Silver is used to coat cutlery. It does not react with the food.

Figure 7 Aluminium is very flexible and it can be rolled out into thin sheets.

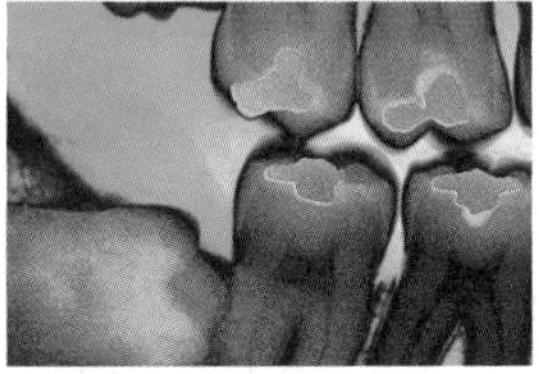

Figure 8 Mercury is used in tooth fillings because it makes other metals into a paste.

- big lumps of metal are hard to test for bendiness;
- bottles and cups go 'ting' when hit, and they are not made of metal.

Testing for metals

Use a simple circuit with a battery and light bulb to test for metals. If the solid material put into the circuit **conducts electricity** and the bulb lights, it is a metal.

Hold the material in your hand. If it is a metal it continues to feel cold. Metals are good conductors

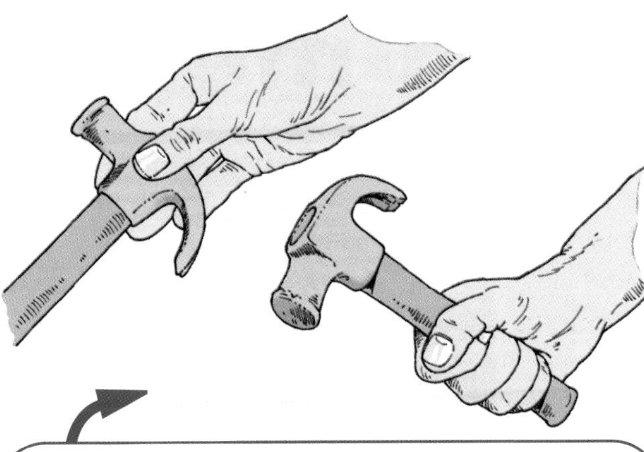

Figure 9 The head of the hammer will feel colder than the handle because it is made of metal.

of heat. They will **conduct energy** from the hand away from the surface and so feel cold. (Try this with the head and handle of a hammer.)

Corrosion

As soon as they are made, metal surfaces start to change chemically. They combine with oxygen in the air to make different materials. This can make the surface go dull. With iron and steel this **corrosion** is called rusting.

Questions

1. Make a list of all the different metals you can think of.
2. Make a list of metal objects that you own. Try to add the name of the metal they are made of.
3. What metals are the Olympic medals made from? What does each metal look like?
4. Describe what a steel object looks like when it is rusty.
5. Draw a cartoon strip of a steel bucket as it gradually rusts away. Explain what is happening.

Dirty work

Toby was going to clean his uncle's darts trophies. He washed and polished the plastic and wooden ones. He used special metal cleaning stuff on the metal ones. The metal ones came up really shiny even though the surface started off very dull.

Figure 10 Which is which?

He was puzzled about what to use on two of the trophies. One was made of 'pewter' and one was made of 'bakelite', but both were black, dull and dirty. Toby had no idea what cleaning method to use on them. He tested them and here are his results.

	Head of hand test	Electrical test
pewter	felt cold for a long time	conducted electricity; bulb lit up
bakelite	quickly felt warm	did not conduct; bulb stayed unlit

Table 1 Toby's results

Questions

6. Which trophy was metal?
7. What would Toby use to clean this trophy?
8. What would the metal trophy look like when clean?
9. Draw pictures to show Toby testing the metal trophy.

Remember

Fill in the spaces using the following words.

conductors corrosion electricity

Metals are good ____1____ of heat. Metals can conduct enough ____2____ to light a bulb.

Metals go dull when they are in air. This is called ____3____. Rusting is a special form of this.

Metals and non-metals

Some substances contain only one sort of atom. We call these 'elements'. Most elements are metals, a few are non-metals.

Metals are some of the most useful materials we have. There are about 70 metallic elements. Most of the time it's fairly easy to tell if a material is a metal, but there are some modern materials that look like metal but are not.

What makes metals useful?

Metals all share certain **properties**.

The less important ones are:

- they are **shiny**, if the surface is clean;
- they make a nice 'ting' if hit.

The more important ones are:

- they are tough;
- they do not shatter;
- they can be shaped by squashing them;
- they do not crack easily;
- they can hold large weights without breaking;
- they don't melt easily (only one metal (mercury) is a liquid; tin and lead melt fairly easily, but most metals are solids that don't melt until they get very hot!);
- some metals are **magnetic**. Iron and steel are strongly magnetic, cobalt and nickel are weakly magnetic;
- they **conduct energy** easily. The particles quickly transfer energy through the solid as heat;
- they **conduct electricity** well;
- they are **malleable** – they can be hammered into shapes;
- they are **ductile** – they can be drawn out into wires.

Figure 1 A steel knife is tough (does not wear away or crack) and strong (thin, but does not buckle).

Figure 2 Tungsten is a metal. A tungsten filament in a light bulb conducts electricity well and has a very high melting point.

The main differences between metals are their heaviness and how quickly they react with other chemicals.

Metals combine several of the properties needed to make an object very useful.

Questions

1 Look at the Periodic Table on pages 16 and 17. Make a list of all the elements which you know are metals.

2 Which metals are magnetic?

3 Copy the table below. Match the correct property to the metal.

Metal	Property
copper	very hard, used for aeroplane parts
gold	very light, used for window frames
aluminium	stays shiny, used for jewellery
titanium	liquid metal, used in thermometers
mercury	conducts electricity well, used for wires

4 Choose some properties of metals from the list. Draw a large picture/poster of metal objects or devices that need those properties to work. Explain why each property is needed.

Non-metals

(a) Carbon

(b) Sulphur

(c) Chlorine

(d) Oxygen

(e) Nitrogen

(f) Phosphorus

Figure 3 Non-metal elements are different colours and several are gases.

There are only about 20 elements that are non-metals. They also have certain properties:

- Many are **gases**;
- The ones that aren't gases all have **low melting points**;
- They are **brittle** if they are solid;
- They do **not conduct energy** well;
- They do **not conduct electricity**.

Very few of the non-metals are useful materials in the way that metals are. All their usefulness comes from their chemical reactions.

Questions

5 Look at the pictures of the non-metal elements in Figure 3.
a) Which are gases?
b) Are the solids shiny like metals?

6 Compare the properties of non-metals with the properties of the metal objects in your poster for Question 4. Explain why non-metals are not used for making things.

7 Match the non-metallic elements with their uses in the table below.

Non-metallic element	Use
carbon	very light gas, used in balloons
chlorine	gas we use in our bodies which is taken in by the lungs
helium	barbecue charcoal; burns well to give lots of heat
oxygen	kills germs in water supply and swimming pools

Remember

Use the following to fill in the blanks.

brittle not low crack shiny magnetic conduct heat gases

Metal elements are ____1____, they do not ____2____ easily, some are ____3____, they ____4____ and electricity well.

Non-metallic elements are not tough, they are ____5____. They are ____6____ or ____7____ melting point solids. They do ____8____ conduct heat or electricity.

Making compounds

Elements can be combined directly to make new compounds. The new compounds are pure substances. They contain a fixed ratio of atoms from the elements that made them.

Atoms join together in different ways to form **compounds**. In compounds the clusters of atoms are called **molecules**. Each molecule is exactly the same.

The letters of the alphabet **combine** to make millions of words. From all the atoms you should be able to make millions of compounds. But there are rules that limit this.

1 For metal atoms to form a compound, they have to combine with non-metal atoms.
2 Non-metal atoms can combine together in groups to make compounds or parts of compounds.
3 Molecules usually contain small numbers of atoms. Carbon atoms are the exception to this. They can make really big complex molecules.
4 When new molecules are formed, the atoms don't vanish, they just get rearranged.

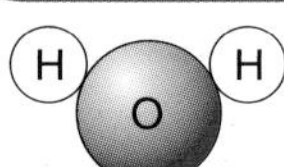

a) Water: two hydrogen atoms joined to an oxygen.

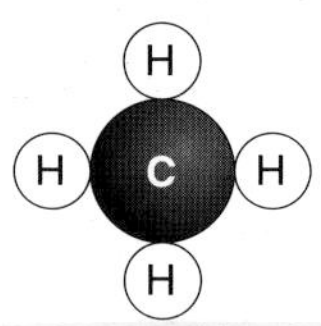

b) Methane (natural gas): four hydrogen atoms joined to a carbon.

c) Sand: a silicon atom and two oxygen atoms (silicon dioxide).

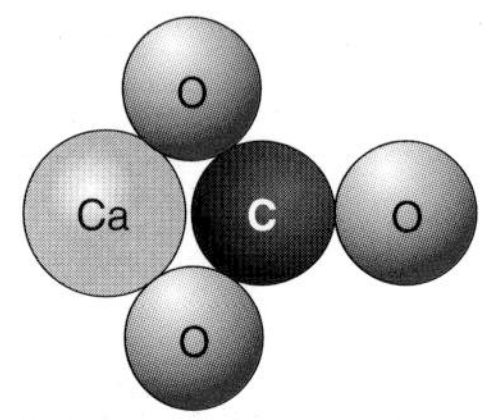

d) Limestone: a calcium atom and three oxygen atoms joined to a carbon atom (calcium carbonate).

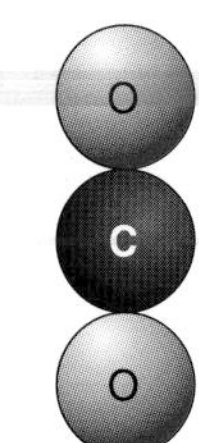

e) carbon dioxide: a carbon atom with two oxygens joined to it.

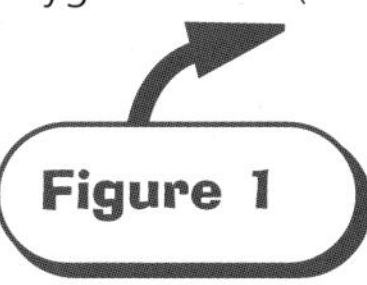

Questions

1 Compounds are pure substances. Explain why.

2 What is the name of a cluster of atoms joined together?

3 What sorts of atoms do metals combine with?

4 In equations, water molecules are written as H_2O and methane molecules as CH_4. This is called their formula. Explain why.

New rock

a) Calcium oxide coming out of the cement kiln.

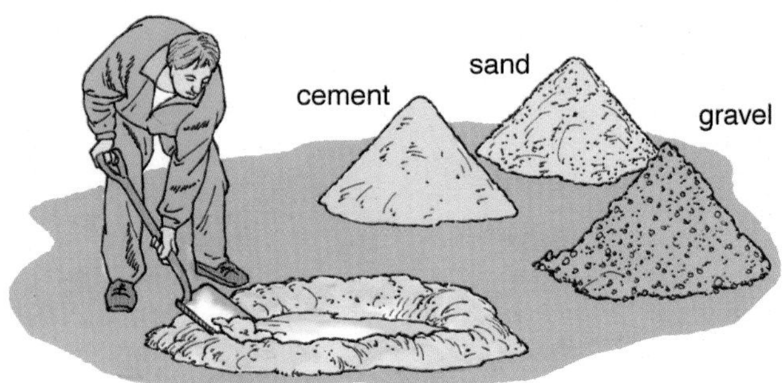

b) It gets mixed with water, sand and gravel.

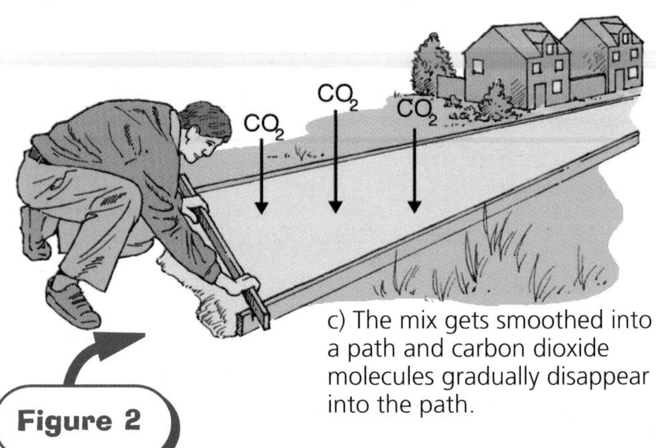

c) The mix gets smoothed into a path and carbon dioxide molecules gradually disappear into the path.

Figure 2

Making cement is a chemical process that goes back many years. Cement is made using limestone that has been crushed to a powder and roasted in a furnace. When the cement is mixed with sand and water it sets really hard. It doesn't just dry out like mud, it changes chemically to a new substance as it sets.

Calcium oxide in the cement absorbs carbon dioxide from the air. Mixing it with water helps this process. Hard calcium carbonate crystals are formed.

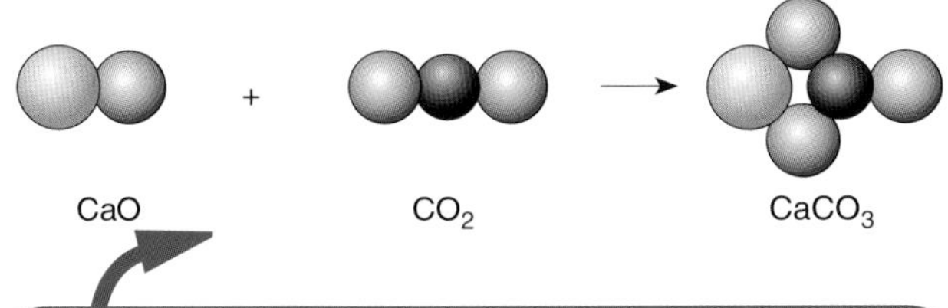

Figure 3 The reaction to produce calcium carbonate

Burning methane

The hydrogen atoms get pinched first to make water molecules. Then the carbon atoms in the methane combine with oxygen to make carbon dioxide gas.

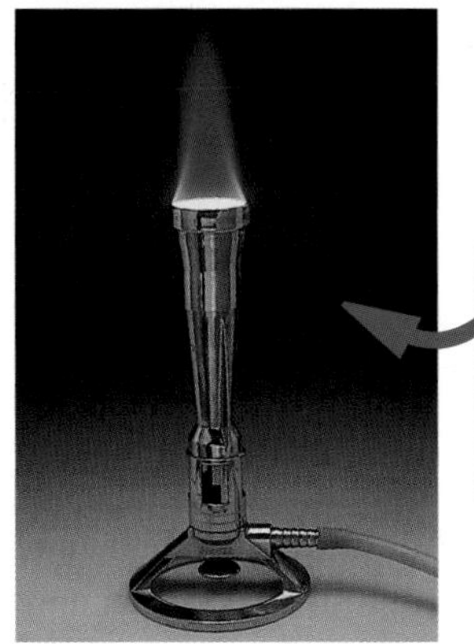

Figure 4 A Bunsen burner burns methane in oxygen to produce carbon dioxide and water.

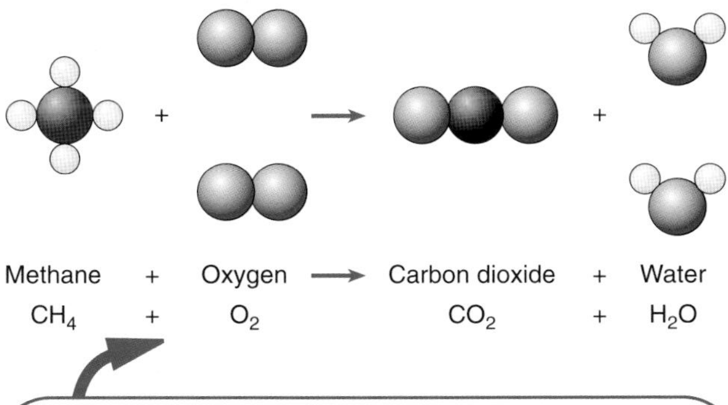

Figure 5 The atoms involved in the reaction between methane and oxygen

Testing a gas: carbon dioxide

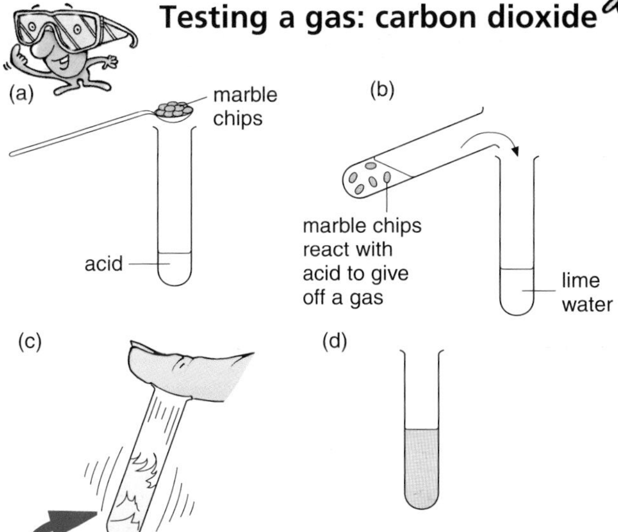

Figure 6 a) Put calcium carbonate chips into some acid. b) When the test tube fills up, pour the gas into a test tube containing a little limewater. c) Shake the limewater and the gas. d) If the limewater goes milky, the gas is carbon dioxide.

Questions

5. What solution do you use to test for carbon dioxide?
6. What do you see during the test?
7. Why does cement set hard?
8. What substance other than carbon dioxide is made when methane burns?

Remember

Use the following words to fill in the gaps.

complex atoms molecules combine compounds carbon

Atoms ____**1**____ with each other to make new substances called ____**2**____. New particles made in this way are often called ____**3**____.

When chemical changes happen, the ____**4**____ get rearranged into different molecules. No atoms get lost.

Most molecules are small. Only ____**5**____ atoms can join to make big ____**6**____ molecules.

Oil and gas

The word 'petroleum' literally means 'rock oil'. Petroleum is the second most **abundant** liquid on Earth. Crude petroleum and natural gas are often found together. The natural gas is dissolved in the liquid oil. We often refer to crude petroleum as crude oil. This material provides two-thirds of the world's primary energy supplies. The oil and gas are **non-renewable** resources and our use of them has increased so much that we have worries about how long they will last.

There is evidence that humans have used petroleum products throughout history. Oil that had **seeped** to the surface would mostly evaporate and leave behind **bitumen** – the tarry component of the mixture of hydrocarbons (compounds containing hydrogen and carbon) from which it is composed. This has been used for thousands of years as a **waterproofing agent** for plumbing, boat building and brick bonding. There is reference to bitumen being used as a coating for Moses' basket and Noah's Ark being 'pitched' inside and out with it.

The Native Americans collected oil for medicines. The American settlers found its presence in the water supplies a **contamination**, but they learned to collect it to use as fuel in their lamps.

Petroleum oil became a valuable **commodity** in the nineteenth century. The whaling industry was failing to provide enough whale oil to light the lamps of the world and a new source was needed. The first oil well was drilled in August 1859.

The uses for oil increased as the supply grew. The invention of the car engine meant that the petrol fraction of the oil mixture was needed for transport. Then the invention of aeroplanes demanded fuel that could be best supplied from oil.

In the 1940s, the development of man-made materials from oil, such as nylon and polythene, gave us the plastics industry.

It is no wonder that oil was called black gold and that discovery of oil and gas could mean riches beyond belief.

Oil is a fossil fuel. When we burn it we are releasing energy first captured from the Sun millions of years ago, mainly by plankton (tiny **prehistoric** plant life, many of which inhabit our oceans today) by the process of **photosynthesis**. The remains of these **microscopic** plants and tiny animals settled on the sea bed. They were buried deeper by sediments like clay and sand as the years went by. The sedimentary layers continued to accumulate and the increased pressure and temperature helped to turn much of the organic matter into the hydrocarbons that make up oil and gas. The oil and gas formed in this way **migrated** upwards. Some of it reached the surface and escaped, some was trapped underground, not as a 'lake' but in the pores of the rock itself.

An oil well is drilled, looking for pockets of **porous** rock that contain the crude oil. When a pocket is found, water is pumped down to push the oil to the surface. The crude oil is then transported to a refinery. At the refinery the oil is vaporised and passed through a fractionating tower. Here the mixture is separated into its component parts by fractional distillation. Each part has a different use. Some of these are petrol and diesel for motor car engines, kerosene for jet engines or bitumen for making roads.

Questions

1 Make a list of the 12 words in bold type and write their meanings beside them.

2 Draw a flow chart to describe how a crude oil molecule gets from deep underground to a car's petrol tank.

3 Write down all the uses of crude oil that are in the text and any more that you know about.

4 'Cars run using energy that came from the Sun.' Explain why this is true or false.

Scientists

Sir Harold Kroto

'I was the kid with the funny name in my form. I now realise that I made a continual effort to blend in as best I could, by making my behaviour as identical as possible to that of the other kids.

My father had to leave Berlin in 1937. He originally wanted to be a dress designer but somehow ended up running a small business printing faces and other images on toy balloons.

He set up his own small factory, to make balloons as well as print them. I spent much of my school holidays working at the factory. I was called upon to fill in everywhere, from mixing latex dyes to repairing the machinery and replacing workers on the production line. I only now realise what an outstanding training this was for the problem-solving skills needed by a research scientist.

As time progressed, I gravitated towards chemistry, physics and maths. I was attracted by the smells and bangs that endowed chemistry with that slight but charismatic element of danger.

I was keen on sport, tennis in school and gymnastics outside school. At one time I remember wanting to be a Wimbledon champion.'

Sir Harold Kroto, Nobel Prize for Chemistry 1996

The Nobel Prize discovery

For centuries it was believed that the element carbon only existed in two very different forms, soft black **graphite** and hard transparent **diamond**. But in 1985 a new form of carbon was discovered, which had a remarkable structure. This form of carbon was composed of hexagons and pentagons of carbon, joined together to form a completely spherical shape – a football!

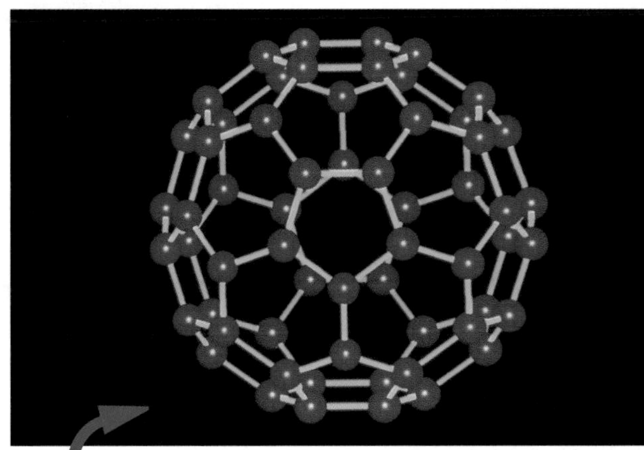

Buckyballs are used as lubricants, for cancer treatment and as tiny chemical sponges, mopping up dangerous chemicals from injured brain tissue.

Buckminsterfullerene was discovered completely by accident during an investigation into the outer atmosphere of stars. An apparatus was used that vaporises graphite with a high power laser and allows it to re-form in vacuum. A variety of materials were formed, including a mysteriously stable material. This material always consisted of exactly 60 carbon atoms. It was named buckminsterfullerene after it was suggested that its structure is similar to that of a geodesic sphere, and that was the reason for its stability.

'A youngster recently asked me what advice I would give to a student who wanted to be where I am now. One thing I would **not** advise is to do science with the aim of winning any prizes. My advice is to do something that interests you, and do it to the absolute best of your ability. If it interests you, explore it because something unexpected often turns up. Having chosen something worth doing, never give up and try not to let anyone down.'

Closer

Has science got atoms right?

Theories about atoms have had to be changed because more advanced experiments showed ideas to be wrong.

Democritus (about 400 BC in Greece)
Atoms are invisible and very small. The name atomon means indivisible.

Dalton 1802
All matter is made of atoms. Atoms are indestructible.

J J Thomson 1897
He discovered the electron. He proposed the 'plum pudding' model, in which thousands of tiny negatively charged corpuscles swarm inside a cloud of positive charge.

Ernest Rutherford 1911
He fired very fast tiny particles at thin gold foil:

- Over 98% of the particles went straight through;
- About 2% of the particles went through but were deflected;
- About 0.01% of the particles bounced off the gold foil.

The atom contains a tiny dense centre called the nucleus. In size, this is like a pea in the middle of a football stadium.

Today we describe a nucleus as made of protons and neutrons, and explain most of chemistry through this atomic model.

Quarks and leptons 1964
A few types of **even smaller** objects can explain neutrons, protons and all the new particles.

These are called quarks and leptons.

String theory (today)
All of these particles can be explained as different 'notes' given out by tiny vibrating strings.

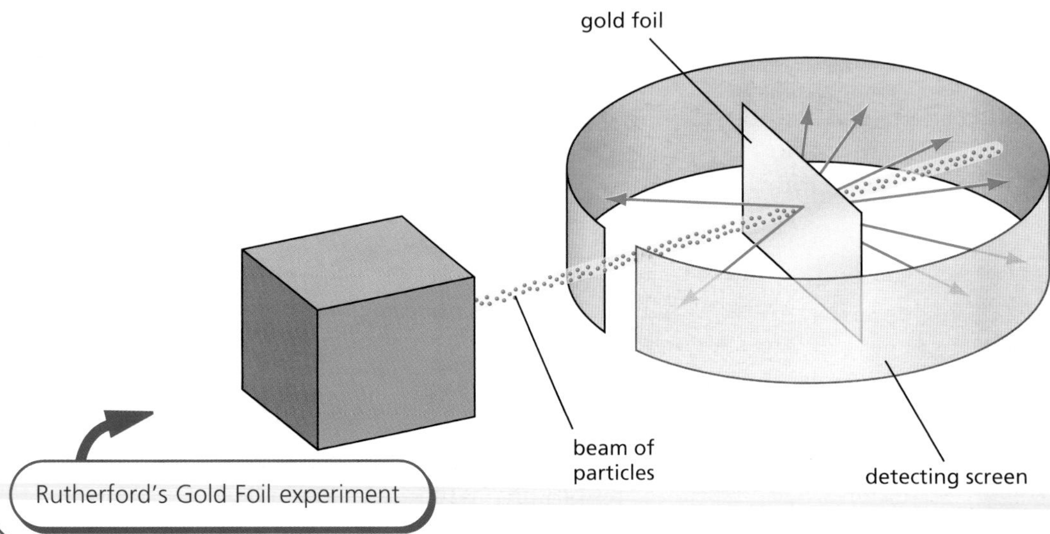

Rutherford's Gold Foil experiment

Activity

Devise a thinklinks chart to relate these terms:

atom **element** **structure** **proton** **neutron** **electron**
nucleus **properties** **Periodic Table** **metals** **non-metals**

Energy and fuels

Opener
Staying warm and going cold

starting temperature = 50 °C

finishing temperature = 18 °C
(the same temperature as the surroundings)

If you make a hot drink and forget about it for half an hour it goes cold. Energy transfers from the hot drink to the surroundings. It warms the surroundings a little bit.

You can forget about your body for half an hour and it stays warm. You transfer energy to your surroundings but you use your food to replace it.

A human body might stop using food to replace the energy it transfers to its surroundings. Then the body does the same as the drink. It warms its surroundings ever so slightly until its temperature is the same as the surroundings.

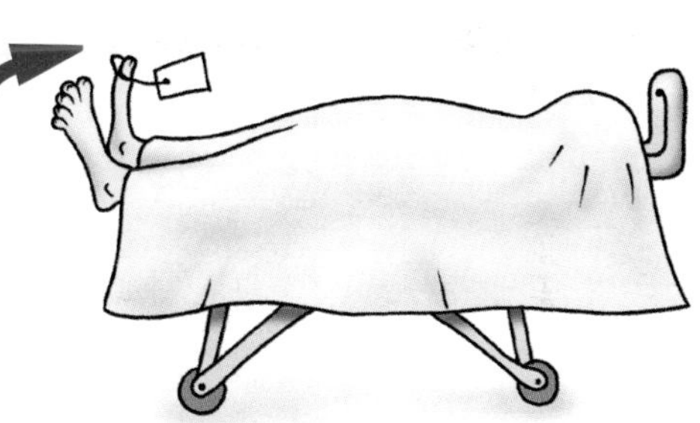

Questions

1 Touch the desk. Touch your forehead. Are you alive? How can you tell?

2 Which has the higher temperature, the desk or your forehead?

3 Which transfers energy continuously to the air around it, the desk or your forehead? Where does the energy come from for this?

4 If a dead body is put into a refrigerated compartment where the air temperature is 4 °C what will happen?

5 It is a bad idea to put a hot drink into a fridge. Why?

6 A cup of tea that has already gone cold has the same temperature as the surrounding air. A typical room has an air temperature of 18 °C. Draw another cartoon like the ones above to show the cold tea. Add the starting and finishing temperatures. Add a caption to explain what does or does not happen.

Temperature differences

Energy transfers into and out of objects, depending on the temperature difference between them and their surroundings.

Winter or summer, a letterbox is just a lump of metal in a useful shape. It doesn't actually *do* anything itself. But its temperature changes. It changes in response to the temperature of its surroundings.

For example, in the evening when the air turns cooler, the letterbox will also start to turn cooler. Whenever the letterbox is at a higher temperature than its surroundings, energy transfers away from it. And when it's cooler than its surroundings, energy transfers into it. Energy doesn't transfer in or out when the temperature of the letterbox is the same as the temperature of the surroundings. There is no overall energy transfer.

Other objects behave in the same way.

Figure 1 A letterbox in winter and summer

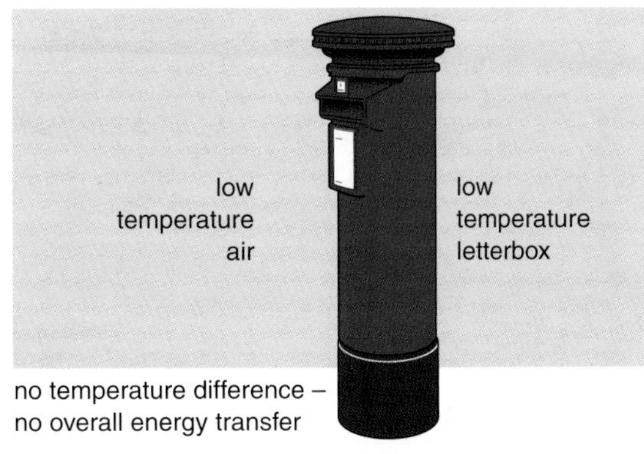

no temperature difference – no overall energy transfer

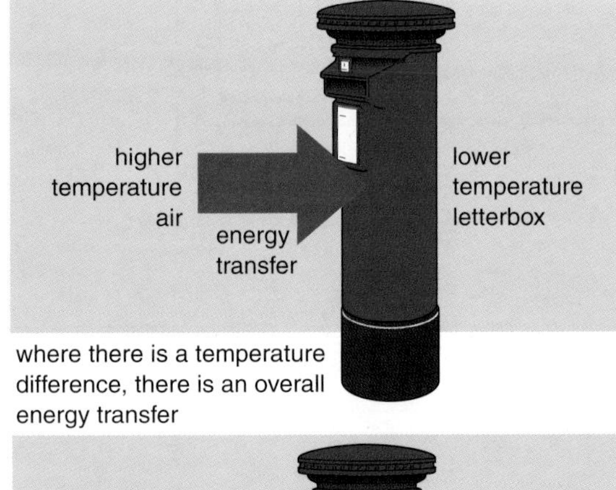

where there is a temperature difference, there is an overall energy transfer

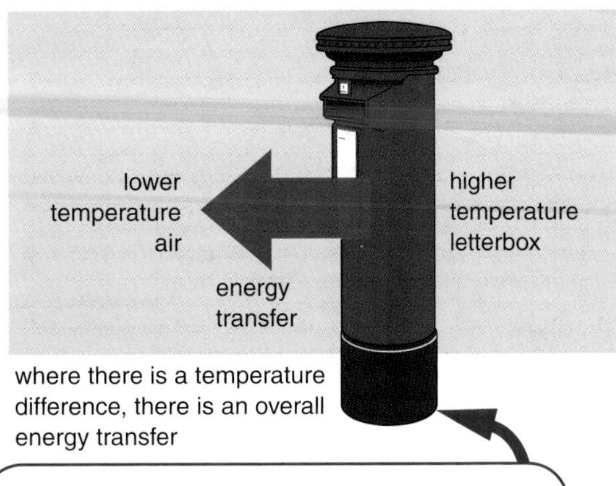

where there is a temperature difference, there is an overall energy transfer

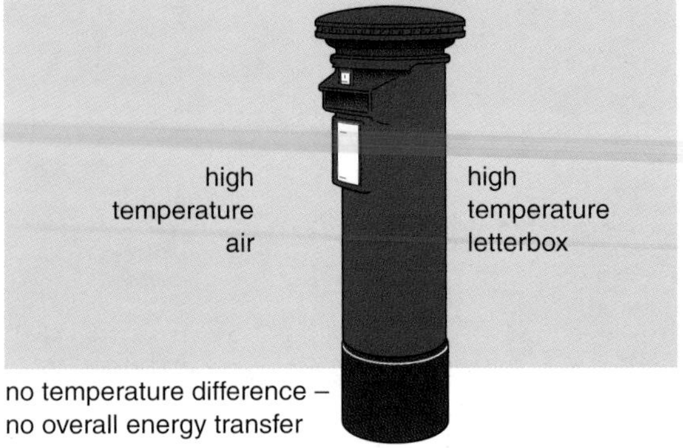

no temperature difference – no overall energy transfer

Figure 2 Energy transfers for a letterbox

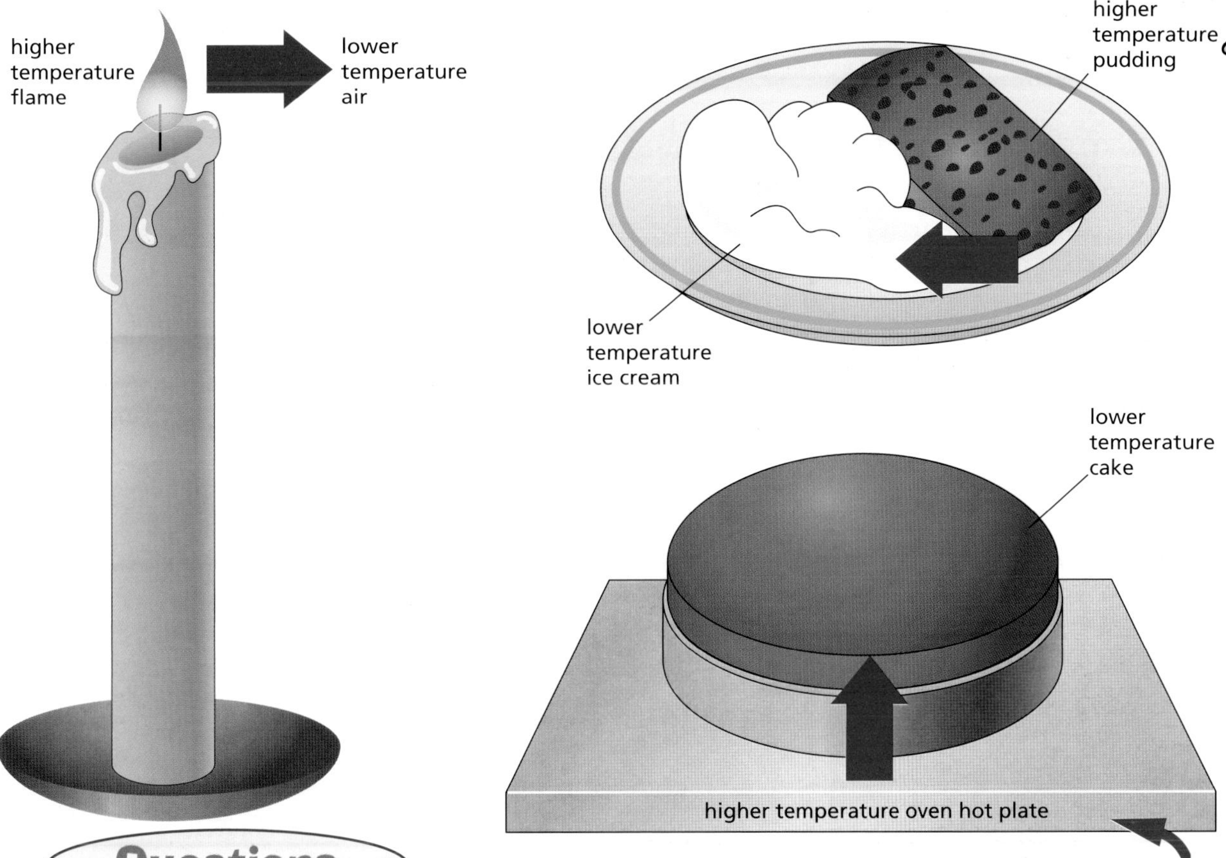

Figure 3 The arrows show overall energy transfer. When there's a temperature difference between the objects in contact, one gains energy while the other loses energy.

Questions

1 What would happen to the temperature of a letterbox when it snows if:

a) the snow was warmer than the letterbox was to start with?

b) the snow was colder than the letterbox was to start with?

2 a) When you run hot water and cold water into a bath, which water warms up and which water cools down?

b) What energy transfer has taken place?

3 Sketch energy transfer diagrams for:

a) an ice cube floating in a glass of lemonade;

b) an iceberg that floats from cold water into warmer water;

c) a pile of cold oven chips when you put them into a hot oven;

d) a bottle of warm milk that's just been moved from a warm room into a fridge.

Remember

Unscramble the words to complete the sentences below.

MET TRUE PEAR difference causes energy transfer. The GREENY transfer takes place from the object at HEHRIG temperature to the object at RE OWL temperature.

There is no overall energy transfer when the objects have the AS ME temperature.

Energy transfers and temperature

Energy from the Sun arrives at planets like Venus, Earth and Mars. The energy warms the planets' surfaces. Planets also transfer energy back out into space.

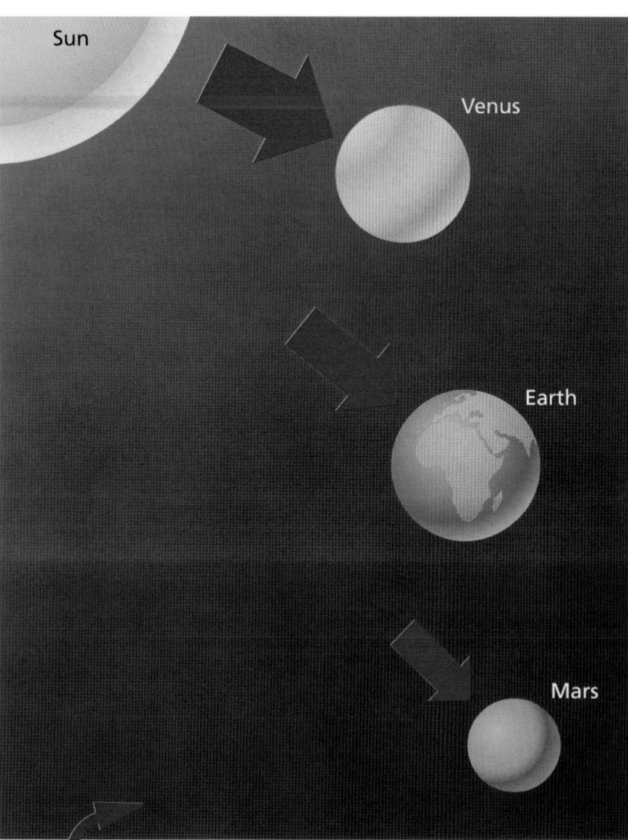

Figure 1 The light of the Sun not only warms the Earth, it also shines on other planets like Venus and Mars. Venus is closer to the Sun than we are, so energy from the Sun arrives more rapidly on Venus than it does on Earth. Mars is further from the Sun so energy that arrives from the Sun is less intense.

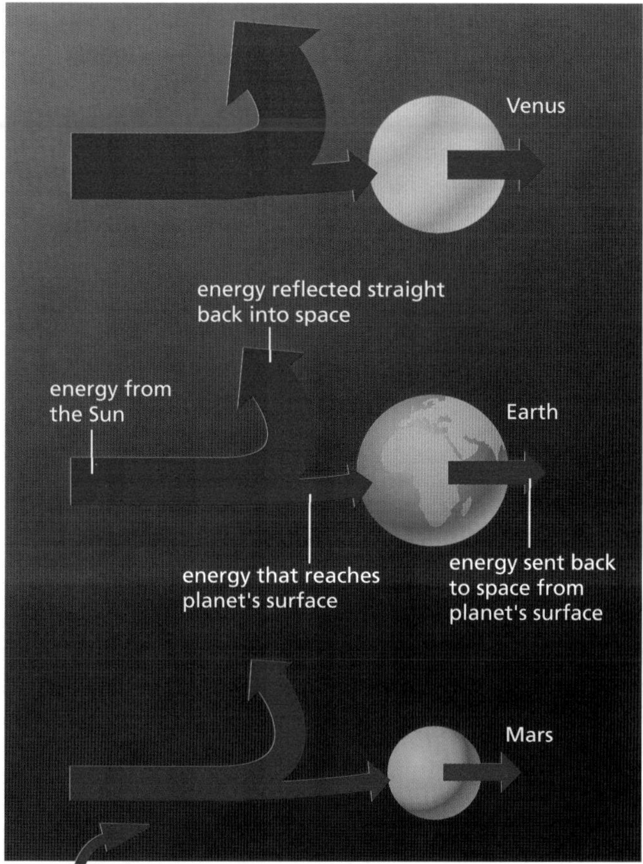

Figure 2 There are no living things on Venus or Mars. They are dead places. But Mars and Venus are like the Earth in some ways. Some of the energy that arrives at each planet is reflected straight back into space and some energy warms each planet's surface.

The Sun warms the surface of a planet. A warmed planet radiates energy out into space. Each of the planets is in **energy balance**. Energy arrives at the same rate as it leaves.

A hotter planet transfers energy back out to space faster than a cooler planet.

A planet that sends out energy faster than it receives it cools down. Or a planet could transfer energy out more slowly than it receives it until it warms up. The temperature of each planet settles to its own energy balance temperature.

This temperature doesn't change unless the atmosphere of the planet changes. On Earth, humans are changing the atmosphere. This makes it harder for energy to transfer back out to space. It disturbs the Earth's energy balance and could change the Earth's average temperature and cause **global climate change**.

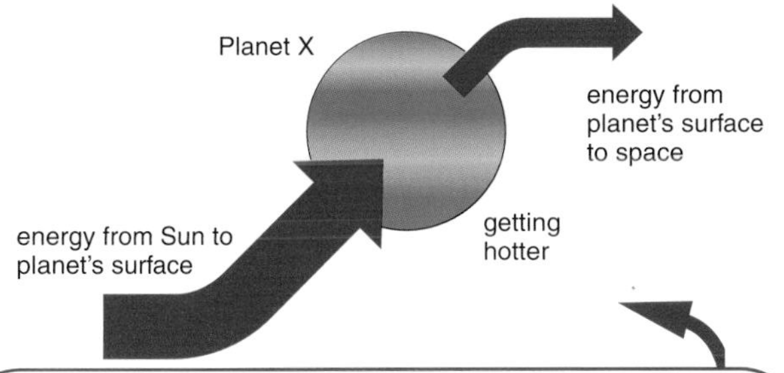

Figure 3 If a planet's surface receives more energy than it sends back into space, it gets hotter and hotter – its average temperature rises.

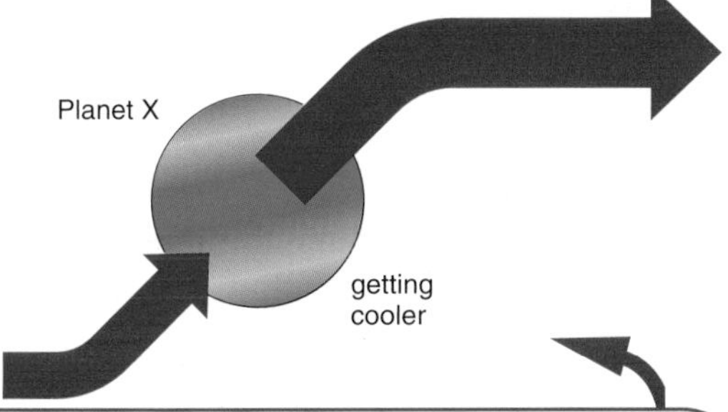

Figure 4 If a planet's surface sends energy out into space faster than it receives energy from the Sun, it becomes colder – its average temperature falls.

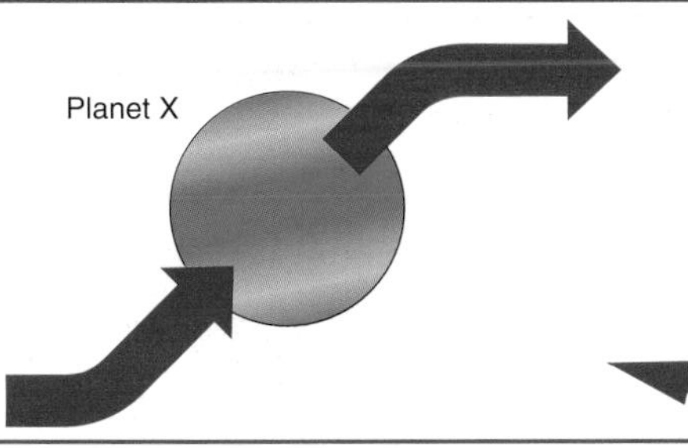

Figure 5 This planet has energy balance. Its temperature stays steady.

Figure 6 Tim Docherty is a climate scientist. He's trying to work out better ways to predict the changes that might be happening to the Earth's average temperature and its climate.

Questions

1 a) Which one of these planets is in energy balance?

b) What does energy balance mean?

c) What could cause a planet to lose its energy balance?

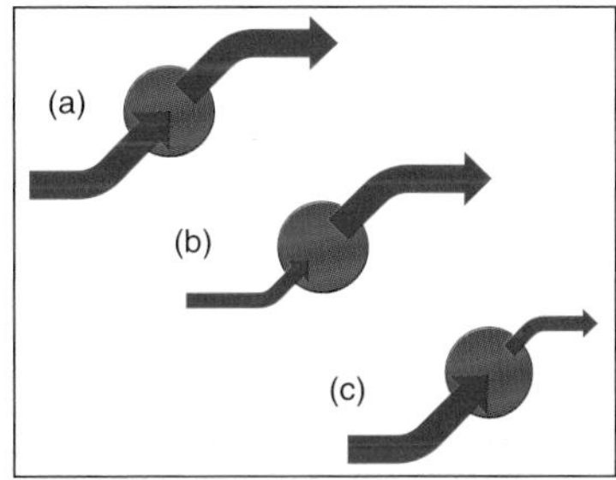

2 What will happen to the temperature of a planet if:

a) energy arrives at the planet faster than it leaves?

b) energy leaves faster than it arrives?

Remember

Use the following words to complete the passage below.

work out **Mars** **planets** **planet** **same** **Sun** **balance** **space** **temperature** **atmosphere** **global climate change**

Energy transfers out from the ___1___. Some energy reaches ___2___ like Venus, Earth and ___3___. The warmed planets send energy back out into ___4___. The amounts of energy they receive and the energy they send back out are the ___5___. They are in energy ___6___. Each ___7___ stays at a steady temperature. But if the ___8___ of a planet changes, then it could lose energy more slowly. This would cause the average ___9___ of the planet to rise. Scientists are trying to ___10___ how changes in our atmosphere could cause ___11___.

Warm bodies in cold places

Human bodies are usually warmer than their surroundings. They transfer energy into their surroundings. The energy must be replaced.

Jane Mitchell is a scientist who has worked at a research station in the Antarctic. She does research on the Earth's atmosphere, helping us to find out more about our planet.

Antarctica is a huge continent and almost all of it is covered in ice. Even in summer the weather is far too cold for snow to melt. In winter it's dark nearly all of the time, and the blizzards last for days.

Figure 1 Jane Mitchell at the Antarctic research station, finding out more about our world

Twenty people live and work at the research station. Fresh supplies have to be carried on sledges from a ship anchored 15 kilometres away.

When Jane went on trips outside the station, two things were really important – plenty of food and special warm clothing.

People have warm bodies. If your body temperature doesn't stay close to 37°C then you die. Even on a warm day, energy transfers out from your body into your surroundings. The bigger the difference between your body temperature and the temperature around you, the faster the energy flows away from your body. In Antarctica where the temperatures are very low, the energy can transfer out very quickly indeed. Good clothes provide **insulation**. Energy can only transfer out through them very slowly.

You can wear insulating clothing to slow down energy transfers from your body. You can also replace the energy that you lose. To replace energy you eat food.

Food carries a store of energy. The energy was stored in the food by plants, using the light of the Sun. Whenever Jane went on journeys into the cold world outside, she took plenty of food. There'd be lots of 'high energy' foods like rice, potato powder and sweet chocolate.

Figure 2 Energy stores can replace the energy that transfers out from a human body into the cold world outside.

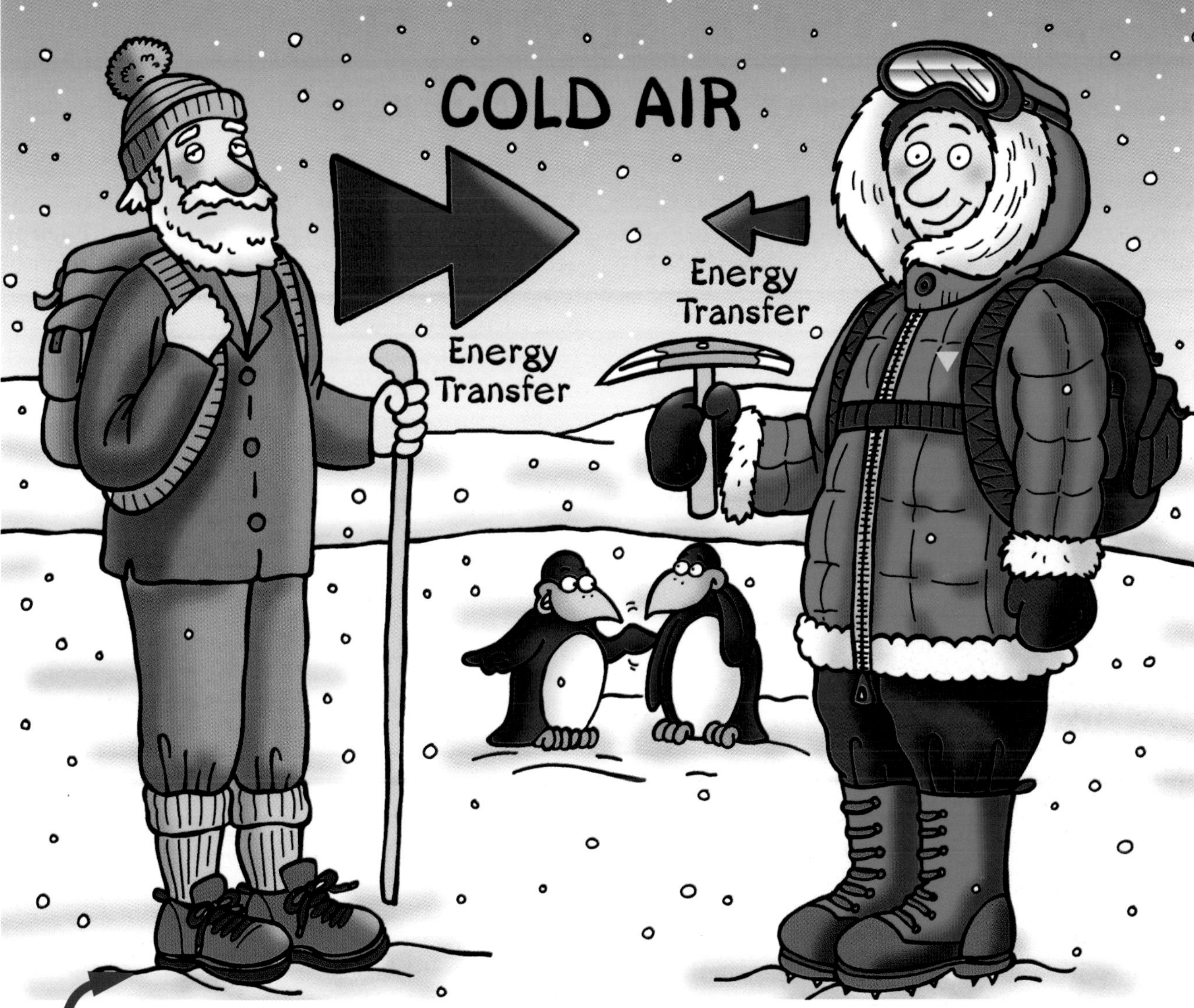

Figure 3 Early explorers, like the man on the left, had poor food and poor clothing, so their bodies couldn't cope with the cold. Modern scientists, like the person on the right, carry good energy stores, like chocolate, and wear clothing that insulates very well to reduce energy transfer.

Questions

1 What is the temperature of your body in °C?
2 What does 'insulation' mean?
3 Explain why you lose energy more quickly when swimming in the sea than when in a hot bath.
4 Can you explain why cold weather makes you hungry?

Remember

Complete the passage below using the following words.

warmer transfers insulate energy reduce temperature

We need food to supply our bodies with ___1___. Our bodies are almost always ___2___ than our surroundings. They are at a higher ___3___. In cold surroundings energy ___4___ out from our bodies very quickly. Clothes ___5___ us, to ___6___ the energy flow away from our bodies.

A closer look at energy transfer

Energy moves or transfers between different materials in different ways.

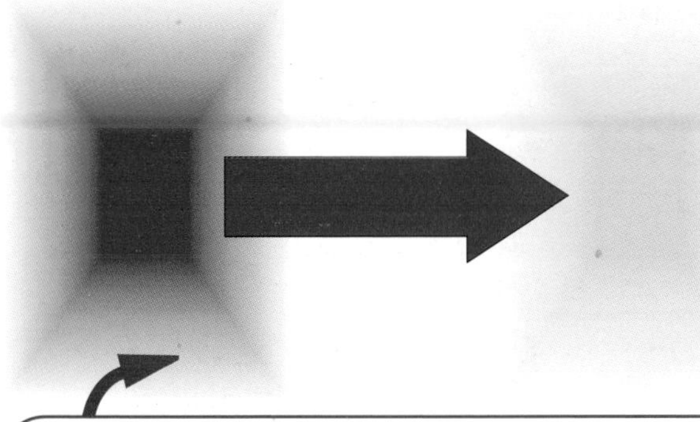

Figure 1 Energy transfers from hot to cold materials

Different energy transfers

Convection

One way to transfer energy from place to place is to actually move hot material from place to place. Hot water moves around central heating pipes to the radiators. It carries energy from the boiler. Most central heating systems need a pump to make the water move. But heated material sometimes moves naturally.

Figure 2 The air is hotter inside this balloon than the air outside it. The air in the balloon has **expanded**. Its particles are further apart than the particles in the air outside. This makes the hot air float in the surrounding cool air and it takes the whole balloon with it.

A hot air balloon provides an example of hot material floating naturally above cool material. The hot air carries its energy with it. It doesn't just happen inside balloons. In liquids like water, hot parts of the liquid rise above cooler parts of the liquid. Transfer of energy by natural movement of gas or liquid is called **convection**.

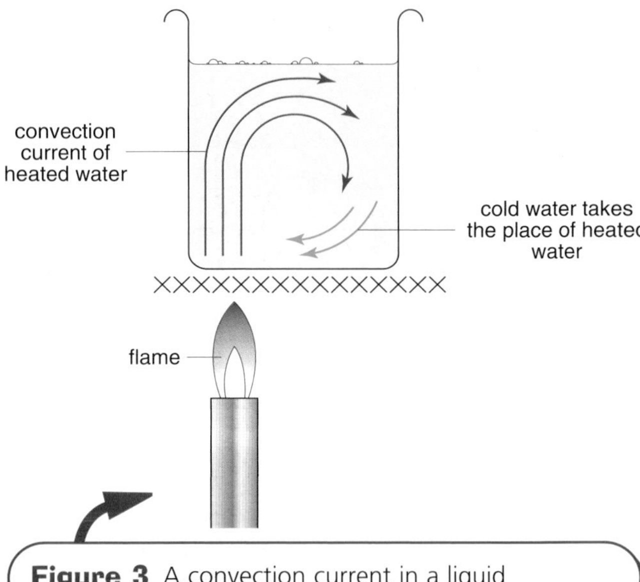

Figure 3 A convection current in a liquid

Evaporation

Have you had an injection recently? Do you remember the cold feeling when the liquid was rubbed on your skin to kill germs? The liquid **evaporated** quite quickly and when it did, it took energy away from your skin. The same thing happens when you sweat. The sweat evaporates into the air and transfers energy in the process. The faster the evaporation, the faster the energy transfers away from your skin.

Figure 4 Sweating and energy transfer

Conduction

Transfer of energy by colliding or interacting particles is called **conduction**. We know that materials are made of particles. In gases, the particles are far apart, but they still collide with each other. Fast particles with a lot of energy can bounce off other particles and transfer energy to them. Collisions between particles transfer energy. But because the particles are far apart in a gas, there aren't that many collisions. There aren't many opportunities for particles to interact. Gases are not very good at transferring energy by conduction.

In solids, the particles are close together and there are strong forces between them. Energy can transfer quickly from particle to particle. Solids are better than gases at conducting energy.

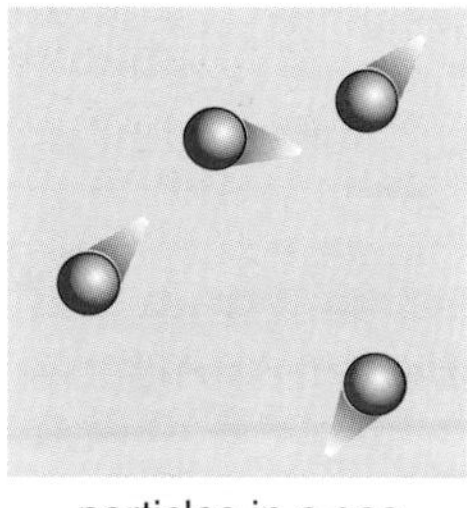

particles in a gas

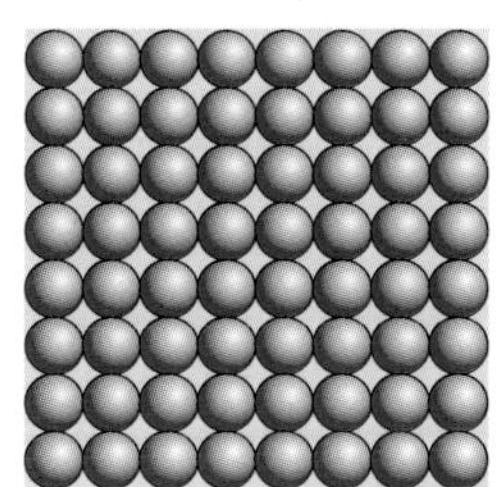

particles in a solid

Figure 5 In solids there are more opportunities for particles to interact.

Radiation

The filament inside a light bulb is so hot that it glows white. It radiates energy to its surroundings.

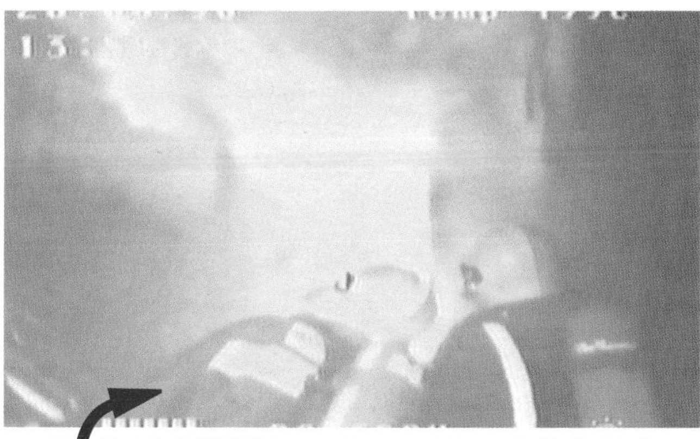

Figure 6 This image of firefighters was taken by an infra-red camera.

Much cooler objects than light bulbs also radiate energy. A table and a brick radiate energy, though only weakly. You radiate energy – more strongly than a brick but less strongly than a light bulb. Special **infra-red** cameras can 'see' this radiation. Rescue services use these cameras when they are trying to find people.

Questions

1 Explain why heating part of a liquid, as in Figure 3, makes the liquid start to move and causes a convection current.

2 Write down an idea about why sweating out of doors on a windy day cools you more than sweating indoors. Discuss your idea with other people.

3 You heat the bottom of a saucepan on a cooker. The liquid inside the saucepan gets hotter. How does the energy transfer through the saucepan?

4 Why don't people glow like light bulbs? Would this be an advantage or a disadvantage?

Remember

Use the words below to complete the sentences.

interact expands evaporating particles convection radiation conduction infra-red

When a material is heated it ____**1**____. This causes ____**2**____ currents.

An ____**3**____ liquid takes energy from part of its surroundings, such as skin.

In the process of ____**4**____, energy transfers between ____**5**____ when they collide or ____**6**____.

All bodies emit ____**7**____. For most everyday objects this is ____**8**____ radiation, but some are so hot that they glow visibly.

Paying the bill for warmth

Warm houses transfer energy into their cooler surroundings. The energy must be replaced. We use many different energy resources for this.

We can use energy resources to keep us warm in our houses. We can burn a gas fire or a coal fire. We can use heaters that run on electricity that's generated in power stations. Central heating might run on oil or natural gas or by using electricity. All of these energy resources cost money, and they all produce pollution.

Previous Bill Balance 0.00
Total Payments Received 0.00
Balance Brought Forward 0.00
Present Gas Charges 51.98
VAT on present charges @ 5% 2.59
Total 54.57

How your bill is calculated

METER READING PERIOD: 19 May 2003 to 31 May
ODP

Meter Serial Number	METER READINGS		GAS USED					
	Present	Previous	Calorific Value MJ/m3	100's Cubic Feet	Cubic Metres	kWh	kWh Cost	Charge £
0000730	4754 E	4734 E	38.20	20.45	57.88	614	1.165	7.15

Daily Standing Charge 12 days @ 7.26p per day 0.87

Payment slip

Figure 1 Most energy resources are expensive. To keep our houses warm takes megajoules of energy every week. Joules and megajoules are units of energy. A megajoule is a million joules.

Problem one: reducing the cost

In winter the air outside is cold, but we want the inside of our houses to be warm. The **temperature difference** makes energy transfer outwards rapidly. Energy flows through the walls, windows and roof. It's a natural process. It's a process we need to control as much as we can if we want to stay warm. For example, we can double glaze our windows, and we can put layers of fibre-glass wool in the loft. These materials act as thermal insulators.

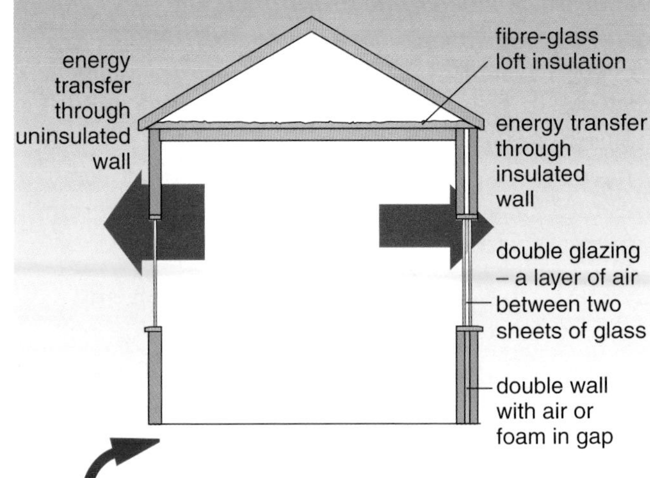

Figure 2 Thermal insulators are materials that reduce energy transfer processes.

Problem two: reducing pollution and saving fuel

Whether we burn fossil fuels at home or in power stations, the process pollutes the atmosphere.

Coal, oil and natural gas are fossil fuels. Sooner or later we'll use up all of the fossil fuels in the Earth.

Future generations could have very serious problems, caused by us. Fortunately, if it's not already too late, there are other energy resources.

Figure 3 Power stations like this release pollution into the atmosphere.

One possible answer to two problems

One energy resource that's becoming more and more important is solar energy. Solar panels generate electricity from the light of the Sun. They are a bit like the leaves on a plant. They soak up energy from the light.

Solar panel technologies are getting better and cheaper. In some parts of the world, people are already using solar panels for energy for their lives – for cooking, lighting and heating, and to run machinery.

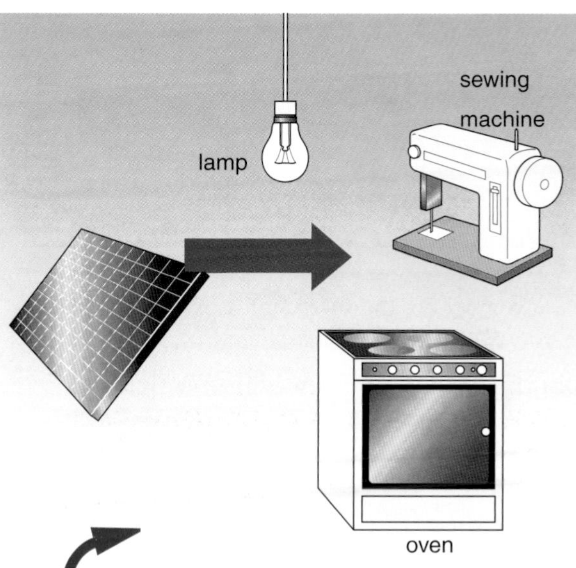

Figure 4 Solar energy can be used for lighting, cooking and running machinery.

Figure 5 A house of the future? It uses solar panels to generate its electricity. It's also very well insulated to reduce the rate of transfer of energy out into the surroundings. It doesn't use fossil fuels at all.

Perhaps sunlight will replace fossil fuels as a main direct source of energy. Once you have the solar panels and the circuits to go with them, sunshine doesn't cost anything. And it is a completely **renewable** fuel – it isn't going to run out.

Questions

1 Name one unit of energy.

2 Describe two ways of saving money on heating bills.

3 Explain the advantages of solar energy over other energy resources for heating. What are the disadvantages?

What is your opinion of how we should use energy resources in future? Write a letter about your opinions to your MP or local newspaper.

4 **a)** Name a renewable energy resource.

b) What does renewable mean?

Remember

Use the following words to complete the sentences below.

coal energy temperature resources oil insulation burn renewable natural gas differences

Temperature ___**1**___ cause energy transfer. The bigger the ___**2**___ difference, the faster the ___**3**___ transfer. We can control energy transfer by ___**4**___.

___**5**___ such as solar energy will not run out. Fossil fuels will run out, so we call them non-___**6**___. Fossil fuels, such as ___**7**___, ___**8**___ and ___**9**___ also produce pollution when we ___**10**___ them.

Closer

What makes sense for you?

These are some different versions of the same thing:

Water in the three states of matter – solid, liquid and gas

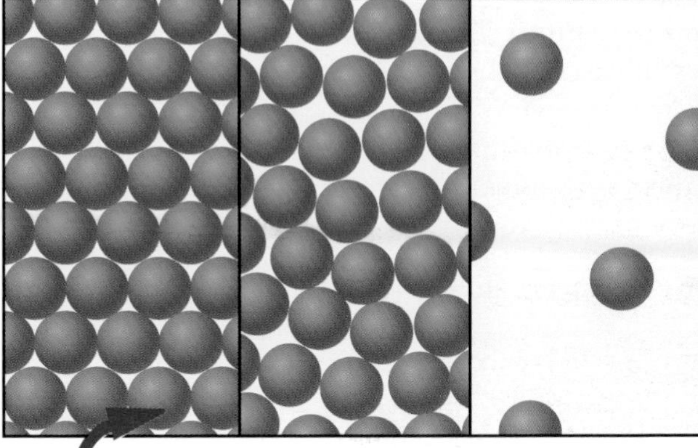

A particle model of the three states of matter

We can make diagrams showing particles as little balls. Alternatively we can pretend that the particles are like something we can easily picture, such as people at a carnival. We are only pretending, but if it helps us to image what goes on in real materials then it is useful. The balls and the carnival people are two different models of real materials.

One way to imagine the particles in the three states of matter – a 'people model'

Questions

1 Use the particle ball model. How does the motion of the tiny particles inside the material change when you:

- heat some water in a beaker with a Bunsen burner?
- mix hot water with cold water in your bath?
- heat an iron rod at one end?
- heat the bottom of a saucepan full of water?
- pour cold water onto very hot iron?

2 Now use the carnival people model to think about the same processes. Does this model match the particle ball model? Does it match what happens in the real world with real objects?

3 A model should help you to understand what happens with real objects. Which model works best for you, the particle ball model or the carnival people model? Explain why.

Respiration

Opener
Fit for life

Most people know if they are better suited to running longer, slower races or shorter faster ones. But is there any science behind this?

The oxygen test

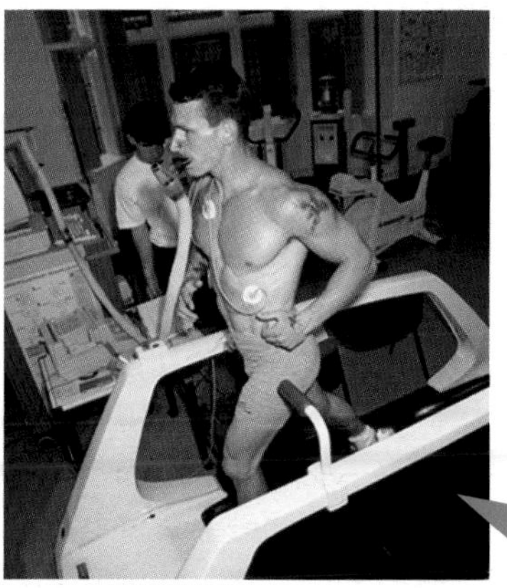

An athlete wearing an oxygen mask

How quickly you can transfer oxygen from your lungs to your muscles is important. If you are fast and efficient at doing this you are more likely to be a sprinter. Marathon runners need a constant supply of oxygen.

The muscle fibre test

- There are two types of muscle fibres, fast twitch and slow twitch. On average we have roughly half and half of these types of muscle fibres.
- Fast twitch fibres contract quickly and do not always need a ready supply of oxygen. Sprinters and high jumpers often have a high percentage of fast twitch muscle fibres.
- Slow twitch muscle fibres need oxygen and are slower to contract. Long distance and marathon runners have a high percentage of slow twitch fibres.

Darren Campbell, sprinter, and Dame Kelly Holmes, middle distance runner

Some facts about muscles and recovery

- Fast or explosive movements require more recovery time than slow movements.
- Fast twitch muscle fibres recover more quickly than slow twitch muscle fibres.
- Women generally need more recovery time than men.
- Older athletes generally need more recovery time than younger athletes.

Questions

For each question explain your answer fully.

1 If an athlete prefers running long races to short ones are they more likely to have a fast rate of oxygen transfer to the muscles or a slow one?

2 An athlete was found to have a fast twitch to slow twitch muscle fibre ratio of 4:1. Would you suggest that they are a long jumper or a 1500 m runner?

3 In the triathlon, competitors have to swim for 1.5 km, then cycle for 40 km and finally run for 10 km, straight after one another. Would triathletes benefit more from slow twitch or fast twitch muscle fibres?

4.1 How do cells use food?

Glucose is our body's main 'fuel'. We use it to release energy in a process called respiration.

Figure 1 Exercising muscles need more energy.

Figure 2 Glucose is our main fuel for energy release.

On supermarket shelves you can see many high-energy foods and drinks. People like them if they are playing energetic sports or even if they are having a busy day and need a bit of extra get up and go. Energy is needed for all the reactions that are happening in your body. New cells need to be made for growth. Old cells need to be replaced. Chemicals have to be made and moved from one place to another. Your body temperature has to be kept normal. The more we exercise, the more energy our muscles need to be able to contract. If we are very ill and cannot eat, then we may need to be 'fed' by putting a solution of glucose straight into our bloodstream.

Glucose is a high-energy chemical and is our main fuel. The energy released from it is transferred and used in different ways in the body. But how does this happen? Glucose doesn't provide energy in a tube of tablets in your pocket. The energy is locked into the tablet and has to be released.

Small glucose molecules are produced when carbohydrate (see page 8) from foods like bread and cereal is **digested**, or broken up, by **enzymes** in the small intestine. Energy is released from glucose in the cells in our bodies in much the same way as energy is released from other fuels. Fortunately for us, however, glucose does not catch fire! If there is a plentiful supply of oxygen, energy is released from glucose and carbon dioxide is produced. This reaction is called **respiration**. A simple equation for the reaction is shown below. When it happens in our cells it is called **cellular respiration**.

Although respiration can be shown by one equation, the breakdown of glucose in cells really takes place in a series of small steps. Each step is made possible by the action of enzymes. In all tissues in the body the overall reaction uses the glucose produced by digestion of food molecules to release energy.

glucose + oxygen → carbon dioxide + water + ENERGY TRANSFER

Isotonic sports drinks

Isotonic sports drinks are specially made to be in balance with your body's fluid. These drinks have carefully selected levels of glucose and salts to help the absorption of fluid from the intestine into the bloodstream. This is how we quickly replace the fluids lost in sweat, and the energy transferred in exercise.

The body needs a constant supply of energy:

- to maintain body temperature – because we are warm-blooded;
- to maintain basic life processes such as breathing, circulation of blood, digestion, brain activity, blinking etc..

Even when a person is at complete rest, energy is still needed. This minimum energy need is often referred to as the resting **metabolic rate**. If we move about, the energy we need increases. For example:

- sleeping — needs 1 unit of energy
- sitting in school — needs 2 units
- a brisk walk — needs 4 units
- and jogging — needs 7 units

To release energy, food needs to be digested to turn the carbohydrate into glucose. But isotonic drinks already contain glucose so need no digestion. They can go straight from the stomach into the small intestine. The glucose and salts easily cross the wall of the intestine and into the bloodstream.

The human body stores only small amounts of glucose. They are stored in the liver as **glycogen**. When you exercise, this is broken down and added to the glucose in your blood to release energy for the working muscles. Soon your body runs low on energy. After exercise, few people feel like eating a large meal rich in starchy carbohydrate, but they are able to drink isotonic drinks, which not only supply fluid but give a boost of glucose energy.

Stop and think!

In everyday language, the word 'respiration' is used differently. Dictionaries will tell you that to respire is to breathe in and out. In science, however, respire means to release energy from glucose in cells. What other words are there that are similar to respire that mean 'to breathe in' and 'to breathe out'?

Questions

1. Name three things that our body does that require energy.
2. Glucose is our main energy-giving fuel. What energy-giving fuel does a car use?
3. Write a simple word equation to show what happens when a car burns its fuel.
4. What do the following terms mean?
   a) Respiration
   b) Cellular respiration
5. How might the energy trapped in a glucose tablet be released into your body? (*Hint*: Think about the work you have done on food and digestion!)

Remember

Complete the sentences using the words given below. Each word may be used more than once.

food glucose respiration
carbon dioxide energy transfer
water oxygen

Staying alive needs ___1___. Our main fuel, ___2___, comes from the ___3___ we eat.

In living cells energy is released when ___4___ reacts with ___5___ from the air we breathe. At the same time waste ___6___ and ___7___ are produced. This chemical reaction is called ___8___ and can be represented by the equation shown below.

___9___ + ___10___ → ___11___ + ___12___ + ___13___

How do oxygen and glucose get to our cells?

Blood is the main transport system for our body, carrying oxygen, carbon dioxide and digested food.

You first become aware of blood when you cut your finger or graze your knee. Most of us know we have and need blood but many people are not very sure of why we need it.

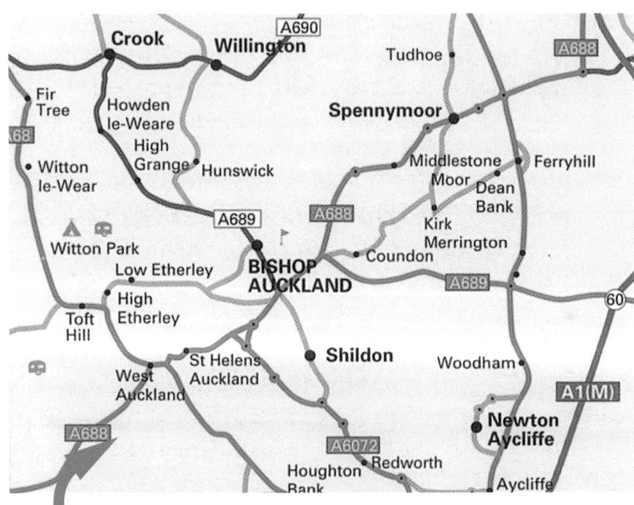

Figure 1 Cars and lorries move around roads to every part of the country.

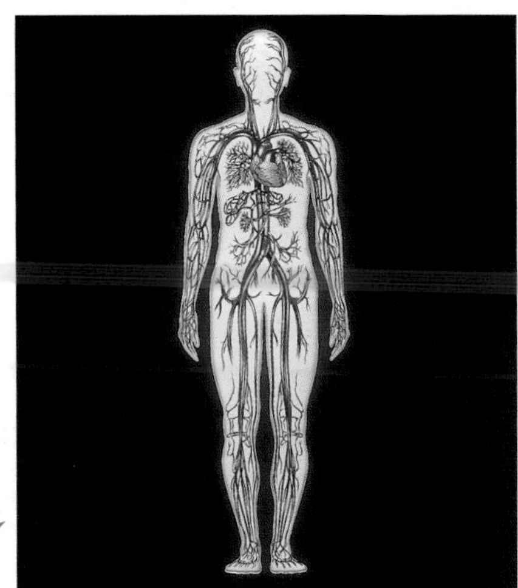

Figure 2 Blood moves in tubes to every part of your body.

Lorries loaded with things we take for granted every day are moved from one end of the country to the other. They deliver essential goods to all our towns, cities and villages. Blood is the main transport system in our body. Oxygen and other substances vital for our well being, like glucose, are transported around our body by blood. Respiration takes place in every cell and so blood has to reach all of them delivering glucose and oxygen.

Blood appears to be a thick red liquid but in fact it contains different types of cells and a pale yellow liquid called **plasma**. The **red blood cells** are the ones that transport oxygen. There are about 5000 million red blood cells in every 1 cm^3 of blood. They contain a dark red substance called **haemoglobin**. As blood goes through the lungs, haemoglobin picks up oxygen from the air we have breathed in. This oxygen is then released where it is needed as blood passes through tissues like muscles and the gut.

Figure 3 This pack contains blood given by a donor. Notice that it has begun to separate out into yellow plasma and a red, thicker layer containing cells.

In diagrams, blood containing high levels of oxygen is coloured red and blood containing low levels of oxygen is coloured blue. Check this in the diagram opposite.

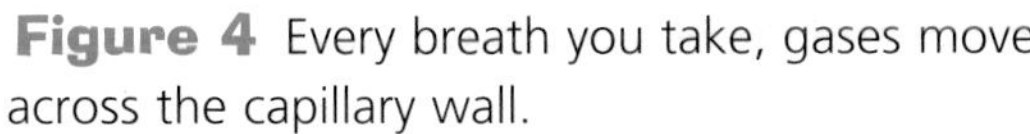

Figure 4 Every breath you take, gases move across the capillary wall.

Figure 4 shows diffusion occurring in the lungs. In the lungs there is a high concentration of oxygen from the air breathed in, so oxygen moves from the lungs into the blood where the concentration of oxygen is lower. Blood going to the lungs from the body tissues contains a higher concentration of waste carbon dioxide than the air breathed in, so carbon dioxide moves from the blood to the lungs to be breathed out. In muscles, the concentration effect makes these gases move the other way. Oxygen moves from the blood capillaries to muscle cells and carbon dioxide moves from muscle cells to the blood.

Blood also carries the glucose needed for respiration. As blood flows around the small intestine, digested food substances, like glucose, move into the blood. Glucose is then transported to respiring cells and moves into them. As blood **circulates**, or moves around the body, all the tissues will have access to a ready supply of oxygen and glucose.

Blood is mainly water and so it is very good at dissolving substances. Waste carbon dioxide is produced during respiration. This gas passes from the tissues into the blood where it dissolves in the plasma. The dissolved carbon dioxide is carried by blood to the lungs where it is released and breathed out.

Questions

1. Red blood cells and plasma are two of the parts of our blood. Think back to work you did last year. What other things do we find in our blood?
2. Diabetics have to be careful about the amount of glucose they have in their diet. They have to check their blood sugar level several times during the day. Why can't they check their sugar levels just once a day?
3. When would you expect a normal person's blood sugar level to go up a little, go up a lot, fall a little or fall a lot?
   - **a)** after eating a light snack mid morning;
   - **b)** after eating a normal school lunch of pizza, chips and a non-diet fizzy drink;
   - **c)** after playing a school football/netball match;
   - **d)** after a friend's birthday party with lots of snacks and drinks;
   - **e)** when walking home after a party.

Remember

Copy the following into your exercise book:

Blood is pumped around the body by the heart. Oxygen and glucose are delivered to the cells and the waste gas carbon dioxide is taken away from the cells back to the lungs where it is breathed out. Remember, however, that blood does much more than just this job and carries many chemicals around our body.

How does blood get around?

Blood is pumped around the body by the heart through a system of blood vessels.

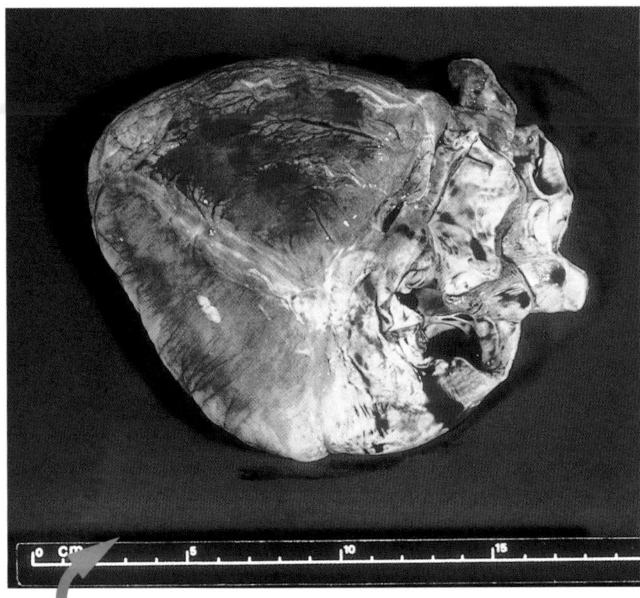

Figure 1 This is what a heart looks like. It's one of the hardest working muscles in your body and so needs a good blood supply of its own.

In 1628, an English doctor called William Harvey showed, using experiments and observations, that blood moves constantly around the body in one direction.

Blood has to be moved to and from every part of your body and it is the **heart** that makes this possible. The heart walls are made from muscle that contracts, or beats, all the time. It squeezes or pumps blood through tubes called **blood vessels** from the heart and back again. You can tell how hard your heart is working by measuring your **pulse**.

There are three main types of blood vessels: **arteries**, **veins** and **capillaries**.

The heart has two pumps that work together. One side pumps blood to the lungs, the other side pumps blood to the other tissues.

Blood is pumped through the arteries, away from the heart, to the tissues. In the tissues, the arteries get narrower and narrower until they form a network of capillaries. Capillaries have thin walls and pass very close to cells. Because of the short distance between the capillaries and the cells, substances can move easily between the blood in the capillaries and cells in the tissues. After moving through tissues, blood moves more slowly through veins back to the heart.

Substances tend to move or **diffuse** from places where there is a high concentration of the substance to places where there is a lower concentration.

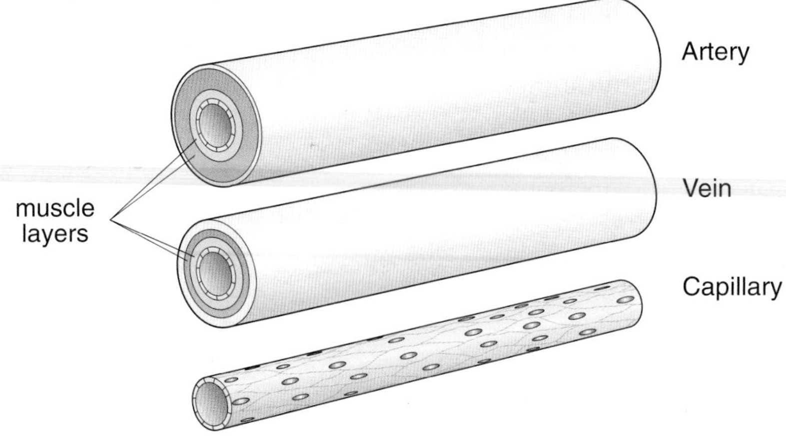

Figure 2 Arteries have thick walls and take blood away from the heart. Veins have thinner walls and take blood back to the heart. Capillaries are tubes with very thin walls. They join arteries to veins.

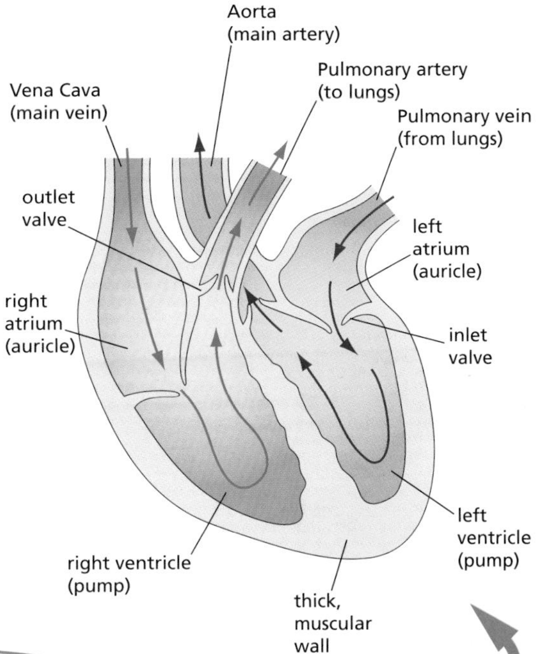

Figure 3 The structure of the heart

Questions

1 In 2AD, a doctor called Galen suggested that blood in arteries ebbed and flowed, like tides in the sea. Write a letter to him, including diagrams, to explain how blood circulates around the body.

2 The heart muscle has its own blood supply through arteries called coronary arteries.

a) Why do you think the heart needs a plentiful supply of oxygen?

b) What do you think would happen if the coronary arteries were blocked?

c) Heart muscle is the same as any other muscle. What gas moves

i) from the blood capillaries to heart muscle?

ii) from the heart muscle to the blood capillaries?

3 Complete this table

Arteries	Veins
	Thin walls for low pressure blood
Carry blood away from the heart	
Carry lots of oxygen	

Remember

A network of arteries carry blood away from the heart and a network of veins carry the blood back to the heart. The capillaries allow the blood to flow through all the tissues and connect the arteries to the veins. The capillaries allow the transfer of substances to and from the cells.

Copy and complete the sentences below choosing from the following words

arteries capillaries heart blood vessels veins

Blood moves around in a system of tubes called ______**1**______.

The ______**2**______ pumps blood around your body. Oxygen-rich blood moves away from your heart in tubes called ___**3**___. Blood containing waste carbon dioxide moves back to your heart in ___**4**___. Thin tubes called ___**5**___ join arteries to veins.

How do the lungs work?

We have to breathe to live. The rate at which we breathe depends on how active we are at the time.

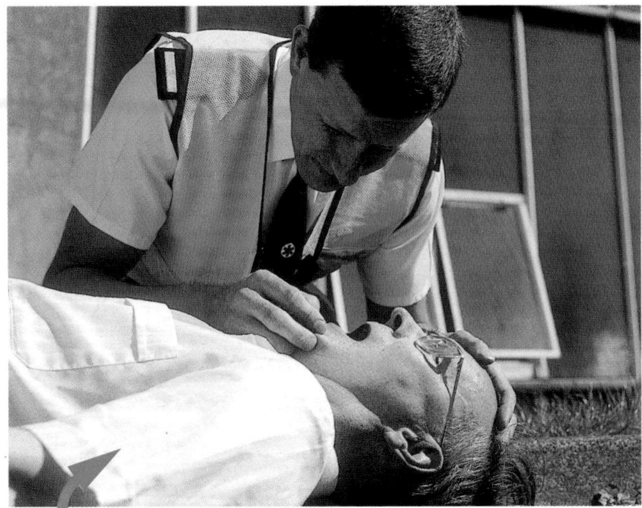

Figure 1 This person is being given mouth-to-mouth resuscitation because he has stopped breathing.

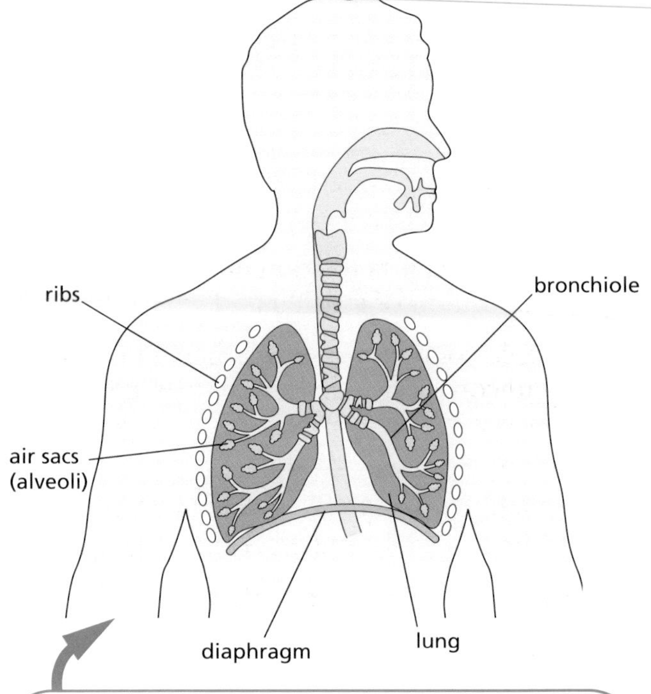

Figure 2 This shows how air passes through your nose down into the deepest part of your lungs.

Most of the time we are unaware of our breathing. It's only when we are 'out of breath' that it becomes an issue. Healthy people breathe faster and deeper when they are exercising in some way, maybe playing an energetic sport.

As you read this page you are probably breathing in about a mugful of air per breath. After an energetic aerobic session this could go up 10 times to 2.5 litres of air per breath. The amount of air breathed in and out depends on what we are doing. The more active we are, the more oxygen we need. To meet this need, we breathe faster and take more air in every breath so that more oxygen reaches deep into the lungs.

We have to breathe in and out to stay alive. Air is drawn in through your nose and mouth, and then down air passages into two **lungs**, one on each side of your body. Figure 2 shows that air goes down a wide tube called the **trachea** which splits into two parts called the **bronchi**, one bronchus for each lung. The bronchi divide into many smaller tubes called **bronchioles**. The bronchioles end in millions of tiny air sacs called **alveoli** (single: **alveolus**). Alveoli are like tiny, very thin, damp balloons at the end of each of the bronchioles. The surface area of all the alveoli added together is very large. If they were spread out flat they would cover a very large area – about the size of a tennis court. Blood flows round the alveoli in a network of fine capillaries.

	Oxygen	Nitrogen	Carbon dioxide	Other gases
Air breathed in (inhaled air) %	21	78	0.04	0.96
Air breathed out (exhaled air) %	17	78	4	0.96

Table 1 The composition of air

Plenty of gas can move between the capillaries and the alveoli because the alveoli …

- can hold large amounts of air;
- have a large surface area;
- have very thin walls;
- have a good blood supply.

Questions

1 Draw a large labelled and coloured diagram to show what happens inside your alveoli.

2 Draw pie charts to compare the composition of inhaled and exhaled air.

3 People sometimes hold a small mirror to an unconscious person's nose and mouth to see if they are breathing. How does this work?

4 Roughly how big is the total surface area of the alveoli in one person's lungs?

5 When you have a lung infection, the alveoli become inflamed. Explain why this makes breathing more difficult.

Oxygen is used in tissues, like muscles and the gut, for **respiration**. This means that blood flowing away from the tissues to the lungs contains low levels of oxygen. Blood moving to the lungs and into the capillaries surrounding the alveoli contains less oxygen than the air drawn into the lungs so oxygen tends to pass from air to the blood by diffusion.

Blood flowing into the alveoli contains carbon dioxide, the waste product from respiration. A very small amount of carbon dioxide is present in the air breathed in (see Table 1) so carbon dioxide tends to diffuse from the blood to the air. It then leaves the body when the air is breathed out.

Remember

Make a flow diagram showing the pathway of an oxygen molecule from the air to an alveolus. Use the words:

bronchus nose trachea alveoli bronchiole

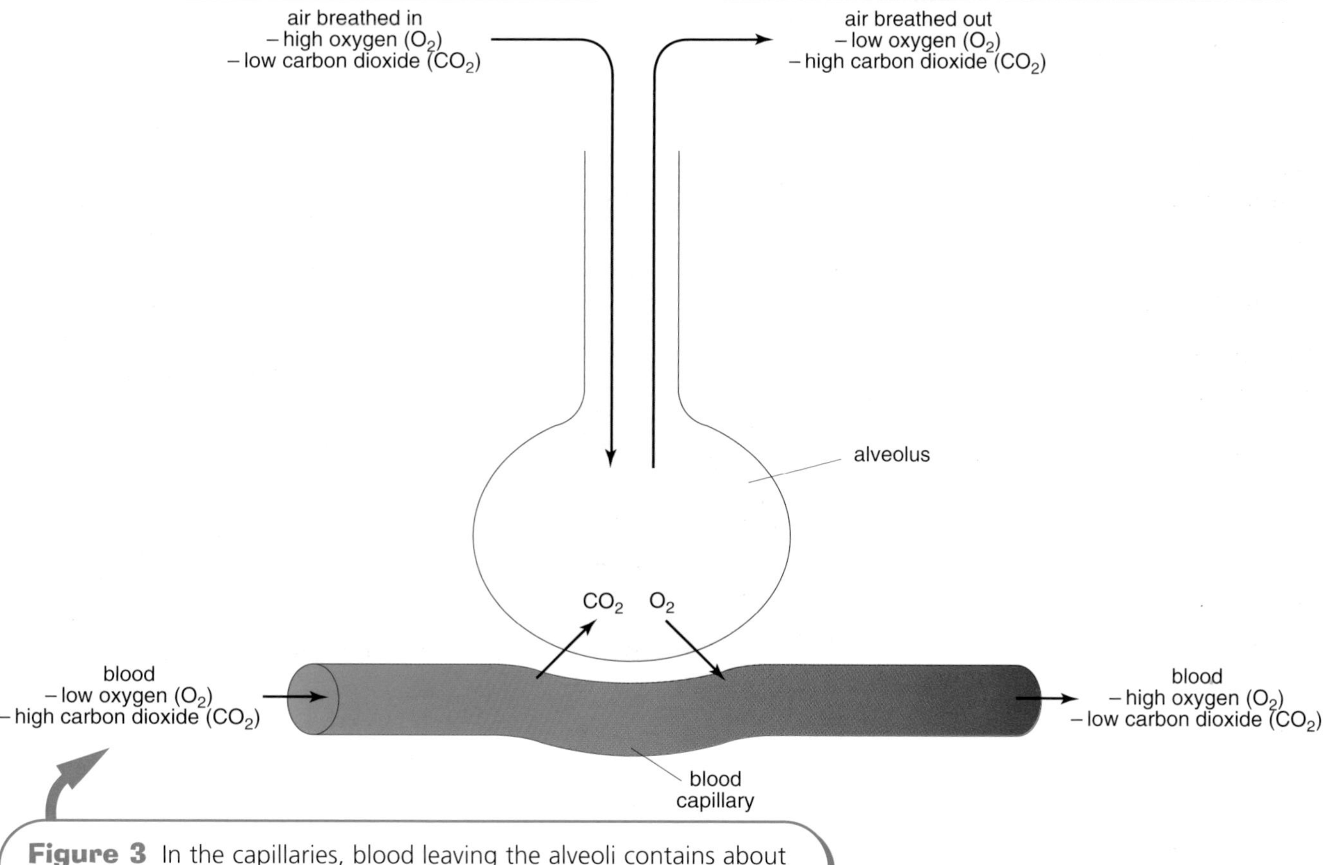

Figure 3 In the capillaries, blood leaving the alveoli contains about the same amount of oxygen and carbon dioxide as the air breathed in.

4.5 Getting enough oxygen

There are two types of respiration: aerobic and anaerobic. Anaerobic respiration occurs when the tissues can't get enough oxygen. Aerobic literally means 'with oxygen' and anaerobic means 'without oxygen'.

Not getting enough oxygen can have some very serious effects. Fit people climbing high mountain ranges like the Himalayas can become exhausted, unwilling to do anything energetic and also confused. High above sea level, the oxygen content of the air is much lower than in the air around you now. So although their lungs are perfectly healthy, climbers can't breathe in enough oxygen to meet their needs.

Figure 1 Inhalers deliver liquid droplets of medicine to widen air passages by relaxing the muscle wall.

People who suffer from **asthma** can become 'short of breath'. They often have to use an **inhaler**. Muscles in the air passages sometimes contract, making the tubes much narrower. This can be caused by stress, fear or allergies to pollen or house dust, for example. The substance in the inhaler relaxes the muscles, opens up the air passages and allows the person to breathe freely again.

Sometimes air passages get infected, causing **bronchitis**. People with bronchitis find it difficult to breathe and cough a lot. Their bronchial tubes are inflamed and lined with a sticky substance called **mucus**. Trying to cough up mucus can break down the thin walls of the alveoli. If this continues, permanent damage to the lungs, called **emphysema**, can occur. Breathing in dust can also cause emphysema. Inhaled dust builds up on the lining of air passages causing irritation and coughing.

Figure 2 People with severe lung damage need to breathe air enriched with oxygen.

Damaged lungs means less surface area for gas exchange. The oxygen supply is cut down and carbon dioxide builds up in the tissues. People with emphysema find even simple actions like getting dressed exhausting.

Plenty of oxygen

For healthy people there is enough oxygen in the air around us to keep us going. Oxygen from air breathed in reacts with glucose from our food releasing the energy for all the activities we need to stay alive. In cells, glucose and oxygen react together in the very complicated series of steps called **aerobic respiration**.

If we take strenuous exercise, more energy must be released to make our muscles contract. As respiration increases, more oxygen is needed. To meet this demand we breathe faster and deeper. More oxygen moves into the blood from the lungs and so the heart has to work harder to move this increased supply to the muscles. Usually the heart pumps about 10 litres of blood per minute around the body. During activity, this can increase to about 30 litres. You have probably measured your pulse rate during and after exercise and know that the heart rate can rise from around 60 beats per minute to around 200 beats per minute during exercise. At the same time, the heart nearly doubles the amount of blood pumped out at each beat.

Without oxygen

Sometimes not enough oxygen reaches tissues like muscles. This can happen to a sprinter

glucose → lactic acid + ENERGY TRANSFER

during a 100 m race. It can also happen to anyone during an exhausting activity. In the absence of oxygen, glucose is broken down in a different way, releasing energy and producing a substance called **lactic acid**. If lactic acid builds up, you get painful muscle pains called **cramps** and your muscles don't work properly.

Respiring without oxygen is called **anaerobic respiration**.

Plants and animals

Other living things respire in the same way as we do. When oxygen is available, they respire aerobically, producing carbon dioxide and water and releasing energy from their food as described earlier.

Animals eat plants and sometimes other animals. Plants make their own glucose but respire in the same way as animals. The energy released from respiration in plants is used to draw substances in through the roots and move them around the plant. Energy is also used for growth and movement.

Questions

1 Draw a poster to explain to a junior school pupil what happens to them when they have bronchitis and can't breathe properly.

2 If you run fast for a few seconds during a football game, you don't breathe because of the effort you make. Explain how this can lead to cramp in the muscles.

3 'Aerobics' is called that because the exercises are specially designed to have a steady pace that enables people to breathe properly. Design a simple leaflet to tell people what happens to their heart rate, to their breathing, in their muscles and in their heart during aerobics. Explain also why it is essential to breathe properly during the exercises.

Remember

Copy and complete the sentences below, choosing from the following words:

more faster more glucose deeper increases energy

During strenuous exercise, ____1____ oxygen is needed to react with ____2____ to release ____3____ to make our muscles work efficiently. There is ____4____ carbon dioxide to be removed. To meet these needs, our breathing rate becomes ____5____ and ____6____. At the same time the heart rate ____7____.

Closer

Climbing Everest

Mount Everest was first conquered on the morning of 29 May 1953 by Edmund Hilary and Tenzing Norgay.

Everest is 8850 m high and apart from having to bear the cold, climbers also need to take oxygen because breathing is difficult.

People can suffer altitude sickness if they climb high mountains, so they need to take special equipment and medication to help them.

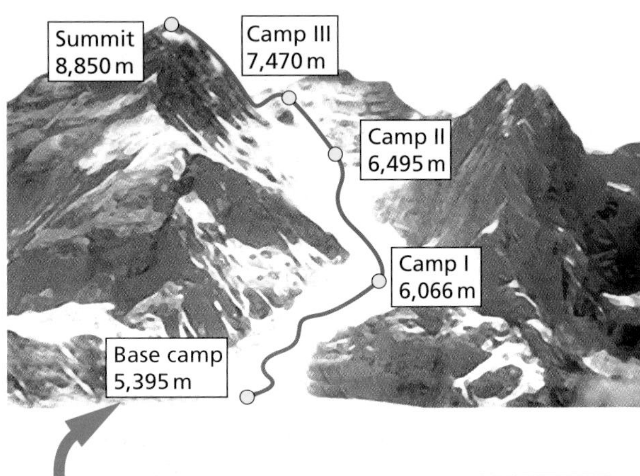

A climbing route on a mountain

Some facts about altitude sickness:

1 At sea level the air is 21% oxygen and 78% nitrogen. The air pressure at sea level means that air is helped into our lungs when we breathe;

2 Most people can climb to about 2500 m with no altitude problems, even though air pressure drops as you go higher;

3 At over 3000 m the drop in air pressure means that most people will have some altitude sickness. It starts about one to two days after reaching this height and lasts for up to three days.

The symptoms are headaches, dizziness, shortness of breath, loss of appetite and sickness.

1 At 3600 m, the air pressure will have dropped so much that although there is the same concentration of oxygen in the air, there is less air and we find it more difficult to get the oxygen into our lungs and our bloodstream. The air pressure is 40% less than at sea level so with each breath you get 40% less oxygen.

2 The higher you go, the more sickness, dizziness and shortness of breath you have. You also begin to lose co-ordination making walking more difficult.

3 If you climb too high too quickly you can suffer from fluid leaking into either the lungs or the brain. This can result in coughing up white, watery, frothy fluid.

4 The lack of oxygen can lead to confusion, disorientation, loss of memory, hallucinations, coma and finally death.

Questions

1 Nitrogen and oxygen make up 99% of the air that we breathe. What makes up most of the other 1%?

2 What would the percentage of nitrogen be at 3600 m?

3 The base camp at Everest is at about 5395 m. What symptoms of altitude sickness might climbers get here?

4 Apart from the lack of oxygen, what other problems will climbers have that could affect how their body functions?

5 Why do routes up Everest have a number of camps along the way?

Reactions and mixtures

Opener
Elements and compounds

Making materials is like making sandwich fillings, some combinations go together well to make a good material:

- Cheese and pickle
- Peanut butter and jam
- Chicken tikka

But other combinations don't work at all:

- Cheese and jam
- Peanut butter and pickle

Some combinations are materials that are easy to separate:

- Ham and cheese
- Chicken salad

But the best are materials that join well and cannot be easily separated, these are like compounds:

- Egg mayonnaise
- Banana and sugar
- Coronation chicken

Compounds often have better properties than the elements from which they are made.

Elements contain only one type of atom. Compounds are substances made from different types of atoms joined together. When compounds are made, the properties of the elements are changed to make a useful material.

For example:

Corrosive gas (Oxygen) + Explosive gas (Hydrogen) → Liquid that keeps us alive (Water/hydrogen oxide)

Reactive metal (Magnesium) + Corrosive gas (Oxygen) → Substance that cures indigestion (Milk of magnesia/magnesium oxide)

Poisonous gas (Chlorine) + Explosive gas (Hydrogen) → Substance that breaks down food in the stomach (Hydrochloric acid)

Activity

1 Look at the copy of the Periodic Table on page 151.

Make a list of ten elements that are used to make objects without having to be changed, e.g. gold is used for necklaces.

Write down the use in the list as well.

2 Look at the Periodic Table again and find five pairs of elements that you know join together to make compounds. Write down the name of the compounds. Find out what use these compounds have. For example H_2O, CO_2, NaCl, CH_4.

5.1 Pure thoughts

Pure substances contain only one sort of particle. Mixtures can be separated by various scientific methods.

Scientists have lots of problems with the word '**pure**'.

To most people a pure substance means one that contains no harmful substances, such as pure orange juice, or pure Devon butter.

Typical composition – mg/litre

Calcium	35.0	Sulphate	6.0
Magnesium	15.0	Nitrate	1.5
Sodium	12.0	Fluoride	<0.2
Potassium	1.3	Iron	<0.03
Bicarbonate	179.0	Aluminium	<0.005
Chloride	10.0		

Table 1 Ingredients found in a bottle of pure mountain spring water

Look at the ingredients label for pure mountain spring water in Table 1. You would expect it to have nothing but water in it – but it has! It contains substances that have dissolved in the water as it flowed through the mountain rock. It's nearly pure water, but there are other particles in the mixture as well as water particles.

In science, pure means containing only one type of particle.

These are pure substances:

- pure water – contains only water particles
- copper metal – contains only copper particles
- sugar crystals – contain only sugar particles
- oxygen gas – contains only oxygen particles

Really pure water is called **distilled water**. This water has been evaporated and condensed, leaving all the dissolved substances behind. When the distilled water is left to stand, oxygen from the air dissolves in it and it becomes a solution again. All solutions are mixtures because they contain a solute and a solvent.

Questions

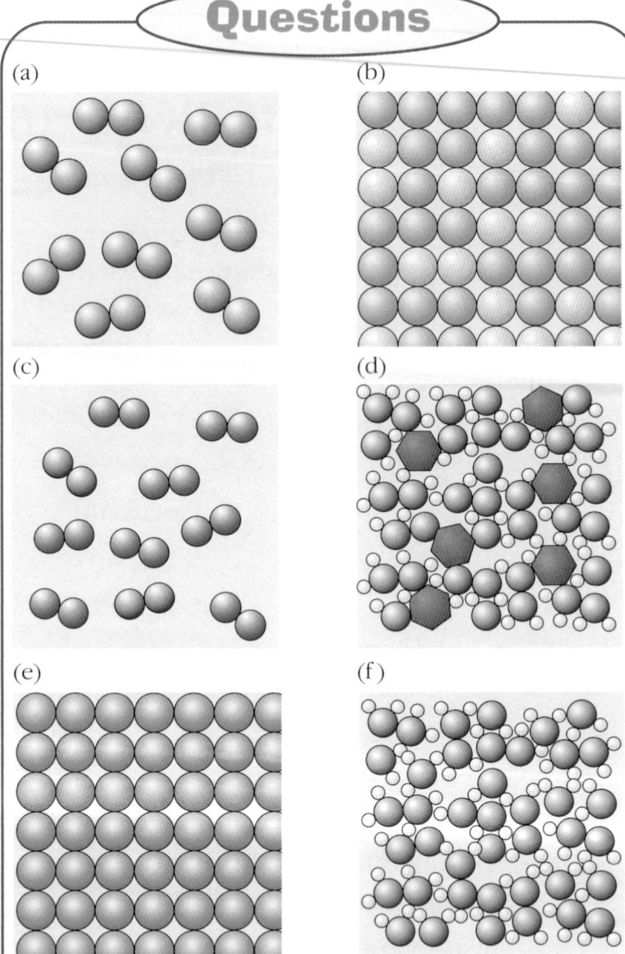

Look at the six boxes in the diagram above.

1. Which two are gases?
2. Which is pure oxygen?
3. Which is air (oxygen and other gases mixed)?
4. Which two are liquids?
5. Which is pure water and which is sugar dissolved in water?
6. Draw a diagram to show the particles in pure solid sugar.
7. Which two diagrams show solid materials?
8. One is pure copper metal, the other is brass – a mixture of copper and zinc metals. Which is pure copper and which is brass?
9. Draw a diagram to show what the particles in pure zinc metal would be like.

In real life we use very few really pure substances. Most materials have better properties if they are a mixture. Mixtures of metals are called **alloys**. These have more useful properties than pure metals.

Figure 1 This is what you need to make a cup of white coffee and a sponge cake.

Nearly all the cooking we do makes **mixtures**. Mixtures can make very useful materials. They often have very different **properties** from the pure substances that make them. All of the materials in Table 2 are mixtures. Some materials only work as mixtures.

Mixture	Made from . . .
black ink	several powdered dyes and water
blood	red cells, white cells, salt and water
butter	milk fat, salt and water
glass	washing soda, sand and lead metal

Table 2 Some common mixtures

Questions

10 What do you mix to make a cup of coffee?

11 Describe a 'mix' that you have made to eat (a pizza topping or a sandwich) that is better than one food on its own. Explain why it is better.

Marta does not like orange flavours. She can easily cope with a box of chocolates.

12 What would she need to do to separate the orange ones from a tube of Smarties?

13 What would she need to do to separate the orange ones from hundreds and thousands (cake decorations)? (When you separate mixtures in the laboratory the particles are so small you can't see them.)

Remember

Use the following words to fill in the spaces.

particle mixtures pure different

When we say something is _____**1**_____, we mean it doesn't harm people. But pure really means substances that contain only one type of _____**2**_____.

Many materials are _____**3**_____. These materials have _____**4**_____ (physical) properties to the substances they are made from.

5.2 Into thin air

The air is a mixture and not a pure substance.

Figure 1 Damage caused by the 1999 hurricane

Where does the push come from to flatten buildings and uproot trees during a hurricane? It comes from moving air.

During the hurricane that swept through France on Boxing Day, 1999, buildings were ripped apart, trees were blown over and there were millions of pounds worth of damage – all caused by thin air.

In fact, thin air is not that thin. It seems thin because we're used to it. In the space under a normal two person school desk there is about 1 kg of air. A school hall contains about 6 tonnes of air. When these large lumps start moving about it's no wonder trees get pushed over.

Where the lost mass goes

In many chemical changes the substances seem to gain or lose mass, but this is not what is happening. The mass is being transferred to and from a store of materials in the air.

Many things use air as a raw material.

Coal is mainly carbon atoms. The carbon does not disappear when it burns. It reacts with the oxygen in the air and makes carbon dioxide. This is a gas, so it mixes back into the air. The air gets heavier because carbon is added to it.

An oak tree starts as an acorn. Two hundred years later it weighs hundreds of tonnes. Trees don't take much material out of the ground – just the water from rain and some minerals. Leaves absorb most of the matter to make wood. Carbon dioxide is taken in by the leaves and water is absorbed by the roots. Photosynthesis turns these two substances into wood.

Figure 2 Does coal burn and disappear?

Figure 3 Do trees appear from nowhere?

These use oxygen	These use nitrogen	These use other gases from the air
cars (to burn fuel)	fertiliser factories	light bulbs (argon)
people	crisp packets	welding (argon)
iron and steel works	hospitals (for freezing warts off and preserving human embryos)	party balloons (helium)
sewage works		deep sea divers (helium)

Questions

1 a) What is the main material in coal?

b) What does it react with when it is hot?

c) What new material does it become?

2 a) Where does the carbon dioxide for making wood come from?

b) What other material is needed to 'make' wood?

c) What do leaves and roots do in this process?

3 Write word equations to explain the changes referred to in questions 1 and 2.

4 How do people use oxygen?

5 The air we breathe out is heavier than the air we breathe in. Explain why.

Investigating air

We often use the word 'pure' to describe clean air. We know air is a mixture of several gases. All the gases are colourless and have no smell, and that's what air is like.

Some of the gases in the air are elements and some are compounds. Particle pictures of the gases (like the one in Figure 4) make it possible to say which is which.

Gases in the air

Oxygen	21%
Nitrogen	78%
Carbon dioxide	0.03%
Noble gases (mainly argon)	approx. 1%
Water vapour	a varying amount depending on the weather

Table 2 Composition of air

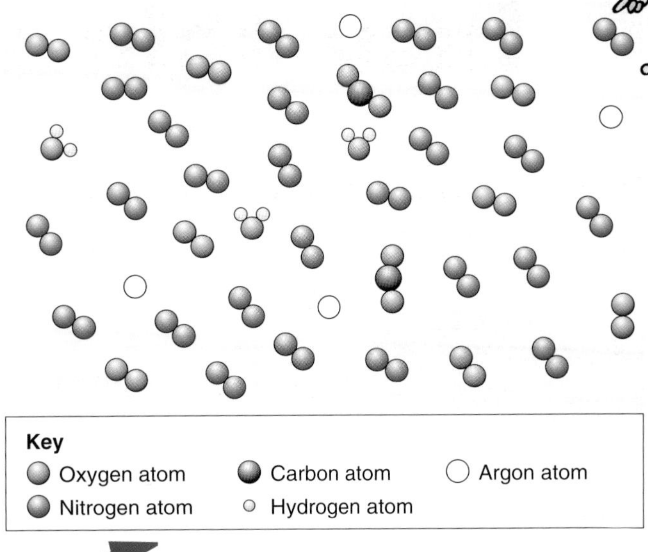

Key
- Oxygen atom
- Nitrogen atom
- Carbon atom
- Hydrogen atom
- Argon atom

Figure 4 The gases in air

Questions

6 What do the following consist of:
a) an oxygen particle?
b) an argon particle?
c) a carbon dioxide particle?
d) a nitrogen particle?

7 Which substances in the air are elements?

8 Which substances in the air are compounds?

Remember

Copy (with tracing paper) and label this pie chart showing the amounts of gases in the air.

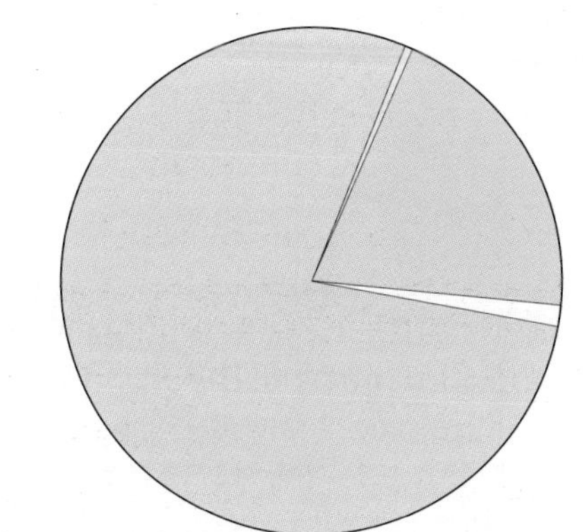

5.3 Strange reactions – no!

There are many different types of reaction and changes. We use them all to make the substances useful to us.

Figure 1 Chemical changes

Strike a match, light the gas cooker, cook a fried egg, digest the food, then use the energy you get to play tennis. All five of these everyday processes use chemical changes to make them work. We expect the changes which happen in matches, gas and eggs to work every time we try them. Chemical changes are predictable – they always happen the same way. These changes also follow **patterns** – for example gas, candles and petrol burn in very similar ways.

Oxidation

When you heat most metals they react with the oxygen in the air. They make new substances called **oxides**. Magnesium burns all the way through and makes magnesium oxide, a white powder. Adding oxygen to a substance is called **oxidation**. **Reduction** is the opposite of oxidation, like when iron oxide is made into iron metal.

Combustion

Combustion is a special sort of oxidation reaction. Oxygen in the air is used to burn a fuel and transfer energy causing heating of the surroundings. Many things will burn, but not all of them are fuels.

Thermal decomposition

Lots of substances decompose when heated. Making toffee is a decomposition reaction. When you heat sugar, some of the particles fall apart to make 'caramel'. Your breakfast toast is made in the same way. Some of the starch particles in the bread are 'caramelised' to make the brown toasty colour. So you get a nice texture and stronger taste.

Precipitation

When you bubble colourless carbon dioxide gas through colourless limewater solution they react and an insoluble substance is made. The insoluble substance makes the liquid cloudy. It is called a **precipitate**.

Figure 2 This pupil is demonstrating a precipitation reaction.

Displacement

To make high performance aeroplane parts, titanium is needed. Titanium ore is turned into metal by using sodium. The sodium steals, or displaces, the oxygen from the titanium ore, leaving only useful titanium metal.

Figure 3 A stealth bomber – a high performance aeroplane

Fizz reactions

Fire extinguishers need to be able to squirt water at the base of a fire. Some use gas pressure to do this.

Figure 4 A fizz reaction

Figure 4 shows sulphuric acid and sodium hydrogen-carbonate being mixed. This reaction makes lots of fizz as carbon dioxide gas is given off.

When you cook scones, a very similar reaction is used to make the scones spongy. Baking powder contains tartaric acid and sodium hydrogen-carbonate. The 'fizz' from the reaction fluffs up the scones as they are cooking.

Enzyme reactions

Enzymes break up big complicated particles into small simpler substances. Enzymes are used in biological washing powders to break down the food that got on your clothes.

Neutralising acids

Acid nettle sting is neutralised by an alkaline dock leaf. The dock leaf is not harmful to us as it is only a weak alkali.

Questions

What type of reaction is happening in Questions 1 to 10? Explain your answers.

1 Charcoal is made by heating wood.

2 Acid indigestion is treated with alkaline tablets.

3 Large food molecules are broken up into simpler substances in the stomach.

4 Petrol burns in a car engine to release heat.

5 Milk goes sour as it reacts with the air.

6 Limestone rock makes bubbles when vinegar is put on it.

7 Baked potatoes in the oven go crispy and dark on the outside.

8 Vinegar is used to stop a wasp sting.

9 Washing soda produces an insoluble scum in hard water areas.

10 Copper metal gets deposited on the surface of an iron knife; iron particles take the place of the copper in the solution.

11 Make a list of the science words on these pages and learn to spell them by the 'Look – Say – Cover – Write' method.

Remember

Use the following words to fill in the gaps.

predictable reactions patterns

Chemical ___1___ follow ___2___ so they are ___3___.

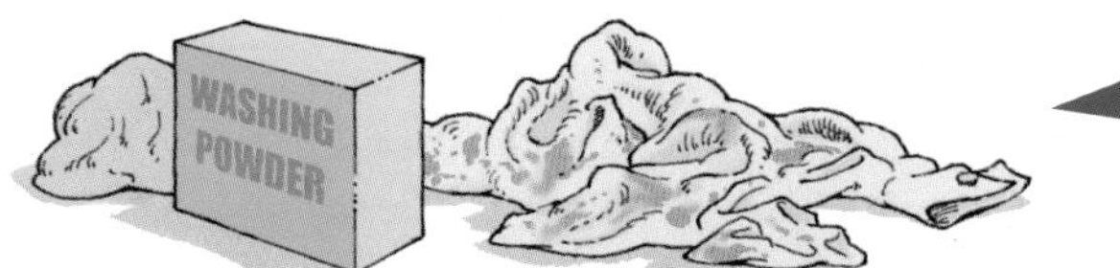

Figure 5 Enzymes are used in biological washing powder.

It's frighteningly tiny

Atoms are like simple creatures. They have only one wish in the world. They want to have an outer shell full of electrons. All chemical changes happen because atoms are trying to achieve this.

The story on this page is a thinking model to help you understand how atoms join together.

Figure 1 An average 60 kg teenager contains two billion billion billion (two followed by 27 zeros) atoms.

Atoms are very small. Very small indeed. In fact *incredibly* small. So small that you can't see them, even with a microscope. Because they are small they are frightened. Can you remember when you were small and went out into crowded places? You kept close together with your friends and held hands. You have two hands. You felt safe if both hands were held. Atoms are the same. They are 'safe' only if all their hands are being held. But atoms have different numbers of hands. The bravest have one hand only. Here are pictures of some of them.

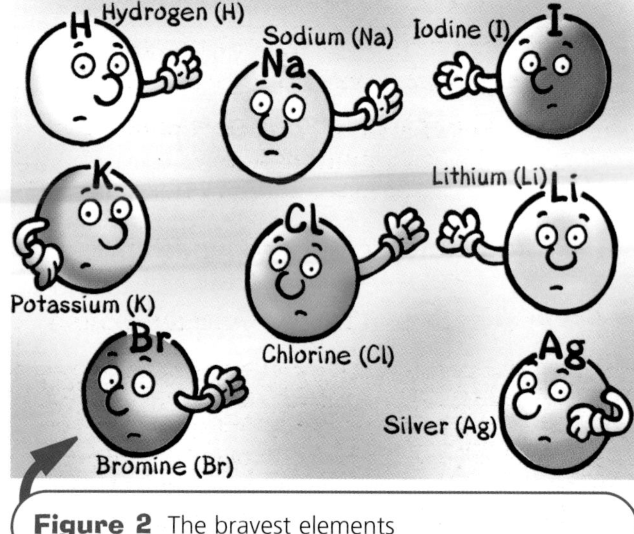

Figure 2 The bravest elements

The atoms in Figure 3 are a bit less brave. They exist with two hands.

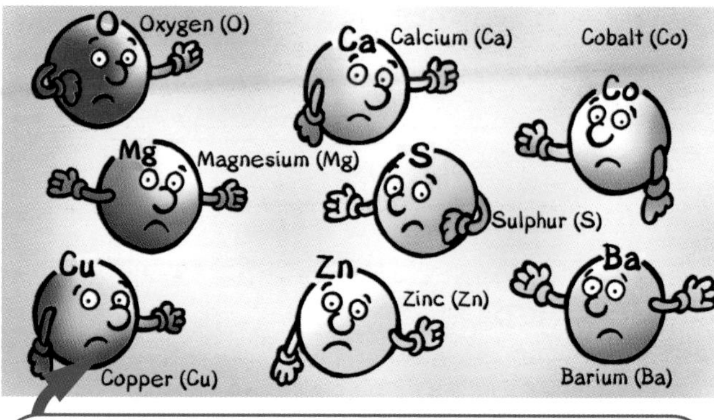

Figure 3 Elements with two hands

Some atoms exist with three hands, like those in Figure 4. They still need all their hands held. They are scaredy.

Figure 4 Elements with three hands

But the scaredyest of all is this one.

Figure 5 Carbon is special. It is very keen to hold onto its mates. That's why pure carbon – diamond – is so hard. It links up in long chains to make really big groups. It is the only atom that does this.

When atoms hold hands with their friends they are happy. They say to each other 'We have reacted. We are safe from change for a while.'

Here are some groups of atoms. They have joined together, we say '**reacted**.' They now feel safe. What a nice group. This group is a **molecule**. It has no free hands so it cannot react any more.

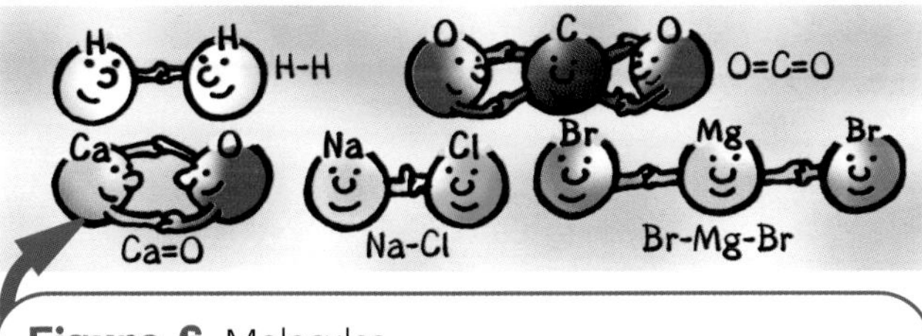

Figure 6 Molecules

The groups in Figure 6 are content. They have all their hands held and feel less small. They are molecules, made up from small groups of atoms.

Carbon forms special molecules. It can form quite large gangs in the end.

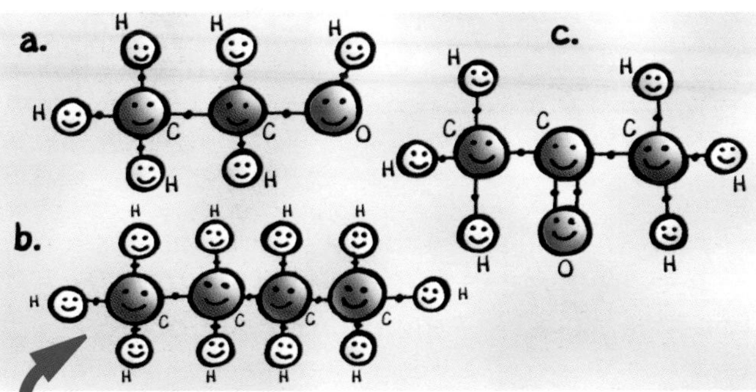

Figure 7 a) The ethanol gang (they live in wine). b) The butane gang (they live in camping gas). c) The propanone gang (they live in nail varnish remover)

Strangest of all, there are some 'dead tough' atoms. They stay on their own all the time. They have no hands at all to hold on to other atoms. They are real loners and form no compounds at all.

Figure 8 No molecules for these atoms

Of course, this is only a story to help you understand. The atoms do form small groups, and with the numbers of 'friends' you have learnt here. The number of hands is called the **valency**. Make sure you know the number of 'hands for each atom'.

Questions

See if you can draw these groups.

1 One atom of carbon being friendly with hydrogen.

2 Nitrogen being friendly with hydrogen.

3 Sodium being friendly with oxygen.

4 Aluminium being friendly with chlorine.

5 Aluminium being friendly with bromine.

6 Magnesium being a group with oxygen.

7 Phosphorus making a group with a formula PCl_3. How many 'hands' has phosphorus?

8 Titanium, making a group with a formula TiO_2. How many 'hands' for titanium?

9 Chlorine on its own has a formula of Cl_2. Why do these atoms go round in pairs?

10 What other gases that are elements have atoms that go round in pairs?

Remember

Copy and fill in this table. Put all the elements mentioned in the questions and text in the right column.

Zero hands so makes no links with other atoms	One hand so makes one link with other atoms	Two hands so makes two links with other atoms	Three hands so makes three links with other atoms	Four hands so makes four links with other atoms
(4 elements)	(8 elements)	(8 elements)	(4 elements)	(2 elements)

Always the same recipe

Cooking and chemistry both have rules about how much of one material will combine with another.

Cooking and chemistry can be dangerous and can have spectacularly pleasing results. Both have very precise rules – follow them correctly and the results are exactly predictable.

Figure 1 These identical cakes have been produced by a trained cook.

Pastry cooks train until they can produce identical, perfect cakes every time, so your doughnut or sponge cake will be exactly the way you expect it to be. To make this happen, cooks combine exactly the right quantities of different ingredients so they react with each other completely. The fat combines with exactly the right amount of flour so the pastry tastes like pastry and not flour or fat.

When chemicals react, they follow exact rules about how much of one element will combine with another and what the compound will be like. Even when chemicals fall apart, they do it according to the same sort of strict rules.

When any chemical gets made or broken up the combining rules must still be followed. The atoms react so that *all* their hands are still held.

One oxygen particle combines with two lithium particles to make one lithium oxide.

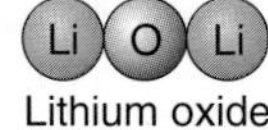

Three oxygen particles combine with six lithium particles to make three lithium oxides.

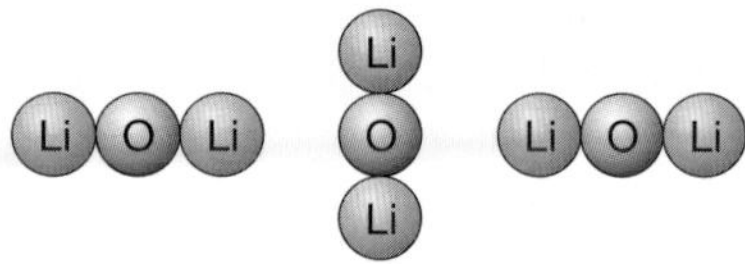

Six oxygen particles combine with 12 lithium particles to make six lithium oxides.

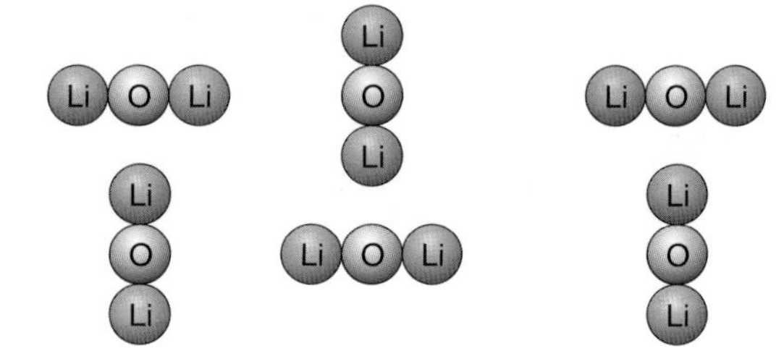

You can see that the ratio of lithium atoms to oxygen atoms stays the same no matter how many 'particles' of lithium oxide are made.

One copper carbonate splits up into one copper oxide and one carbon dioxide molecule.

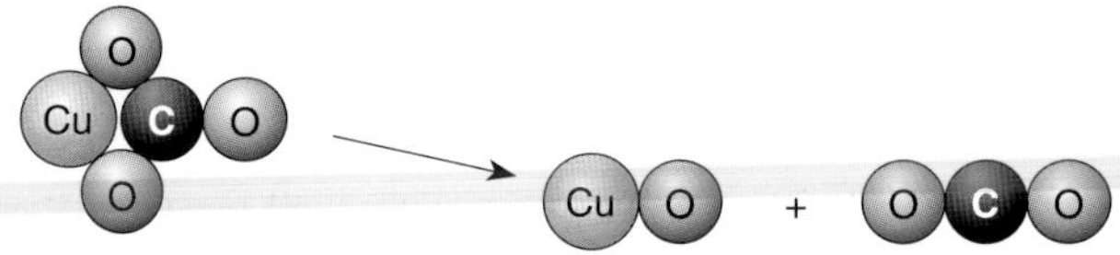

Five copper carbonates split up into five copper oxides and five carbon dioxide molecules.

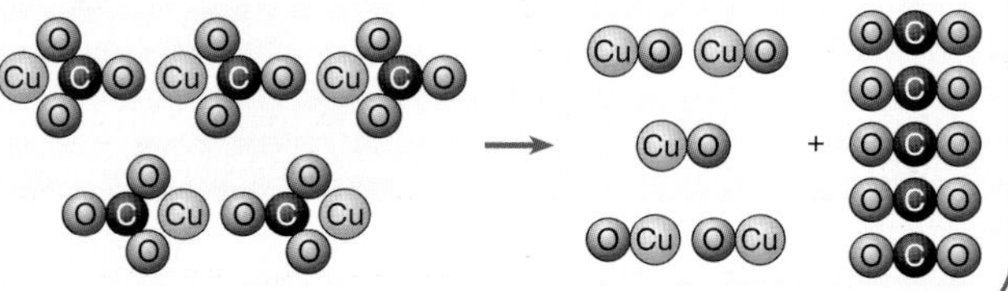

Ten copper carbonates split up into 10 copper oxides and 10 carbon dioxide molecules.

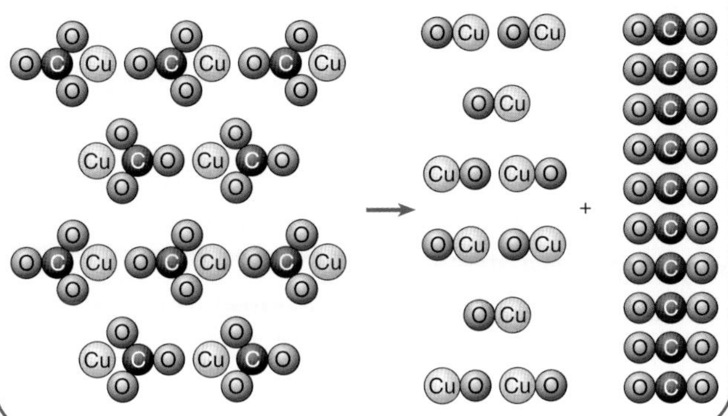

When green copper carbonate was heated it decomposed. Copper oxide was left and carbon dioxide gas was given off.

One carbon dioxide molecule was given off for each copper carbonate molecule that was there at the start.

Remember

Use these words to fill in the spaces.

same ratio formula atoms type compounds

Chemical ___1___ are made of small groups of different atoms. The ___2___ join together in a fixed ___3___ like in a recipe. The percentage of each ___4___ of atom in the compound is the ___5___ no matter how much of the compound is used. The chemical ___6___ represents the ratio of atoms in the compound.

Questions

1 How many atoms of oxygen are there in an oxygen molecule?

2 If 400 magnesium atoms were oxidised, how many oxygen molecules would be needed?

3 Complete the following table for the decomposition of copper carbonate:

Number of particles that fall apart	Number of carbon dioxide molecules produced	Number of copper oxide particles left behind
1 particle		
20 particles		
2 million particles		

4 What new substances are made when calcium hydroxide reacts with carbon dioxide?

5 One magnesium atom has a mass of 24 units and one oxygen atom has a mass of 16 units. What is the total mass of magnesium oxide produced when one magnesium atom joins with one oxygen atom?

6 Complete the table below. The first one is done for you.

Number of magnesium oxide particles	Total mass of magnesium atoms	Total mass of oxygen atoms	Total mass of magnesium oxide	% of total that is magnesium atoms
1	24	16	40	60
3				
20				
100				

Closer

Right mix – correct properties

Building

A concrete and glass stadium

Concrete is made by mixing cement (calcium oxide) and water. It is left for several hours to absorb carbon dioxide from the air. This sets hard to make rock-like concrete (calcium carbonate crystals). Sand and gravel make the mixture harder.

Food

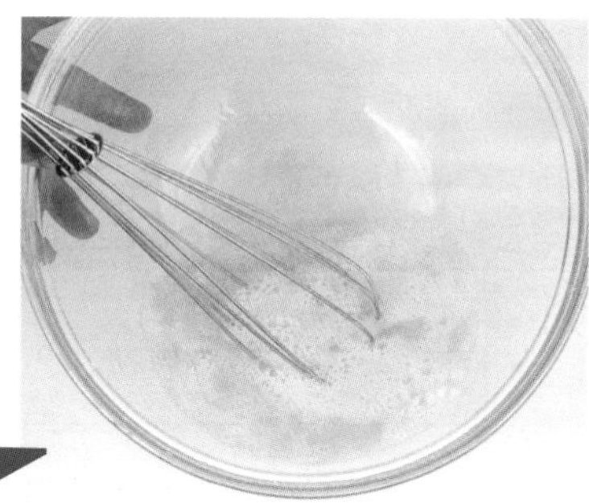

Eggs being beaten by a chef

Eggs are wonderful materials. Egg is made from globules of protein strands rolled up into a ball.

When you cook egg the strands unravel and tangle up with each other making a loose mass of interwoven strands. This can be used to hold other materials together, like in scrambled eggs, quiche or cakes.

Fashion

Clothes are made of fibres

Cloth needs to be made of fibres. Fibres need to be strong when you pull them and flexible when you bend them. The molecules clothes are made from are long, strong but flexible as well. There are plant fibres such as linen, animal fibres such as silk, and manufactured fibres such as polyester.

Questions

1 Kate did some work investigating the amount of 'night light' candles that got burned away and how much they heated water. Here are her results:

Amount of candle burned	0 g	3.0 g	5.0 g	8.0 g	10.0 g	14.0 g
Temperature of 100 g of water	20°C	36°C	46°C	62°C	72°C	92°C

a) Plot a line graph of the results.

b) Put in a line of best fit through the points.

c) What do you notice about the line?

d) How would you describe (in words) the relationship shown in the graph?

e) How much candle would be needed to boil the water?

Magnetism

Opener
Action at a distance

Wizards in stories can exert forces on objects without touching them.

The Earth can pull you down without touching you. Think about what would happen if you jumped from an aeroplane. Gravity acts at a distance. That's a strange thing, if you stop and think about it. You can't do that. You can't lift objects up or pull or push them without touching them.

Magnetic force is like gravity. It can act at a distance. Try holding a couple of strong magnets without letting them touch each other. Feel the force. It feels strange. You don't have to invent magical worlds. There is plenty of real amazement in the real world. Wizards? Who needs them?

Questions

1 Which of these can you control 'at a distance':

- an approaching bus when you are at a bus stop;
- what your friend hears when you talk to them on the phone;
- the sound inside a house when you press a doorbell;
- a raindrop that is falling towards you;
- a dog;
- the TV channel.

Do any of them involve wizards or wizardry?

2 Here are some more amazing observations. They all have something to do with magnetism:

- a compass needle always points in the same direction;
- Earth has a much thicker atmosphere than Mars;
- a piece of cardboard can make sounds that are exactly like human voices or musical instruments;
- a doorbell doesn't make just a single 'ting!' but goes on ringing for as long as you press the button.

What are the causes of these strange phenomena? Discuss some of your ideas.

Magnetic forces

Magnets have space around them where they can exert magnetic force. The space is called a magnetic field. Field lines show patterns of magnetic force.

Magnets are fun. You can stick them on the fridge. You can put two together – sometimes they **attract** and sometimes they **repel**. The force between them feels strange. They can push and pull each other without touching. The force of magnetism acts at a distance. The space around a magnet where its force can act is called its **magnetic field**.

The Earth itself is a very large magnet. All magnets can exert forces on each other and the Earth is no exception. If you hang a magnet up so that it is carefully balanced and free to swing, it will settle so that it points in a certain direction. One end will point towards the North of our planet, and the other end will point South. Chinese sailors discovered this a long time ago. They invented the **compass**.

the Earth's NORTH

the Earth's SOUTH

Figure 1 Compasses all over the Earth point northwards.

A compass is a small magnet that can swing freely. Compasses all over the Earth point from South to North. So wherever you are you can use a compass to tell which way is North and which way is South.

The end of the compass that points North is called its North pole. The end that points South is called its South pole. Every magnet has a North pole and a South pole.

Figure 2 Which way to home and safety? The compass will tell you which way is North and which way is South.

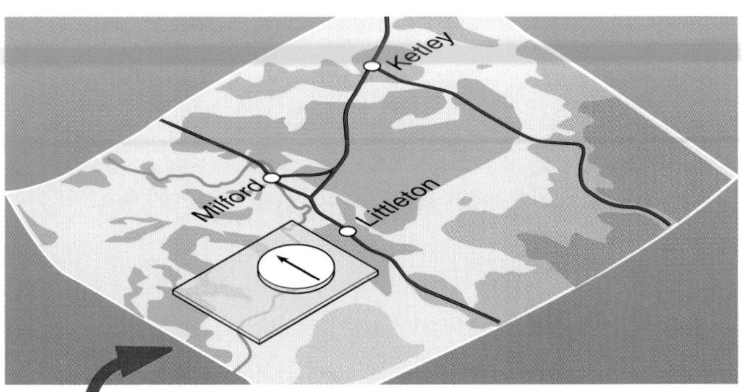

Figure 3 A compass tells you which way is North.

Magnetic field lines

You can use little compasses to trace the patterns of magnetic forces that act in the area around a magnet. You end up with a pattern of looping lines. These are called **field lines**, or sometimes **lines of force**. Arrows on the lines show which way the compass needle points.

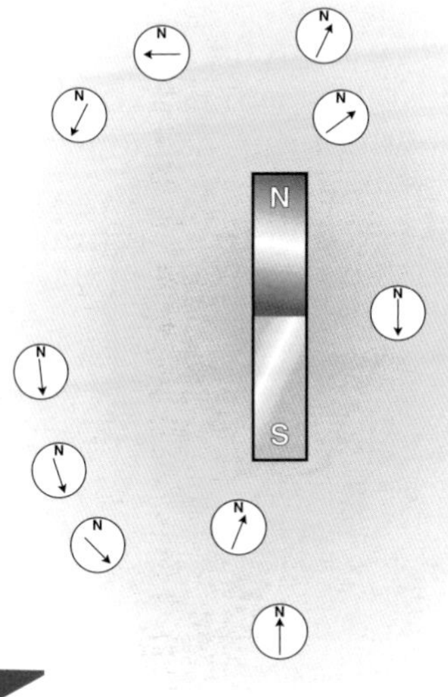

Figure 4 Do compass needles point all over the place when they are in a magnetic field? Or are there patterns in how they behave?

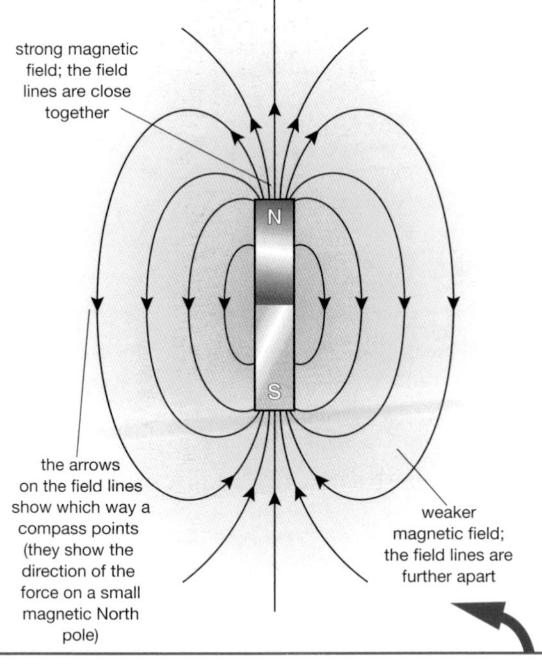

Figure 5 The pattern of field lines around a magnet

Questions

1 What word means the opposite of attract?

2 What is the name of the space around a magnet in which its force can act?

3 Why is it useful that the Earth is a magnet?

4 Look at the compass and map in Figure 3 to answer these questions.

a) Which village is furthest North?

b) If you were at Littleton, which way would you have to go to get to Milford?

5 Copy and complete this diagram to show the complete pattern of field lines.

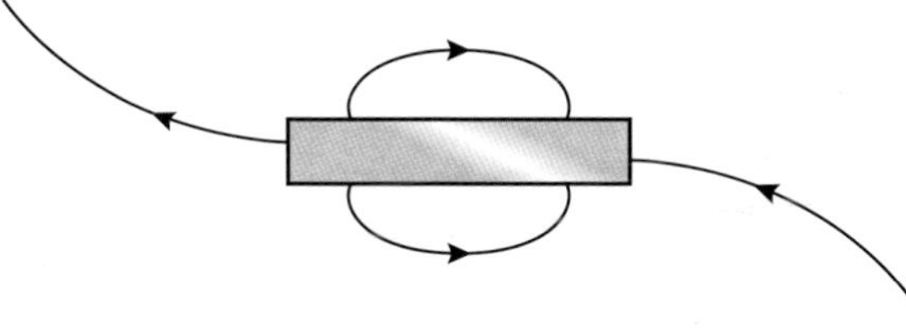

Remember

Unscramble the words to complete the passage below.

Magnetic force can act at a <u>SCAN TIDE</u>. The space around a magnet where it can exert force is called its magnetic <u>ELF ID</u>. The <u>HEART</u> acts as a large magnet and exerts forces on other smaller magnets. Every magnet has a <u>THORN</u> pole and a South pole. Magnets can <u>TAT CART</u> or repel each other.

Lines of <u>F CORE</u> are also called field lines. They show the direction of the magnetic force that can act at different places in a <u>MAGIC NET</u> field.

6.2 Patterns of magnetism

Steel is good for making permanent magnets. A coil of wire in a circuit acts as a temporary magnet.

Patterns of attraction and repulsion

If you hold two strong magnets close together you can feel the force. Sometimes the magnetic force is an attractive force – the force takes over and the magnets pull your hands along. But sometimes the force is repulsive – the magnets push each other away.

There's a pattern to the pushing and pulling. North poles attract South poles, and South poles attract North poles. Two poles that are *different* always *attract*. Two poles that are the *same* always *repel* each other.

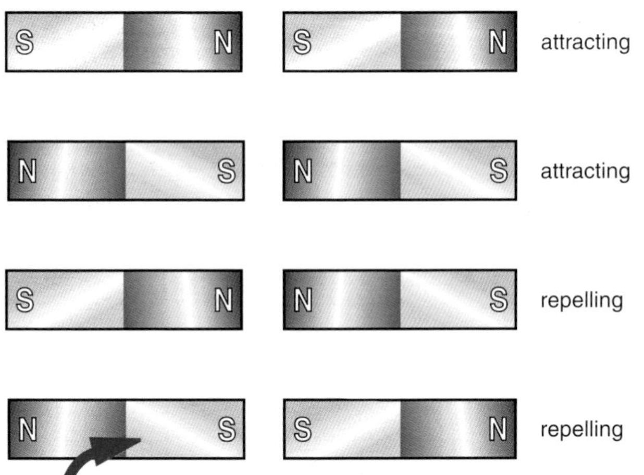

Figure 1 Two different poles attract; two poles that are the same repel.

Magnetic materials

Most materials aren't magnetic. When you hold just one magnet, your hand can't feel any force. Your hand is not made of magnetic material.

The most common magnetic materials are iron and steel. If you hold a piece of iron or steel next to a bar magnet, it will feel the force. Steel is good for making permanent bar magnets. Steel magnets keep their magnetism. Compass needles are made of steel.

Electromagnets

When an electric current flows in a wire, the space around the wire becomes a magnetic field. Electric current seems to create magnetism.

If a wire in an electric circuit is made into a tight coil, the magnetism of each turn of the coil adds to the total strength of the magnetic field. A coil makes a strong magnet that can be switched on and off. It's called an **electromagnet**.

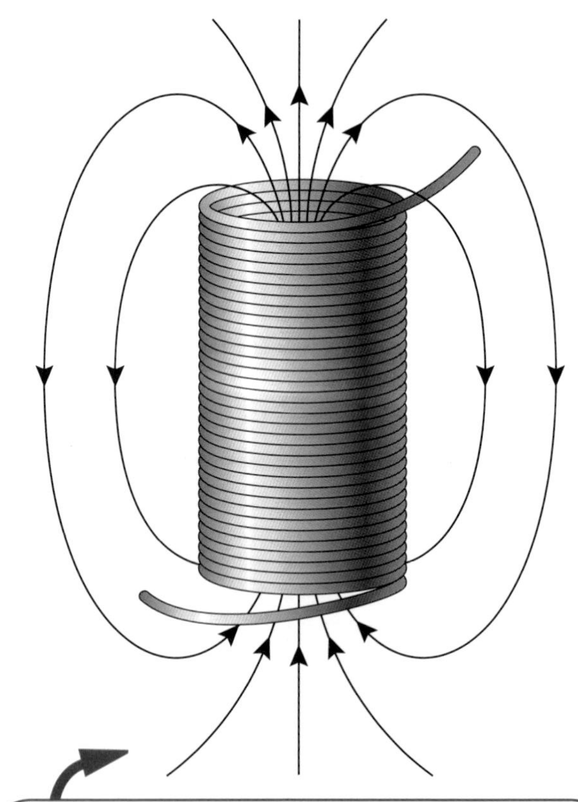

Figure 2 An electromagnet is a coil with an electric current. It has a pattern of field lines around it.

Look at the patterns of field lines around the electromagnet:

- the lines are closer together where the field is stronger;
- the lines and arrows show the direction of the force that acts on the North pole of a magnet.

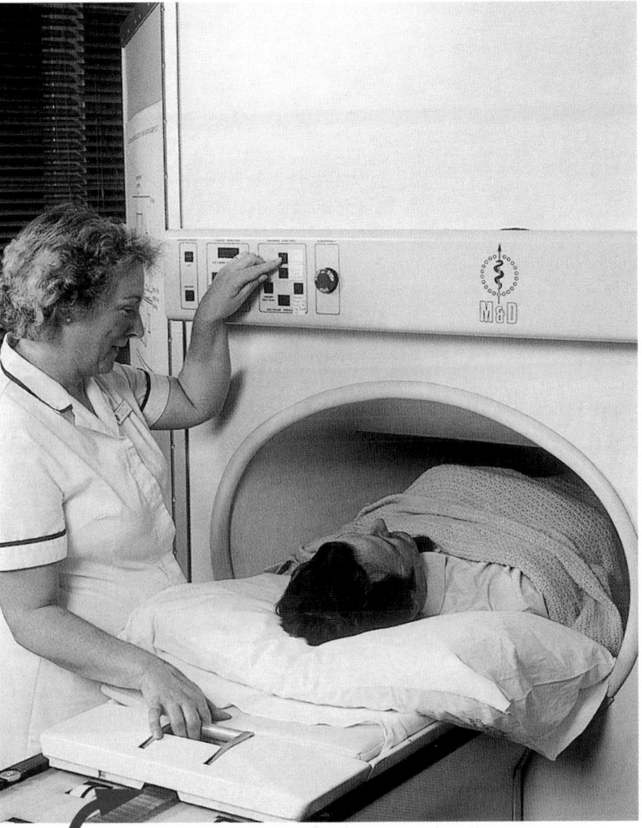

Figure 3 This person is having a body scan. The scanner machine contains coils which act as very strong electromagnets. The person lies in a very strong magnetic field. The magnetism does the person no harm, but it makes the atoms in their body respond by giving out radio waves that the scanner can detect. The scanner produces a picture of a slice through the person's body.

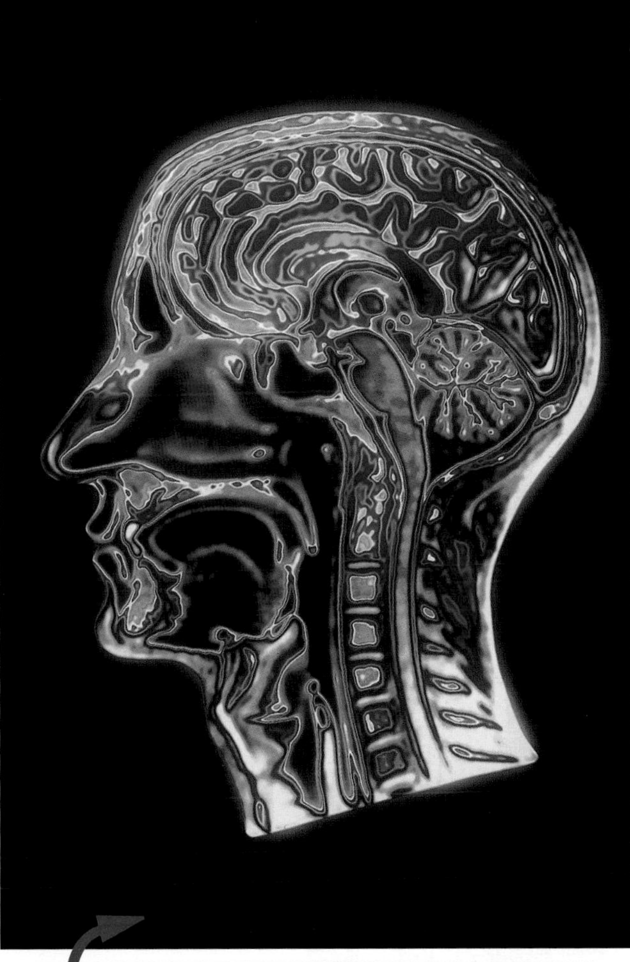

Figure 4 This picture of a slice through a human head has been made using strong magnetic fields in a scanner.

Questions

1 What effect does:

a) a North pole of a magnet have on another North pole?

b) a North pole of a magnet have on a South pole?

2 Why is steel good for making compass needles?

3 In what ways is an electromagnet more useful than a permanent steel magnet?

4 Compare the pattern of field lines around a bar magnet (page 65) and an electromagnet. What do you notice?

Remember

Complete the passage below using the following words.

switched attract same electromagnets permanent

Poles that are different always ____1____. Poles that are the ____2____ always repel. Most materials are no good for making magnets. Steel is useful for making ____3____ magnets. ____4____ are coils of wire. Their magnetism can be ____5____ on and off.

6.3 Power lines

When a current flows in a wire there is a magnetic field around the wire.

Figure 1 Power cables in Aberffordd

TV presenter: Here in the village of Aberffordd the local doctor, Dr Mair Roberts, has brought attention to a very high rate of cancer. Dr Roberts, is this really anything unusual?

Doctor Roberts: Well, everybody knows that cancer is a common disease, but here in Aberffordd it's more than three times as common as the average for the whole of the UK.

TV presenter: So what can be the cause of this?

Doctor Roberts: Nobody can be sure. We've tested the water and that's completely normal. Many people here work on farms and it could be that some of the pesticides they use have harmful effects. Though in similar farming villages there isn't the same high rate of cancer. One suggestion is that the problem is caused by the high voltage power cables that pass over the village from the power station two kilometres away.

TV presenter: But they look like ordinary power cables to me.

Doctor Roberts: Yes, but all power cables carry quite strong electric current, and that means that there are strong magnetic fields all around them.

TV presenter: Are you saying that the magnetic fields in the space around the cables are causing cancer?

Doctor Roberts: We can't say that for sure, and the electricity company say that there's no evidence that magnetism causes cancer. But that doesn't stop people worrying.

TV presenter: Is there anything about these particular magnetic fields that could be a problem?

Doctor Roberts: Well, the current in the cables is large, and that makes strong magnetic effects. Also the current isn't steady, but vibrates backwards and forwards 50 times per second. It's **alternating** current. That means that the magnetic fields are also vibrating, and perhaps the vibrations can affect the complicated chemistry in a human body.

TV presenter: Also with me is Nigel Morris, who works for the electricity company. He's the man responsible for operating these cables. Mr Morris, how can you answer these allegations that it's your power cables that are making people ill, and causing some of them to die?

Nigel Morris: Over many years, we've made detailed studies on possible effects of power cables. There's simply no known way in which the magnetic fields in the space around power cables can cause cancer. This situation in Aberffordd is a mystery to everybody, but I'm absolutely confident that our power cables are not causing the problem.

TV presenter: Nobody denies that there's a problem here in Aberffordd, but nobody has any idea about the cause, and still less about what can be done. This is Gita Patel, News at Nine, Aberffordd.

Questions

1 Why is it unlikely that the problem at Aberffordd is caused by:

a) the water supply?

b) pesticides from farms?

2 a) Why are the magnetic fields around power lines strong?

b) Why do the magnetic fields 'vibrate' rapidly?

3 As far as we know, magnetic fields are harmless to people. What research could scientists do to try to find out more about this?

Magnetic field around a wire

Every wire with an electric current has a magnetic field around it. You can use a compass to follow the pattern of the magnetic field lines as in Figure 2. The bigger the current, the stronger the magnetic field. If the current varies, the strength of the magnetic field varies in just the same way.

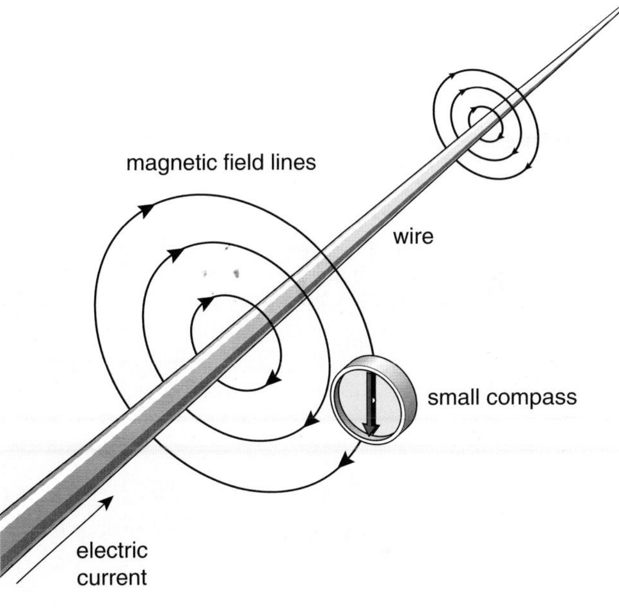

Figure 2 A compass lines up along magnetic field lines around a wire that has an electric current.

Remember

Complete the spaces using the following words.

lines magnetic field current electric

There is always a ____1____ field around a wire when it is carrying an ____2____ current. The bigger the ____3____ in the wire, the stronger the magnetic ____4____. A pattern of field ____5____ shows the directions of the magnetic forces.

6.4 Bells

An electric bell is an electromagnetic device. It uses an electric current to create a magnetic field. Magnetic force creates movement of the hammer to hit the gong.

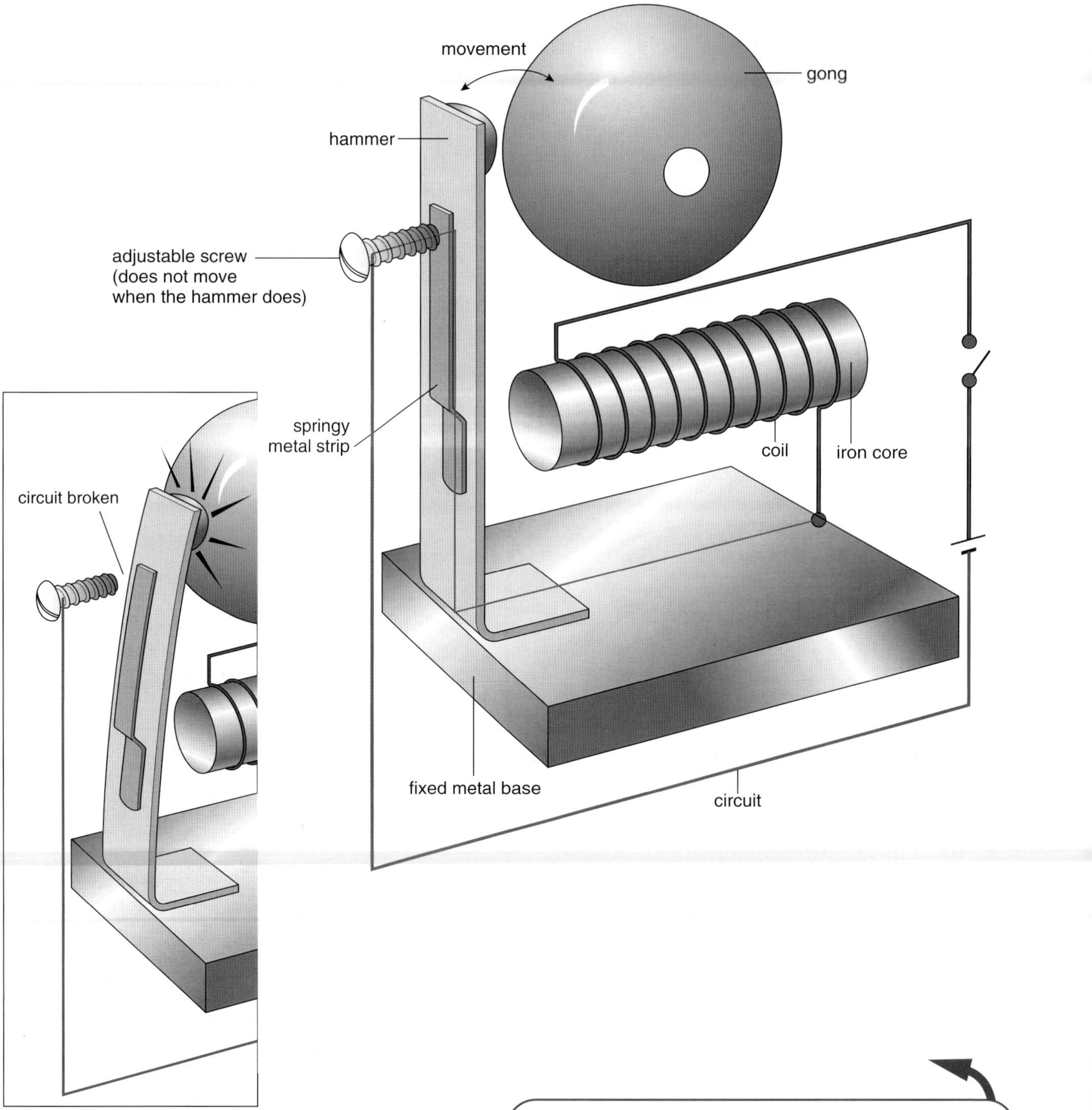

movement
gong
hammer
adjustable screw (does not move when the hammer does)
springy metal strip
coil
iron core
circuit broken
fixed metal base
circuit

Figure 1 The workings of an electric bell

The **electromagnet** in an electric bell is a coil of wire. When a current flows in the coil it becomes a magnet. The coil has a **core of iron** to make the magnetism as strong as possible. When the current stops, the magnetism very quickly fades away. That's what makes electromagnets so useful – the magnetism is under control.

The coil exerts a magnetic force of attraction on the iron of the **hammer**. The hammer moves and hits the **gong**. But the **springy metal strip** fixed to the hammer also moves. It moves away from the **adjustable screw**. The springy metal strip and the adjustable screw are both part of the electric circuit. Together they act like a switch. When they move apart they break the electric circuit. So the coil loses its magnetism.

When this happens, there's nothing to attract the hammer across to the gong. So the hammer drops back to where it started. Of course, it takes the springy metal strip with it. The springy metal strip again makes contact with the adjustable screw and so the current is switched back on. The current flows in the coil and the whole process starts over again.

The hammer dashes backwards and forwards, several times every second. Each time it hits the gong there's another little ringing sound. The bell rings and rings.

Electromagnetic relay

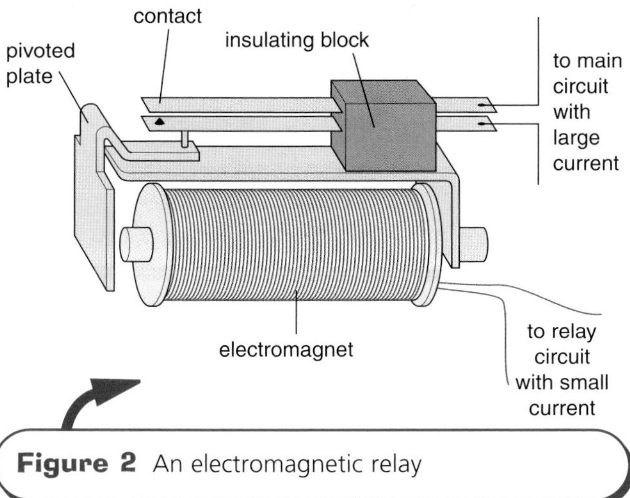

Figure 2 An electromagnetic relay

Have you ever heard a quiet click or clunk when the central heating or washing machine turns on? This is usually a sign that an electromagnetic **relay** is switching on part of a circuit.

A relay is an electromagnetic switch. It works in a very similar way to an electric bell.

There is a coil with an iron core. When a current flows through the coil, it turns the iron core into an electromagnet. The electromagnet attracts the pivoted plate. As this moves, it closes the switch contacts.

With an electromagnetic relay, a very small current in the coil can be used to switch on a large current in a separate main circuit.

Car starter motors use a relay. A small current of less than 1 amp is switched on by the ignition key. This closes the contacts in the relay connected to the starter motor and makes a current of 50 or 60 amps flow.

Questions

1 In an electric bell ...

a) why does the hammer move towards the gong?

b) why does it move away again?

c) what is the iron core for?

d) which parts act as a switch?

Remember

Fill in the spaces in the passage below using the following words.

lose hammer on adjustable metal strip electromagnet repeats current

An electric bell works by using a coil as an ___1___. The electric ___2___ in the coil makes it magnetic, so that it attracts the ___3___. The hammer hits the gong. The movement breaks the circuit between the springy ___4___ and the ___5___ screw. That makes the coil ___6___ its magnetism. The hammer moves back, switching the circuit back ___7___ again. The process ___8___ itself many times every second.

Loudspeakers

Loudspeakers can create high amplitude vibrations in the air. Most loudspeakers contain electromagnets.

For some kinds of music, amplitude is what matters most.

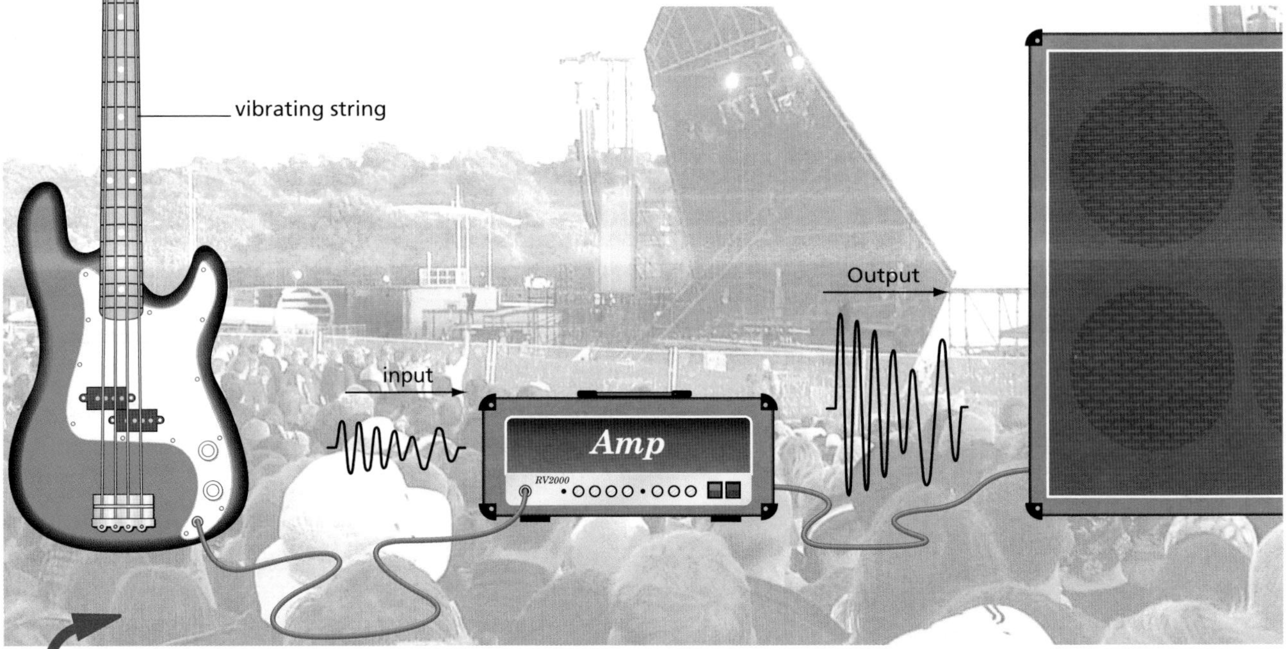

Figure 1 The patterns of vibration of the guitar string make patterns in the electric current in the guitar's electric circuits. The current passes through an amplifier which makes a bigger current with the same pattern. The amplified current passes through the coil in a loudspeaker. The loudspeaker vibrates. The sound that travels through the air carries the same patterns as the sound made by the guitar string but now it's LOUDER.

Amplification

The metal string of an electric guitar doesn't make a very loud sound. It doesn't produce vibrations with very high amplitude in the surrounding air. But the vibrations of the string generate electric currents in the guitar's circuits. These electric currents are still quite weak. The currents flow to an **amplifier** which makes bigger currents with the same patterns in them. The bigger currents are enough to make a loudspeaker vibrate with high amplitude. Then the quiet guitar is as loud as you want it to be. The process of making loud sounds from quiet ones is called **amplification**.

Inside a loudspeaker

The main parts of a loudspeaker are a cardboard **cone**, a **coil** and a **fixed magnet**. The coil is attached to the cone. It's the coil and the cone that vibrate to make the high amplitude vibrations in the surrounding air.

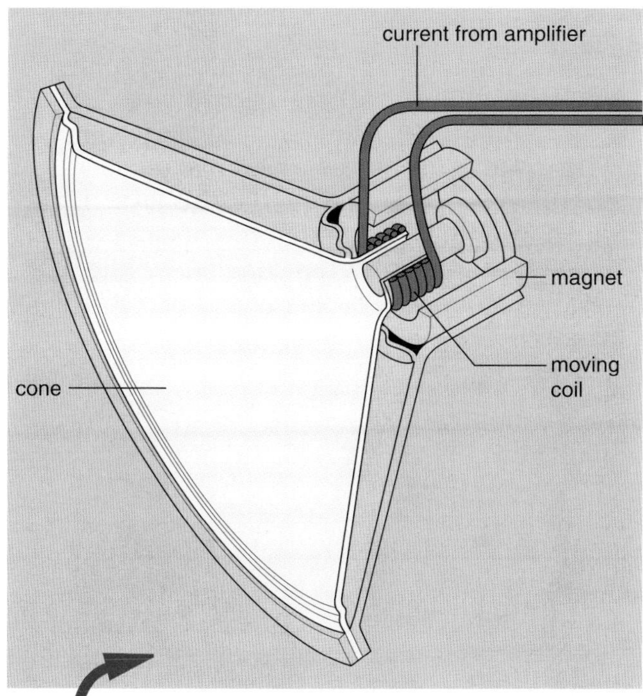

Figure 2 In a loudspeaker, magnetic force creates vibration of the coil and the cone.

The electric current from the amplifier flows through the coil. The coil becomes magnetic. That creates force between the coil and the fixed magnet. The pattern in the electric currents makes the force stronger and weaker, varying rapidly. So the coil moves rapidly backwards and forwards, and the cone moves with it.

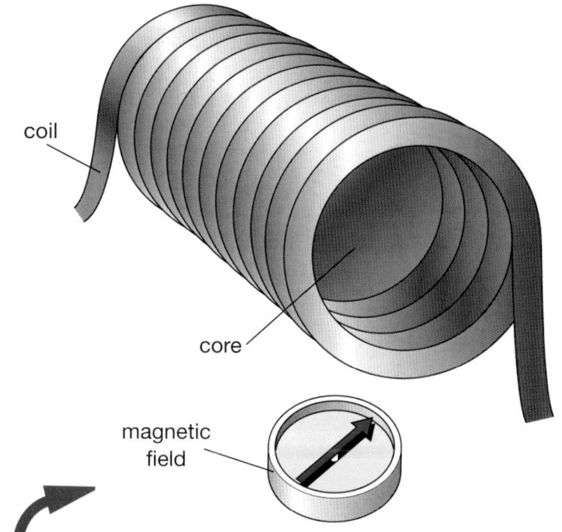

Figure 3 Any coil of wire becomes an electromagnet whenever a current flows through it. The strength of the electromagnet depends on: the kind of core inside it, the current in the wires, the number of turns of wire in the coil and the dimensions of the coil. In a loudspeaker the current varies so the magnetic force varies.

Questions

1. Explain what an amplifier does.
2. What's the difference between the vibrations of a string of an electric guitar and the vibration of the loudspeaker that provides an amplified version of the same note?
3. Describe what each of these does to make a loudspeaker produce sound:

   amplifier coil fixed magnet cone

Remember

Use the following words to complete the passage below.

cone current magnetic amplitude amplifier loudspeaker magnet

When an electric ____**1**____ flows in a coil, the coil becomes ____**2**____. A varying current in the coil of a ____**3**____ creates varying force between the coil and a fixed ____**4**____. The varying current makes the coil vibrate. So the ____**5**____ of the loudspeaker vibrates. It can vibrate with high ____**6**____ to make loud sounds. An ____**7**____ takes the small electric current from a guitar pick-up and creates bigger currents that are strong enough to drive a loudspeaker.

Closer

Reality checks

Science is about reality. It is about using your eyes. It is about thinking. Here are some things to look at and think about:

- What happens to a compass needle when it is in between two similar magnets? Does it depend on the orientation of the magnets?
- Is wood a magnetic material?
- Is a 2p coin made of magnetic material? Is a 2p coin a magnet? [Hint: If it is it will be able to repel other magnets, and not just be attracted by them.]
- What about a £1 coin?
- How can you use magnetism to sort steel cans from aluminium drinks cans? (This is important for recycling metals.)
- Tape some strong (ceramic) magnets to both ends of some 'dynamics trolleys'. Line up several trolleys so that the magnets on the ends are always repelling. Move the end trolley closer to its neighbour. Observe and explain.

Questions

1 These are some words and ideas about magnetism:

- action at a distance
- attraction
- compass
- electric current
- electromagnet
- field lines
- gravity
- iron
- magnet
- magnetic field
- magnetic material
- North
- repulsion
- steel
- South

Make your own big thinklinks chart to show how the words are connected to each other.

Now add these words to your chart:

- coil
- Earth
- electric bell
- iron core
- loudspeaker
- relay switch

2 These are some search words that you could use on the Internet to find out more about why magnetism matters. You could use the information you gather to make a small poster:

- geomagnetism
- aurora
- how a loudspeaker works

Choose your information carefully. Do not use information that you do not understand yourself. If a website is too technical, find a simpler one.

Micro-organisms and disease

Opener
Superbugs!

When we have an infection, the doctor can give us antibiotics to kill off the bacteria causing the infection. Some bacteria have evolved to become resistant to antibiotics.

What is MRSA?

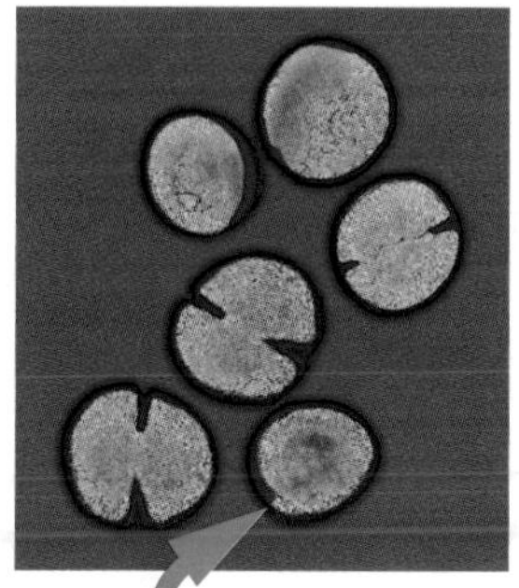

The MRSA superbug

MRSA is a bacterium that is resistant to antibiotics. MRSA stands for **M**ethicillin (a type of antibiotic) **R**esistant (is not easily killed) ***S**taphylococcus* ***a**ureus* (the name of the bacterium). It lives on your skin and 20–30% of the population have it inside their nose. If it gets into an open wound it can cause a very serious infection.

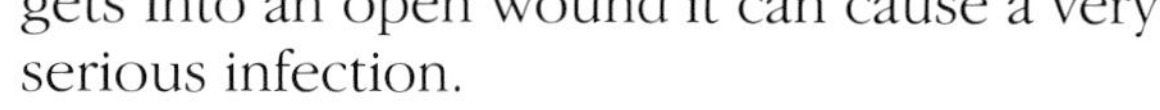

MRSA has been in the news with some people dying after being infected and others left with serious illnesses. Poor hygiene in hospitals is often blamed. Doctors and surgeons must wash their hands thoroughly.

Washing your hands after going to the toilet or before handling food is also important.

Procedure for washing hands

1. First rub your palms together.
2. Rub the palm of your right hand over the back of your left, then your left over your right.
3. Interlock your fingers and twist your hands, rubbing the palms together.
4. Curl the fingers of your left hand around the fingers of your right hand and rub together.
5. Grab the left thumb in your right hand and twist, then grab the right thumb in your left hand and twist.
6. Rub the fingers of each hand across the bottom of each palm.
7. Grab the left wrist in your right hand and slowly work up to the elbow.
8. Grab the right wrist in your left hand and work up to the elbow.

Questions

1 Learn the sequence that surgeons use to wash their hands. Give yourself five minutes to learn it, then close the book and turn to the person next to you. Show your partner the sequence (they can look at the book to check if you are correct). Now test your partner to see if they can repeat the sequence.

Microbes

Germs are microscopic organisms called viruses and bacteria.

Figure 1 Germs are everywhere.

Just what is a germ and can you really pick it up? What are commonly called germs are in fact **micro-organisms**, like **bacteria** and **viruses**. They are living things that are too small to see with the naked eye. Not all micro-organisms are harmful as you will find out. Some are useful to us.

There are millions of different types of bacteria. In fact, if we were to judge who ruled the Earth by the numbers of individual living things present on Earth at any one time, the bacteria would win hands down (at least they would if they had any hands!). There are also many different types of virus.

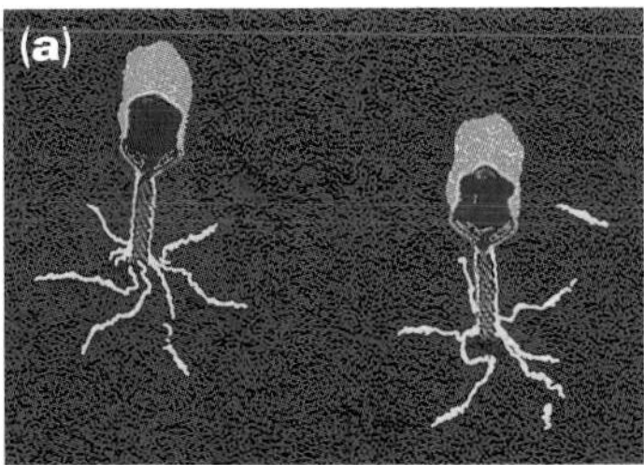

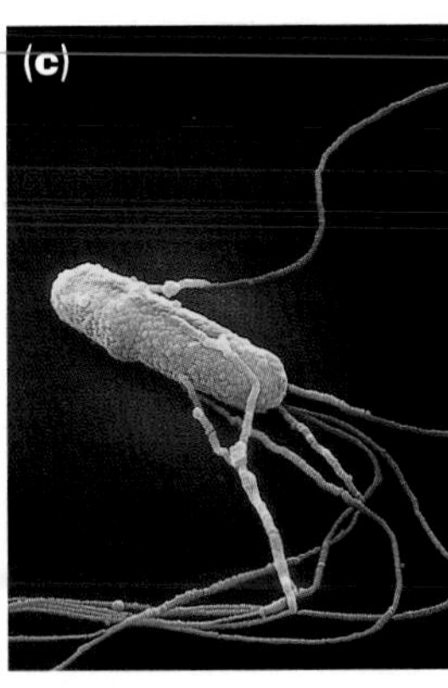

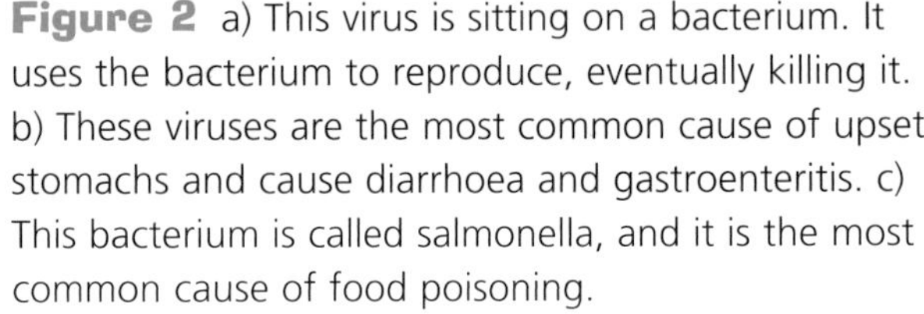

Figure 2 a) This virus is sitting on a bacterium. It uses the bacterium to reproduce, eventually killing it. b) These viruses are the most common cause of upset stomachs and cause diarrhoea and gastroenteritis. c) This bacterium is called salmonella, and it is the most common cause of food poisoning.

If you compare a bacterium (plural: bacteria) to a virus, there are a number of differences. Look at Figure 2. A bacterium is much bigger than a virus. Bacteria have a similar structure to a normal cell, but they do not have a nucleus. Bacteria contain strands of **DNA** instead. These control what happens in the bacterium and how it reproduces. Bacteria need a food supply to give them energy to enable them to grow and multiply. Many bacteria are involved in the decomposition (rotting) of dead plants and animals.

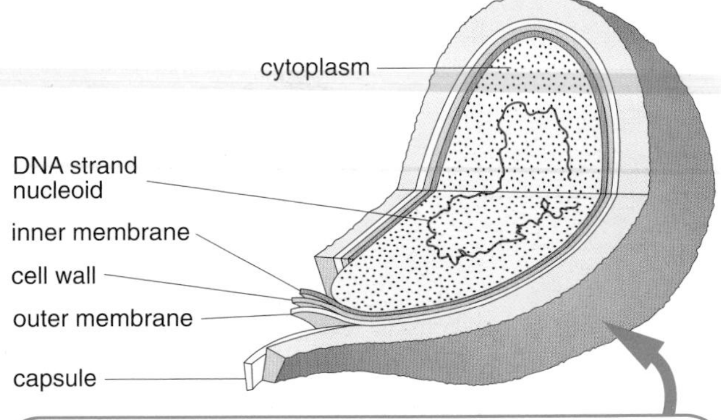

Figure 3 A simple bacterium

Viruses do not have any of the structures found in normal cells. They do not need food to supply them with energy. They contain a strand of DNA and need to enter a cell of another organism to reproduce. Instead of a membrane surrounding the virus, they have a coat or shell made of protein. A virus can exist for thousands of years unchanged and inactive. Once it finds a new host cell it can become active again. The DNA strand then tells the host cell to make copies of the virus.

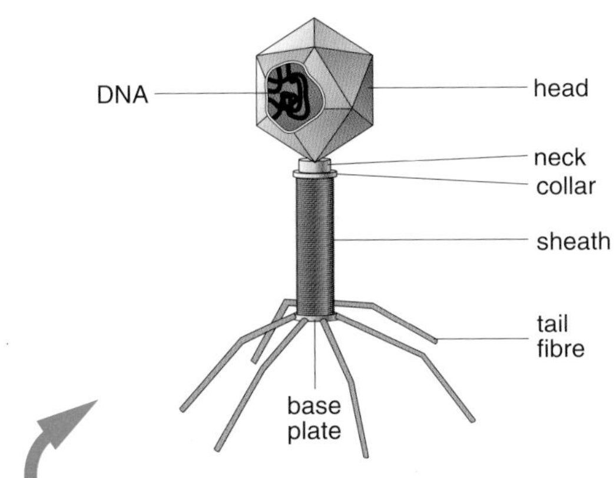

Figure 4 A T2 phage virus, which attacks bacteria

Because micro-organisms are so small they can spread easily. There is an old saying 'coughs and sneezes spread diseases, catch them in your handkerchief'. If you look at Figure 5 showing a person sneezing, you can see tiny water droplets spraying out from their nose and mouth. These droplets can contain millions of bacteria or viruses. The water spray doesn't immediately fall to the ground, so anyone breathing in the droplets can become infected. Lots of diseases can be spread this way, including colds and 'flu.

Figure 5 A single sneeze produces a jet of water droplets that could spread the 'flu virus.

Stop and think!

Bacteria and viruses can cause disease and are spread between humans and animals in a number of ways. List as many ways as you can by which bacteria and viruses can be spread between humans.

Questions

1. Some scientists say that a virus is not a living organism. Which of the characteristics of living things does a virus have and which is it lacking? (Think back to work you did last year on living things!)
2. Bacteria and viruses do not have a nucleus. What controls how they reproduce?
3. When we catch a cold, we often begin sneezing and get a high temperature. What is the body trying to do when we sneeze and when our body heats up?
4. Bacteria are involved in the decomposition (rotting) of dead plants and animals. Why are bacteria involved in this and not viruses?
5. Which parts of the cell are not present in a virus?

Remember

Use the following words to fill in the spaces below.

micro-organisms millions reproduce small bacteria viruses

____1____ and viruses are ____2____. They are so ____3____ they can't be seen without a microscope.

These living things can ____4____ rapidly so there are soon ____5____ of them. Bacteria and ____6____ are the cause of disease.

7.2 More micro-organisms

Yeast, penicillin and the cause of athlete's foot are also micro-organisms. They are all members of the fungus family.

As we have mentioned, some micro-organisms can be helpful. **Yeast** is particularly helpful, in more ways than one. It is a very simple organism that can quickly reproduce by dividing into two. As it grows and respires it produces two waste products, the gas carbon dioxide and alcohol. We can use the carbon dioxide when baking bread to cause the dough to rise and to give the bread a light fluffy texture. When we brew beers, wines or spirits, yeast produces the alcohol present in these drinks.

Figure 1 Yeast has helped the bread to rise.

Figure 2 The alcohol in this beer was produced by yeast.

Yeast is a type of **fungus**. Some types of fungus can cause us problems. Athlete's foot, for example, is caused by a fungus. A fungus is a type of mould that lives in dark, warm, moist areas. On the feet, the fungus can grow on and between toes, as well as on soles and toenails. Athlete's foot is often spread in places where people go barefoot, such as public showers or swimming pools. It can start with mild itching but can result in painful inflammation and blisters if it is not treated. It usually starts between the toes or on the arch of the foot and may spread to the bottom and sides of the foot.

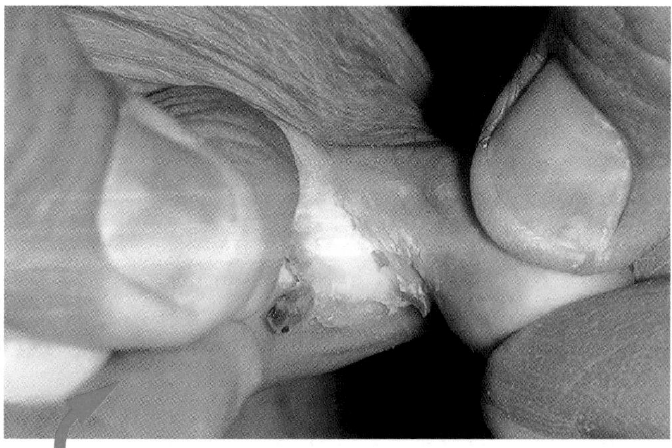

Figure 3 Athlete's foot

How to avoid athlete's foot:

- Wash your feet daily.
- Dry your feet thoroughly, especially in between your toes.
- Avoid tight footwear, especially in the summer.
- Wear sandals in warm weather.
- Wear cotton socks and change daily or more frequently if they become damp.
- Don't wear socks made of synthetic materials like nylon.
- Go barefoot at home if possible.
- Dust an anti-fungal powder into your shoes in the summertime.
- Use foot powders to help absorb moisture and kill any fungus.

Penicillin: a modern miracle

Other types of micro-organisms can actually protect us and keep us healthy. One type of mould that commonly grows on stale bread is **penicillin**. This mould can prevent us from becoming infected by certain types of bacteria and will even kill off bacteria. It was the first really effective treatment for bacterial infections.

Penicillin was discovered by accident when bacteria being grown in a laboratory were infected with the penicillin mould. Alexander Fleming (1881–1955) noticed that the bacteria were killed close to where the penicillin was growing. Fleming couldn't, however, produce enough of the chemical that killed the bacteria without killing the penicillin. In the 1940s two other scientists, Howard Florey (1898–1968), an Australian, and Ernst Chain (1906–1979), a German Jew, managed to produce larger amounts of the chemical. Florey deliberately infected eight mice with deadly bacteria. Four of the mice were given penicillin and lived, the other four, not treated, died after 15 hours.

The first human to be treated was Albert Alexander, a policeman who was dying from a serious bacterial infection. After being given penicillin his condition improved, but supplies of the drug ran out and he eventually died.

In order to make enough penicillin, Florey had to go to America, away from the heart of World War II. The production of penicillin saved many soldiers' lives during the war. In 1945 Fleming, Florey and Chain were all awarded the Nobel Prize for medicine.

Figure 4 Alexander Fleming

Figure 5 Howard Florey **Figure 6** Ernst Chain

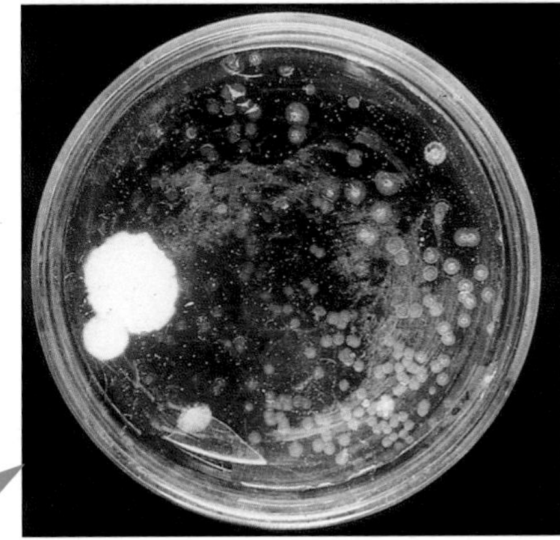

Figure 7 The penicillin (white) growing on a plate of bacteria

Questions

1 Yeast is a type of fungus used in baking and brewing. What other type of fungus is often used in cooking?

2 Athlete's foot is another type of fungus. What living conditions do yeast and athlete's foot both enjoy?

Remember

Produce a leaflet that could be distributed to swimmers at your local swimming pool warning about athlete's foot and giving advice on prevention.

7.3 Spreading disease

Coughs and sneezes may spread diseases but just how do you catch them? More to the point, how does your body react and try to protect you from disease?

Table 1 shows you some common diseases and explains how they are spread between people and how your body tries to protect you from the disease. First of all we need to look at how disease can be spread between people. There are a number of different ways that this can happen. They include:

1 **Person-to-person:** The spread of infection may involve the passing of bacteria and/or viruses by blood or saliva or, for very contagious (easily caught) diseases, through the air (see below).

2 **Food-borne infection:** Food poisoning caused by bacteria is an example of this. Bacteria can contaminate rice and survive boiling. If the rice is cooled and reheated, the bacteria may grow and produce a poison that makes you vomit.

3 **Water-borne infection:** Contaminated water can spread diseases such as typhoid, cholera, dysentery and polio.

4 **Airborne infection:** *Legionella pneumophila* causes Legionnaire's disease. It can be found in many natural water sources but is normally found in poorly-maintained air-conditioning systems or rarely-cleaned shower heads. Airborne droplets of water can be breathed in causing Legionnaire's disease.

5 **Insect-borne infection:** Many diseases are spread by insects. The plague, for example, was carried by rat fleas.

Questions

1 Looking at Table 1, which causes of common disease are the most difficult to treat?

2 Colds and 'flu are more common in the winter than in the summer. Being cold doesn't mean that you will necessarily catch a cold. Why are people more likely to catch colds in the winter? (*Hint*: think about how people behave in the winter months.)

3 Water-borne diseases are much more common in Third World countries. Why might this be the case?

4 Most people confuse a common cold with 'flu. What are the similarities and differences between a cold and 'flu?

5 What should be done to prevent the spread of food poisoning? (*Hint*: think of things you may have covered in food technology.)

Type of infection	What causes it?	How is it spread?	Who is most at risk?	What are the symptoms?	How does the body defend itself?	How is it treated?
Impetigo	Group A streptococcus bacteria	Person-to-person, by contact with infected blisters	People who suffer from cancer, diabetes and kidney disease, because their resistance to disease is lower	Blisters on the skin that weep	The skin normally prevents the bacteria entering the body. If it does enter through sores or cuts, white blood cells fight off infection.	Antibiotic cream or tablets
Strep throat	Group A streptococcus bacteria	Person-to-person, by kissing or coughing	People who suffer from cancer, diabetes and kidney disease, because their resistance to disease is lower	Sore throat	White blood cells fight off infection	No treatment is normally given for mild cases but antibiotics can be used for severe cases.

Meningitis (an infection of the fluid surrounding the brain)	Group B streptococcus bacteria	Most people carry the bacteria but do not get ill. It can be spread from person to person by coughing and kissing, but not as easily as a cough or cold.	Newborn babies, pregnant women, the elderly, adolescents, young adults and people with kidney or liver disease	Fever, severe headache, feeling sick and vomiting, stiff neck, dislike of bright lights	The bacteria are present in a large number of people in the throat and do not cause problems. If they enter the bloodstream, white blood cells kill them off.	Antibiotic injections or tablets **Bacterial meningitis is very serious and must be treated immediately.**
Food poisoning	Salmonella Campylobacter *E. coli*	By eating infected, undercooked food	Young children and the elderly	Headache, stomach pain, diarrhoea, sometimes shivering and fever	By excreting the bacteria in waste and raising the body temperature to try and kill them off	Antibiotics are given only if the bacteria is thought to have spread to the blood.
Common cold	Caused by over 200 different viruses	Person-to-person contact, coughing, sneezing, kissing. Easily passes from person to person in crowds via airborne droplets	Everybody	Sore throat, runny nose, coughs and sneezes	White blood cells fight off the virus and kill it.	No cure, only relief from the symptoms
Influenza ('flu)	Virus, type A, B or C	Airborne droplets from coughing and sneezing, also kissing	Everybody	Fever, chills, aching joints and muscles, sore throat, runny nose, usually much more intense than a cold and sufferers need to spend time recovering in bed	White blood cells fight off the virus and kill it.	No cure, only relief from the symptoms
Measles	Measles virus	Airborne droplets	Mainly children but can affect anyone.	Fever, rash, cold-like symptoms	White blood cells fight off the virus and kill it. A vaccination can be given to young children.	No cure, only relief from the symptoms
Chickenpox	Chickenpox virus	Airborne droplets, direct contact with infected people	Mainly children but can affect anyone.	Slight fever, rash that develops into sores and blisters	White blood cells fight off the virus and kill it. A vaccination can be given to young children.	No cure, only relief from the symptoms
Malaria	Single-celled organism	Insect-borne, the mosquito injects the single-celled organism into the body with its saliva as it bites humans.	Travellers to Central and South America, Central Africa, Asia and the Far East	Shaking, chills, fever	The body finds it difficult to defend itself as the infection happens in the red blood cells.	Antimalarial drugs

Table 1 Types of infection

Internal army

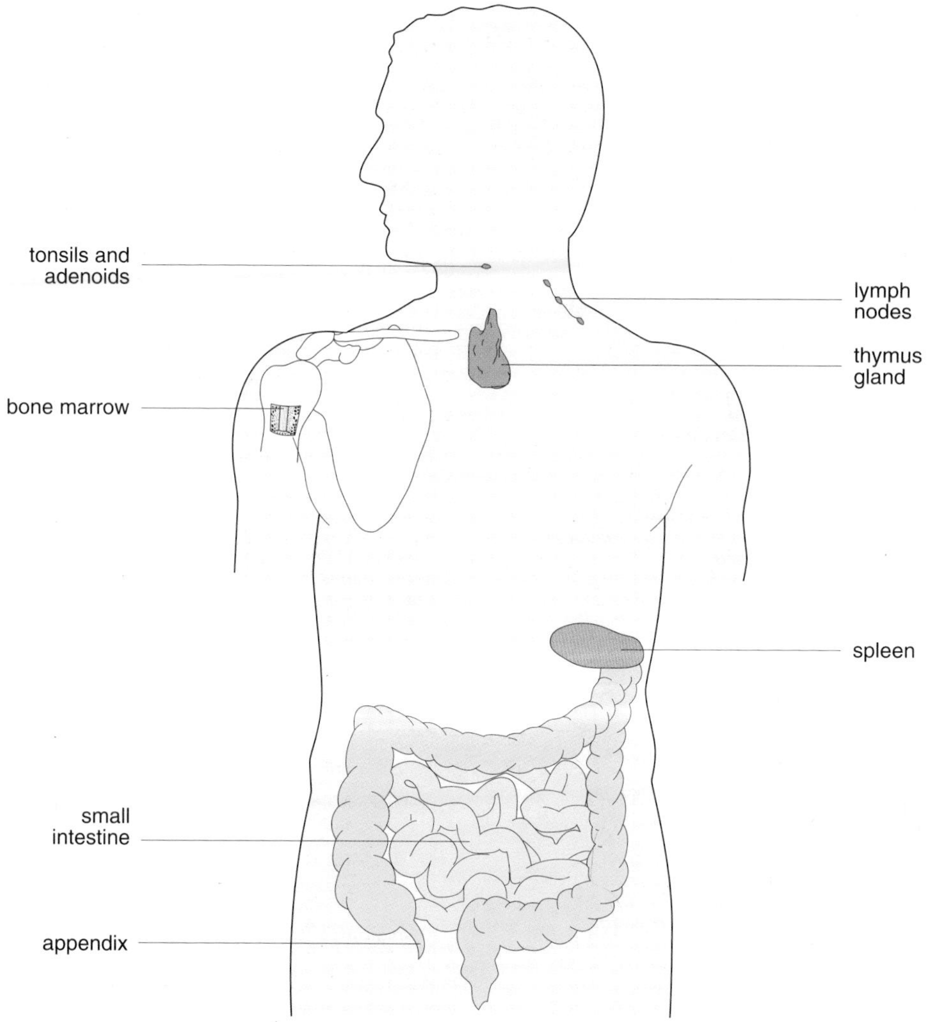

Figure 1 Disease-fighting organs

There are lots of things that can make us ill, but luckily our body can fight off a lot of the micro-organisms that cause infection. If you look at Figure 1 you will see that there are special organs and cells in our body that help to protect us and fight off disease.

Soldier cells

Blood is a sticky red liquid. It is probably the most important liquid in your body besides water. Your blood transports things around your body and acts as a defender against infection. Almost half of your blood is made up of cells – **red blood cells**, **white blood cells** and fragments of cells called **platelets**.

White blood cells are made in your **bone marrow**. Some of them are then changed by the **thymus gland** into different types of white blood cell to help fight off different types of infection. White cells can gather together in your spleen, tonsils, adenoids, appendix and small intestine. They can also gather in the lymph nodes. The **lymph system** contains a colourless fluid which transports white blood cells to the site of infection and micro-organisms and dead cells back to the lymph nodes where they can be broken down and removed from the body.

Your body's defences

Your immune system has developed a number of ways of defending against invading micro-organisms. One of the first barriers is your skin. In case you breathe in any micro-organisms, hairs in your nose and tiny hair-like projections on the surface of cells lining the entrance to your lungs are coated in a sticky mucus. This traps the invaders and passes them upward and out of the body when you cough, sneeze and blow your nose (see Figure 2).

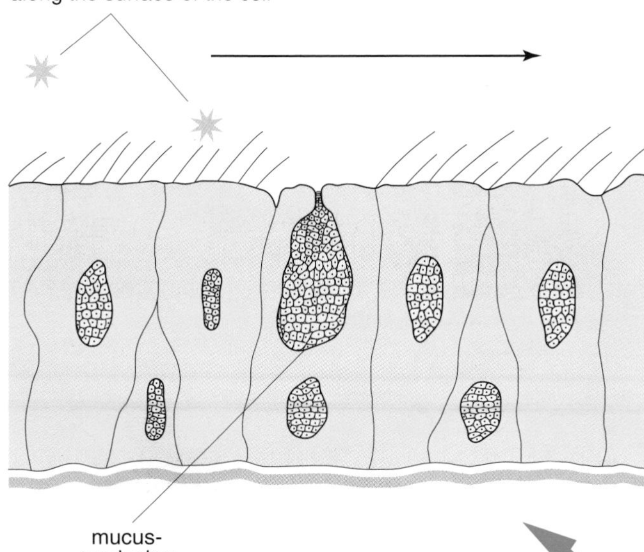

Figure 2 Hair-like projections and mucus trap micro-organisms.

If you breathe in any micro-organisms or get any blown into your eyes, enzymes in your saliva and tears will destroy them. If you eat or drink something that contains small numbers of bacteria, the acid in your stomach will kill them. If you cut yourself and bacteria get into the cut, they will quickly divide and multiply. To try and stop them getting into your bloodstream, your body increases the supply of blood to the injured area, making it appear red and warm, bringing white blood cells to destroy the invaders. Fluid leaks into the surrounding tissue which is why you get a swelling. To stop the blood from continuously leaking, platelets gather around the wound and begin to form a small clot. This plugs the hole in the blood vessel and forms a scab on the surface of the skin. The scab also helps to stop other micro-organisms from entering the body.

Whenever a micro-organism enters the body, white blood cells race towards the site of infection. Different types of white blood cell attack infections in different ways. Some produce protective chemicals called **antibodies** that overpower the micro-organism and destroy it. Others surround the invader and destroy it by chemically breaking it down. White blood cells only live for a short time, from a few days to a few weeks. A small drop of blood (1 mm^3) can contain anything from 7000–25 000 white blood cells. The more difficult an infection is to deal with, the more white blood cells are present in the blood.

Doctors can count the number of red and white blood cells in 1 mm^3 of blood and this can help them decide how healthy you are.

Questions

1 If you accidentally cut yourself, describe what would happen and explain the following:

a) why you stop bleeding after a while;

b) why the area around the cut goes red;

c) why the area around the cut feels warm.

2 List the organs and glands in the body that are there to try and protect you from disease.

3 Blood travels all around the body. How might this help to protect us from infections and disease?

4 Apart from special organs, in what other ways does our body protect us from getting infected with a micro-organism?

Remember

The body has special glands and cells to help us fight infection. Infections can be spread in a number of ways (remember the five ways!).

White blood cells help us fight off infection. Your nose acts as a filter trapping particles of dust and some micro-organisms, so you should breathe in through your nose and out through your mouth!

A shot in the arm

Smallpox is a deadly disease spread by a virus.

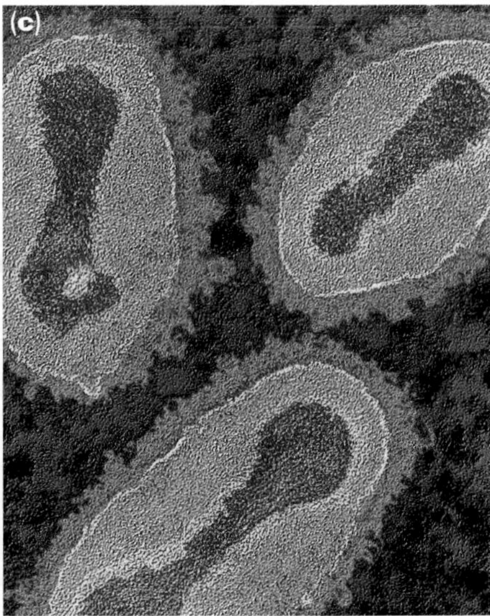

Figure 1 (a) Lady Mary Wortley Montagu, who protected her son from smallpox (b) Edward Jenner, who developed vaccination (c) The smallpox virus

Read the following account of smallpox and its prevention and discuss the questions at the foot of the next page in small groups.

The disease smallpox has been known for over 2000 years. When people catch smallpox, sores erupt on the surface of the skin and in and around the mouth. These were called 'pocks'. They are produced by a virus. Smallpox was a deadly disease that killed many millions of people, rich and poor. Only the very lucky ones survived an attack of smallpox.

Smallpox first appeared in China and the Far East. It is believed that the Pharaoh Ramses V died of smallpox in 1157 BC. The Chinese developed a way of vaccinating people called **variolation**. This involved picking the scabs off infected people, drying them, then grinding them up into a fine dust. This dust was then blown up the noses of healthy people. People protected in this way rarely caught smallpox. If they did, it was not as severe and did not always result in death.

The disease reached Europe around 710 AD and was transported to South America by Hernando Cortez in 1520. After this deadly virus was released into a newly discovered country, over 3 500 000 native Aztecs died in a very short time. Smallpox has now been eradicated. The last naturally-occurring outbreak was in Somalia on 26th October 1977.

Edward Jenner (1749–1823), a country doctor, is credited with having discovered vaccination. In 1796 he injected a 9-year-old boy, James Phipps, with the fluid from cowpox sores by making a small scratch with a thorn on his arm. He then deliberately infected James with smallpox. Luckily James survived. Jenner had noticed that milkmaids who caught cowpox seemed to be protected against smallpox. He took pus from a cowpox sore that had grown on a milkmaid called Sarah Nelmes.

Although Jenner did not know of the practice of variolation, it had been going on for many centuries in the Middle East. A type of protection against smallpox was, however, witnessed by **Lady Mary Wortley Montagu** (1689–1762) 78 years before Jenner made his discovery.

Lady Mary Wortley Montagu was a prominent member of society, the wife of the British Ambassador to the Ottoman Empire. She travelled with her husband and entertained foreign diplomats. In 1715, she contracted smallpox. She survived the disease but her face was badly scarred by the sores and she lost her eyelashes!

In 1718, while living in Turkey, she had her 6-year-old son protected from smallpox. Women in the villages used to collect the pus from sores developed on infected people in walnut shells. They would then dip a needle or sharp point into the pus and puncture the skin of the healthy children of the village. As she had suffered from smallpox and knew exactly how dangerous this was, she decided to try to protect her son. In 1721, a smallpox epidemic broke out in Great Britain and Lady Mary helped to get several children of the aristocracy protected. This came to the attention of the College of Physicians and these 'experiments' met with disapproval from the medical profession. Many people died in the 80 or so years until Edward Jenner's work. Perhaps they could have been saved.

Scientists

Dr Rosemary Leonard, MBE

Dr Rosemary Leonard is best known as a television doctor for programmes such as the BBC's Breakfast News. She also works as a GP (a General Practitioner, or family doctor) in south London, where she has a special interest in women's health problems. Before becoming a GP, she worked in several teaching hospitals, where she specialised in obstetrics, the care of women during pregnancy and birth, and gynaecology, which involves the care of disorders of a woman's reproductive system.

Rosemary trained to be a doctor at Cambridge University and St Thomas's Hospital Medical School in London. She has written on health issues on a wide variety of national newspapers and magazines, and also sits on several government health advisory committees. Apart from her work as a doctor, she enjoys ski-ing, hiking and sailing with her two sons. In 2004 she was awarded an MBE (Member of the Order of the British Empire) for her services to healthcare.

Questions

Think about the following questions. Discuss the issues in groups.

Edward Jenner was a physician or doctor who carried out an 'experiment' on James Phipps. Do you think he would be allowed to do the same today? Was his 'experiment' a proper one to do? What could have happened to the boy?

Doctors had to be paid by patients for each visit and treatment in Lady Mary's day. Why do you think that they were not happy with the treatment she brought over from Turkey for preventing smallpox?

Remember

Prepare a written statement to the General Medical Council. Your statement must either defend Jenner's actions in developing the vaccine or condemn his actions. Remember to use evidence to support your viewpoint. Just saying 'I think Edward Jenner was right' or 'wrong' is not enough. You must say why you think he was right or wrong.

AIDS

What is AIDS?

AIDS was first reported in the United States in 1981 and has since become a major worldwide **epidemic**. AIDS stands for Acquired Immune Deficiency Syndrome. It is caused by the human immunodeficiency **virus** (HIV). HIV is spread most commonly by sexual contact with an infected partner.

Once the virus has **invaded** the body, it enters the cells of the human **immune** system. It then reproduces to create millions of identical viruses inside the host cells. When the infected cells burst open, the viruses escape into the blood and invade millions more cells. The virus goes on to destroy the body's immune system and so individuals diagnosed with AIDS are susceptible to life-threatening diseases. These are caused by microbes that do not usually cause illnesses in healthy people as they are normally controlled by a healthy immune system. It is these diseases that eventually cause death.

HIV can also be spread through contact with **infected blood**. There have been many reported cases of people catching the HIV virus from blood transfusions. Now transfusion blood is checked for HIV infection. In 1985 heat-treating techniques were introduced to destroy HIV in blood products.

Drug users are also prone to infection from HIV because of the practice of sharing needles or syringes. These become **contaminated** with minute quantities of blood from someone infected with the virus.

Transmission from patient to health-care worker or vice versa via accidents with contaminated needles is rare.

Studies of families of HIV-infected people have shown clearly that HIV is not spread through casual contact such as the sharing of food utensils or towels and bedding, swimming pools, telephones or toilet seats. HIV is not spread by biting insects such as mosquitoes or bedbugs.

Origins

Doctors are not sure how HIV first appeared. They think that a polio **vaccine** made using tissue from apes could have been behind the leap made by the virus from monkeys to humans. In the vaccine, the chimpanzee form of the virus could have been transferred to humans and become HIV.

Many scientists doubt this. They say '*the virus had existed in monkeys for millions of years, and in that time, monkeys and chimpanzees had been hunted for food. People who were exposed to the blood of these animals while chopping and processing them for the table, should have got infected a long time ago.*'

Samples of the vaccine under suspicion still exist, and there have been calls for it to be tested, if only to put the theory to rest once and for all. The theory also alarms those who believe the future of medicine is likely to include **xenotransplantation**, where organs from an animal – such as a pig – are placed in a human. The World Health Organisation stresses that all polio vaccines currently in use are rigorously screened and are safe.

Early symptoms

Many people do not develop any **symptoms** when they first become infected with HIV. Some people, however, have a flu-like illness within a month or two of exposure to the virus. People are very infectious during this period, and HIV is present in large quantities in their body fluids.

The severe effects may not surface until a decade or more after HIV first enters the body in adults. During this period, however,

HIV is actively multiplying, infecting and killing cells of the immune system. HIV's effect is seen most obviously in the decline in the levels of one type of white blood cells in the blood, T4 cells – the immune system's key infection fighters. The virus destroys these cells without causing other effects. Eventually an infection such as pneumonia can kill because the immune system has no defences left to fight it.

People with AIDS are particularly prone to developing various **cancers**, especially those caused by viruses. One common example is a skin cancer that is very difficult to treat called Kaposi's sarcoma. In light-skinned people it causes round brown, red or purple spots that develop on the skin or in the mouth.

Treatment

When AIDS first surfaced in the United States, no drugs were available to combat the underlying immune deficiency and few treatments existed for the diseases that resulted. Over the past 10 years, however, therapies have been developed to fight both HIV infection and its associated infections and cancers.

There are now a number of drugs for the treatment of HIV infection. The drugs interrupt an early stage of the virus **reproducing** itself. The best known of these is AZT, which is very expensive. These drugs may slow the spread of HIV in the body but they do not prevent transmission of HIV to other individuals.

Illnesses common in people with AIDS result in symptoms like coughing, shortness of breath, seizures, mental symptoms such as confusion and forgetfulness, severe diarrhoea, fever, vision loss, severe headaches, weight loss, extreme fatigue, nausea, vomiting, lack of co-ordination, coma, abdominal cramps, or difficult or painful swallowing.

A small number of people (less than 50) initially infected with HIV 10 or more years ago have not developed symptoms of AIDS. Scientists are trying to find out why. It is possible that their immune system, or their **genetic** make-up, protects them from the effects of HIV. Scientists hope that understanding the natural method of control may lead to ideas for HIV vaccines.

Prevention

Since no vaccine for HIV is available, the only way to prevent infection by the virus is to avoid behaviours that put a person at **risk** of infection, such as sharing needles and having unprotected sex. Because many people infected with HIV have no symptoms, there is no way of knowing with certainty whether a sexual partner is infected, unless he or she has been repeatedly tested for the virus or has not engaged in any risky behaviour. Authorities recommend that people either abstain from sex or protect themselves by using male latex **condoms** whenever they have sex.

Questions

1 Make a list of all the words in bold type. Beside each word explain what it means.

2 Explain how the HIV virus destroys the immune system.

3 How can the virus be spread?

4 In what ways can the virus not be transferred to others?

5 How can you protect yourself from getting AIDS?

6 What is the difference between HIV and AIDS?

7 What special problems exist in Africa?

8 What illnesses are associated with:

a) early HIV infection?
b) the later stages of AIDS?

Closer

Cholera in London

Cholera is a very nasty disease. In 1854 outbreaks of cholera in London were making hundreds of people ill and many of them died. The disease starts with an upset stomach, then you get diarrhoea. If it is severe you vomit and get bad leg cramps. Eventually you become dehydrated and can die.

During the 1830s and 1840s in London, raw sewage was pumped straight into the River Thames. This killed off all the fish and caused a smell Londoners called 'The Great Stink'. Many doctors, except John Snow (1813–1858), thought that bad air carried disease. The map shows where the outbreaks of cholera happened.

Snow believed cholera was carried in water, not air. He showed that cholera occurred much more frequently in customers of a water company that drew its water from the sewage-contaminated lower Thames. Snow concluded that the infection came from one water pump. He had the pump handle removed and stopped the spread of the disease.

John Snow

0 50 100 150 200
yards

P Pump
∵ Deaths from cholera

Oxford St.
Dean St.
Regent St.
Broad St.

Map showing where outbreaks of cholera happened

Questions

1. Which pump in the map is the most likely source of the infection?
2. How did taking the handle off the pump stop the spread of infection?
3. Cholera can be treated today using antibiotics. What is the most likely cause of cholera, a bacterium or a virus?
4. How do you think that people living a long way from the infected pump still got cholera and died?
5. Find out what happens to the sewage we produce today in our towns and cities.

Weathering and erosion

Opener
The power of rain and sea

Water has the mass and energy to move large chunks of land about. It is the main factor in changing the shape of our land.

Village up to its waist in mud

Flood damage in Cornwall

A 3 m wall of water crashed through a Cornish village in August 2004 when 77 mm of rain fell in three hours.

Cars in the car park were thrown into the sea and people on rooftops were airlifted to safety. Fifty two cars were later pulled up from the mud. The museum had up to 1.2 m of mud in its ground floor rooms.

The local geology contributed to the flooding. That part of Cornwall is made up of shale covered by impermeable clay. Rainwater ran off fields quickly, adding to the torrent.

Huge waves eroding the British coast

Piles of boulders hurled by the sea

In the Western Isles (in Scotland), in Summer 2004, storm waves over 20 m high ripped boulders the size of cars from cliff faces and hurled them up to 50 m inland.

Because sea levels are continuing to rise and larger waves are hitting the cliffs, the rate of erosion of the coastline is increasing.

Questions

1 Write down the meanings of these words:

silt impermeable torrent
storm boulder hurl

2 Why did the rain run off the Cornish land so easily?

3 Where did the mud come from?

4 Why was the mud left behind after the flood?

5 A 1 m cube of rock has a mass of 2 tonnes. Estimate or calculate the mass of a rock the size of a car. (A car is approximately 5 m × 2 m × 1.5 m).

6 Find out where the energy comes from to make the waves in the sea.

The scrubbed face of Britain

The surface of the Earth is constantly being changed by physical and chemical processes.

Have you ever sanded a piece of wood? The rubbing grinds away the surface as tiny dusty particles, until eventually it is completely flat.

The solid surface of the Earth is constantly being scoured away and changed as well. The harsh wind and beating rain both wear away the surface. Physical processes, such as expansion and freezing, split the rocks up; wind and water then carry the bits away. Nothing remains the same for very long.

Box 1

These mountains in Scotland used to be part of North America. The process of **continental drift** carried the rocks here and has been slowly squashing the mountains into the rest of Britain. That's why they have been pushed up higher than the surrounding countryside.

Wind, rain and running water have scoured the rest of Britain practically down to sea level. Our highest peaks are those that were formed most recently.

These mountains were as high as the Himalayas when they were young, but have been eroded away. The peaks left are granite left over by erosion of the softer rock. These mountains were formed only 400 million years ago.

Box 2

Under this bleak moorland, the rock is full of caves and caverns.

Rainwater is a very weak acid, because it contains dissolved carbon dioxide. Rainwater falls on to the limestone and finds its way underground through tiny cracks. As it flows through these cracks, it chemically **dissolves** the rock away very slowly. Eventually, under the ground, huge spaces are left in the rock. People climb down and explore these 'pot holes', as they are called.

Box 3

Great Britain has not always been a quiet place. In the past there have been volcanic eruptions and lava flows. Edinburgh Castle is built on a lump of very hard **volcanic rock** left behind when the softer rock surrounding it was eroded away.

Box 4

The Earth's surface is not really 'rock solid' – it's moving about all the time. Sometimes these movements are quick jerks. These are what we experience as **earthquakes**. Other rock movements are slow, steady pushes that take millions of years. These fold the rock layers into new shapes.

Box 5

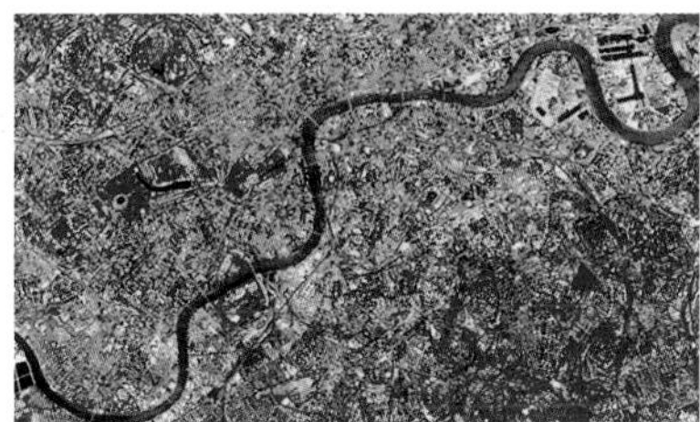

As the River Thames passes through London, its flow gets slower and slower and the river gets wider and wider. The river meanders as it gets slower. As it slows down all the tiny sand and mud particles it has carried begin to **settle** out. These particles make the huge mud flats of the Thames Estuary.

Questions

Box 1 Why are the highest mountains in Britain found in Scotland?
Box 2 How are potholes formed?
Box 3 Why has a lump of rock been left in Edinburgh, sticking up above the surrounding landscape?
Box 4 What caused the folding of the rock layers (strata) in Lulworth?
Box 5 Look at the picture of the River Thames. Why do you think this shows a slow moving river rather than a fast river?
Box 6 What processes break rock fragments from a mountain side?

Box 6

Why a danger notice? The clue is that a huge pile of stones of similar sizes can only be formed by a natural process. All of these stones were once attached to the mountainside above.

As the rocks get heated and then cool they expand and contract. As water in the rocks freezes and thaws it also expands and contracts. These processes cause lumps of rock to crack from the mountain, and gravity eventually sends them tumbling down.

This causes a pile of rocks to accumulate at the bottom of the slope. This is called a **scree slope**. The falling rocks notice warns travellers of the danger of large rocks tumbling down at any time.

Remember

Each of the boxes contains an example of a different process. Fill in the missing letters to complete the words.

Box 1 C _ _ T _ _ENT _ _ D _ _ _ _

Box 2 CH _ _ _ _ AL DIS _ _ _ V _ _ _

Box 3 E _ _ _ _ _ _ of softer rocks

Box 4 F _ _ _ _ _ _

Box 5 S _ _ _ _ _ NG OUT

Box 6 EXP _ _ _ _ _ _ and CON _ _ _ _ _ _ _ _

8.2 Rocks and minerals

A mineral is just one pure substance. Rocks are a mixture of lots of bits of minerals together.

Our planet has a liquid iron and nickel **core**. Surrounding this is a layer of rock called the **mantle**. Only the outer 30 km of this has cooled to become solid rock. Our planet is more like a ball of porridge with a dried crust than the third 'rock' from the Sun.

The Earth has been here for 4600 million years. In this time, weather has made a lot of changes to that 30 km depth of solid rock on the thin outer skin of our planet. Rock is hard but millions of years of rain and wind wear it away very well. Rocks are made from grains of minerals.

The biggest clue that helps you decide whether a material is a mineral is that a mineral is made up of just one colour. Rocks are not just one colour. Because they can be formed from lots of minerals, they often look speckled. The process of **erosion** has mixed the minerals to make rock.

quartz		silicon dioxide
olivine	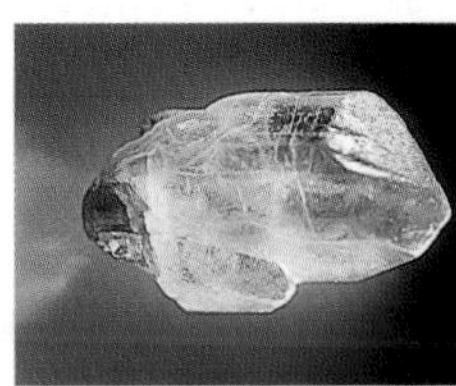	magnesium iron silicate
feldspar		potassium aluminium silicate
malachite		copper carbonate
iron pyrites		iron sulphide
calcite		calcium carbonate
diamond		pure carbon
rock salt		sodium chloride

Table 1 Some common minerals

Questions

1 Put the minerals in Table 1 in groups according to their colour.

2 What are the textures of the minerals like?

3 What are the three main types of rock?

4 Draw what you would expect a conglomerate to look like.

5 Which rocks would you expect to soak up water?

6 What rocks would you not use for building a wall?

7 What would the texture of these rocks be like?
a) sandstone
b) mudstone
c) marble
d) obsidian

8 Is there a pattern linking type of rock and density?

Rock type	Description	Type	Density	One source in UK
Conglomerates	A rock containing many large particles held together by a finer-grained cement; looks a bit like concrete	Sedimentary	Medium	Devon
Sandstone	A rock made of sand-sized particles stuck together	Sedimentary	Low	Just about anywhere!
Limestone	A hard solid rock composed almost entirely of calcium carbonate	Sedimentary	Medium	Portland
Chalk	A soft crumbly rock composed of the calcium carbonate shells of prehistoric sea animals	Sedimentary	Low	Dover
Mudstone	A soft rock composed of particles less than one tenth of a millimetre in diameter	Sedimentary	Medium	Just about anywhere!
Shale	A highly laminated mudrock	Sedimentary	Medium	Pembroke
Slate	Very hard black layered rock. Metamorphosed shale	Metamorphic	High	Pembroke
Marble	Very hard. Completely metamorphosed limestone or chalk	Metamorphic	High	Skye
Granite	A hard acidic coarse grained rock. Generally high in silica, quartz, feldspar and mica	Igneous	Medium	Wales
Gabbro	A basic coarse grained rock. High content of feldspar and pyroxene	Igneous	High	Lake District
Pumice	Highly porous igneous rock, like a rock sponge	Igneous	Low	None
Obsidian	Solid glassy igneous rock. Formed by ultra rapid cooling. Very dark in colour (almost black)	Igneous	High	Isle of Arran

Table 2 Some common rock types

The surface of the Earth is constantly being ground down to a powder, washed away, spread out, buried under more layers, cooked and compressed by heat from below. It can even be pushed down into the magma and re-melted.

These processes drive the **rock cycle** (see pages 126–127) and give rise to three classes of rock types.

These are:

- **igneous rocks** – formed from molten material from inside the Earth;
- **sedimentary rocks** – formed when water deposits layers of material;
- **metamorphic rocks** – formed by the action of heat and pressure on other rocks.

Remember

Write definitions for these words:

mineral

rock

igneous

sedimentary

metamorphic

A million year mixer I

Weather and water break up materials on the surface of the Earth and mix them together to make rock. This breaking up is called 'weathering'. The process of weathering and the water and wind carrying the particles away is called 'erosion'.

Weathering

Cathedrals, statues, buildings and headstones can all be affected by the weather. The Greeks and Romans used lots of marble and limestone in their buildings. Over the centuries weather breaks up stone.

Weathering is a process that breaks up and mixes bits of material. Eventually these become new rocks. There are two types of weathering, **chemical weathering** and **mechanical weathering.**

Mechanical weathering

Freezing

a) Water can fill cracks in the rock. If it is cold, the water will freeze.

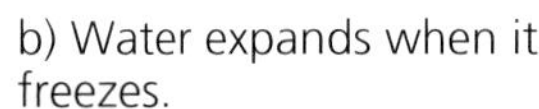

b) Water expands when it freezes.

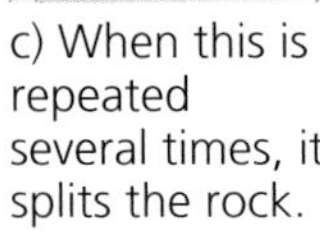

c) When this is repeated several times, it splits the rock.

Figure 1 Freeze–thaw weathering

Expansion

The process shown in Figure 2 is called onion skin weathering. Layers peel off the rock a little at a time. The force of the expansion causes the layer to split off with a crack. This sometimes throws fragments of rock several metres away.

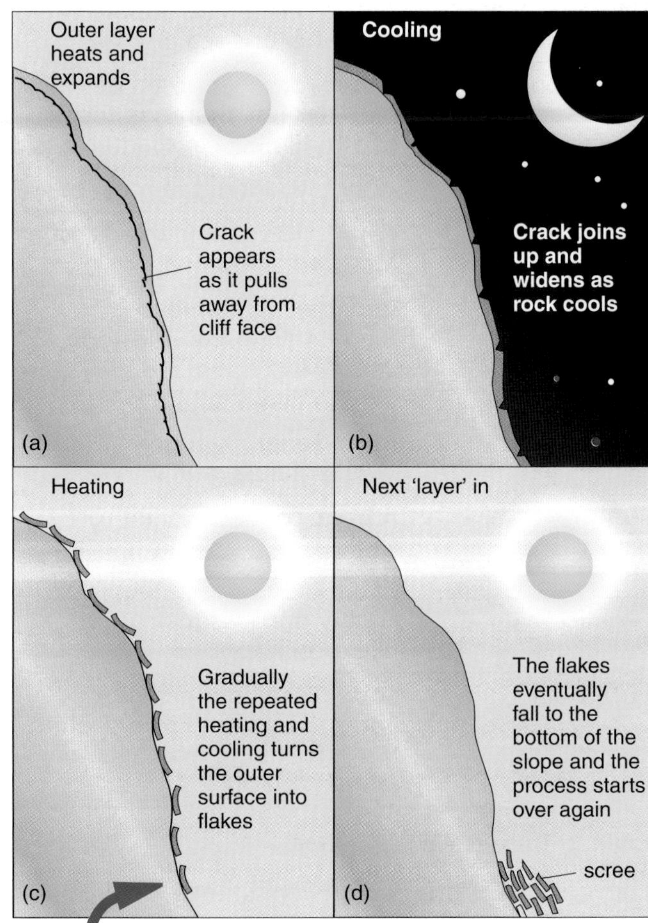

Figure 2 In the hot sun, one side of a rock can heat and expand while the other stays cool. The expansion can cause the rock to split.

Powerful plants

Seeds that are blown by the wind or dropped by birds can grow in the cracks of rocks. The roots force themselves into the cracks, making them bigger. Next time you walk down a tree-lined street, look at the roots of the trees. They often crack paving stones and force pavements up as they grow. They can do the same to rocks. All of this is part of mechanical weathering.

Wind

Figure 3 shows a typical film set landscape seen in many American films. The odd shapes of the rock are caused by strong winds blowing sand over the rocks and wearing away softer rock from below harder rock.

Figure 3 Wind eroded rock

Questions

1. What are the two main types of weathering?
2. When water freezes it expands, and this is why rocks can split apart. Why could freezing water be a problem at home?
3. What causes 'onion skin weathering'?
4. Make three drawings to show the effect of plant roots. Picture A should show soil in a crack in a rock. Picture B has a seed germinating in it. Picture C has the big plant roots forcing the crack wider.
5. Write a short story about how a house or the ground it stands on was eroded away. Use one of these titles.

   'It all started with a seed in a crack in the wall.'

   Or 'The crashing of the waves often woke me when I was young.'

   Or 'We always knew the ice sheet was moving. We could hear it grinding over the rocks in the distance.'
6. Take a different title from Question 5 and draw a picture to illustrate the process.

Sea

The constant beating of the waves eventually breaks off parts of the cliffs. Then the waves roll the rocks back and forth, making them into smaller and smaller pieces.

Glacier

Huge heavy sheets of ice called **glaciers** break up rock and carry it away. The landscape produced has steep-sided 'U' shaped valleys rather than 'V' shaped valleys produced by river erosion.

Figure 4 This valley in Switzerland was shaped by the movement of a glacier.

Remember

Use the following words to fill in the gaps.

rocks carries freezes slow crack running peel away

Mechanical weathering happens when:

- water ____1____ in cracks in the rock and splits the rock.
- heat expands one side of a rock and not the other, making it ____2____.
- plant roots can force a ____3____ in a rock apart.

Most weathering is very ____4____ and takes years to split up ____5____. Once the rocks are split up, ____6____ water or wind ____7____ the pieces away.

8.4 A million year mixer II

Chemical weathering

Chemical weathering is the process by which rock is turned into new materials by chemical change.

Acid attack

Put an aspirin in a glass of water and watch what happens. You will see a speeded up version of what happens to limestone in the rain.

Water slowly dissolves stone? No, some types of water (in this case water that has become slightly acid by falling through the air) dissolves some types of stone (in this case limestone which is alkaline).

Rainwater is naturally slightly acidic. Carbon dioxide from the atmosphere dissolves in rainwater to make a weak acid called **carbonic acid**.

Limestone caves

Limestone is a very alkaline rock so it is quickly attacked by any acid.

Limestone is a rock that contains a lot of **calcium carbonate**. This dissolves in cold rainwater to make calcium hydrogencarbonate solution. This reaction is shown in the equation below:

calcium carbonate	+	carbonic acid	→	calcium hydrogen carbonate
(solid)		(rainwater)		(solution)
$CaCO_3$	+	H_2CO_3	→	$Ca(HCO_3)_2$

Figure 1 Limestone caves in Barbados

As rainwater trickles through cracks in the limestone over many years it can dissolve millions of tonnes of rock to make huge caves like those in Barbados (Figure 1).

The calcium hydrogencarbonate solution in the underground water is not a very stable substance. Often a steady drip from the ceiling of the cavern will allow the solution to decompose back into solid calcium carbonate. This solid slowly forms the stalactites in the photo. These deposits grow at a rate of 1 cm every 100 years.

Hard water

This is an odd sounding idea, but actually this is water with dissolved rock in it. Just as explained earlier, calcium compounds in rock get dissolved in the water. These same calcium compounds get into the water supply to houses.

Hard water is very healthy to drink as we need calcium and the other minerals in our bodies. But hard water does cause problems. It forms scum with soap and leaves the 'limescale' that is found in kettles and other water heaters. Many houses are built with 'water softeners.' These remove the calcium salts from the house's water supply.

Acid rain pollution

If the rainwater has pollution from the burning of fossil fuels dissolved in it, then it becomes much more acidic.

Sulphuric acid and **nitric acid** are made when gases such as sulphur dioxide and nitrogen oxide dissolve in rain clouds. This adds greatly to the slight natural acidity of rainwater.

'Acid rain' has become a severe problem over the last hundred years. It has little effect on how fast limestone caves get created, but the much stronger acid rain severely damages buildings and monuments, particularly those made out of limestone or marble.

But it's not just limestone and marble that get attacked. Many other rocks contain minerals that are based on metal salts (see Table 1).

Rock	Metal salts present
granite	calcium, sodium, potassium
gabbro	magnesium, iron
dolomite	magnesium
gypsum	calcium

Table 1 Metal salts present in common rocks

The natural acidity of rainwater will dissolve these minerals out of rocks and gradually change the appearance and nature of the rock. This makes it softer and so erosion is easier.

Questions

1 Why is rain slightly acidic?

2 Write a word equation for the reaction between an acid and an alkali.

3 Why is limestone attacked more than other types of rock?

4 Put the garden statues in date order starting with the oldest one. The dates are: 1789, 1852, 1906, 1979.

(a) (b)

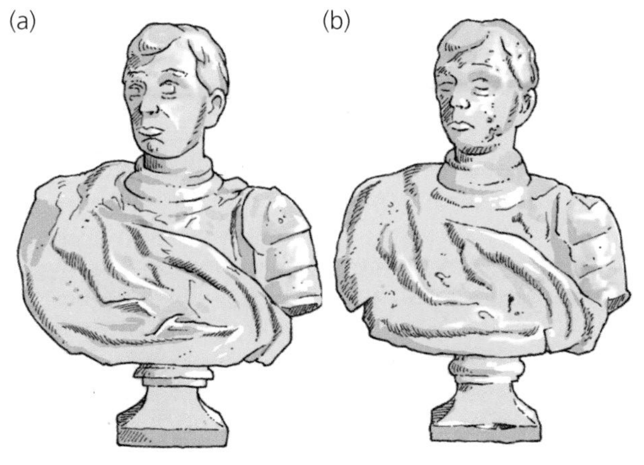

(c) (d)

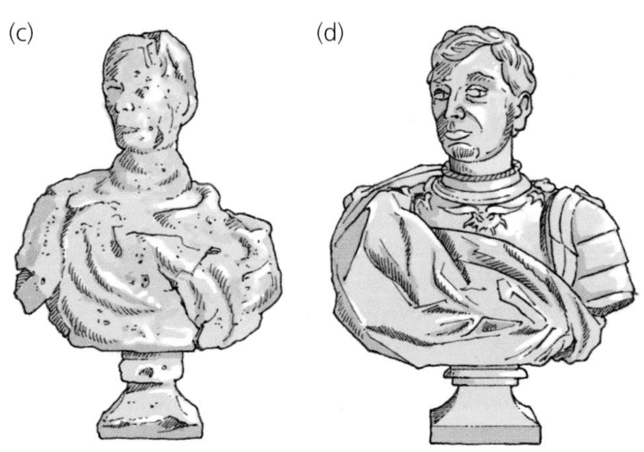

5 What extra substance does hard water contain?

6 What is good about hard water?

7 What problems does hard water cause?

8 What material are stalactites made from?

9 Rainwater is normally slightly acidic. What can make it more acid?

10 Look carefully at how acid pollution has damaged one of these monuments. Which needle stands in Central London?

Remember

Use the following words to fill in the spaces.

acid **dissolve**

Chemical weathering happens when water or dilute acids slowly ____1____ rock.
____2____ rain speeds up the process.

8.5 Grand Canyon story

The Colorado River has dug itself a very famous trench over the last 20 million years. It is up to 30 km wide and 450 km in length. But most remarkably its depth is 1.5 km – a trench a mile deep!

How was the Grand Canyon formed? The powerful force that dug the Grand Canyon is erosion, primarily by water (and ice) and secondly by wind. Water seems to have had the most impact, basically because our planet has lots of it and it is always on the move.

The soil in the Grand Canyon is baked by the Sun and tends to become very hard. It cannot absorb water when the rains come. When it does rain, the water comes down in torrents which only adds to the problem of the rapid erosion of the land.

The plants that grow in the Grand Canyon have very shallow root systems. Unfortunately these root systems are too short to hold the soil in place and so do nothing to deter the soil being quickly washed away.

If you've got lots of water, no place for it to go but down to the Colorado River, and nothing holding the soil and rock in place, the result is frequently a flash flood roaring down a side canyon that can move boulders the size of cars, buses and even small houses. No-one builds houses in the Grand Canyon so that's not a problem but a few holidaymakers have had their cars washed away. The mass that moves down a side canyon during a flash flood is more like fast-flowing concrete than water and it can be very dangerous.

Before the building of the Glen Canyon dam, the Colorado River had spring floods that would exceed a flow of 10 000 tonnes of water per second. This means that if you were standing near the river, 10 000 tonnes of water would flow past you per second! All the water from the melting of the snow in the Colorado Rockies came pouring down through the Grand Canyon in late Spring, every year, as regular as clock-work.

The Colorado's spring floods used to carry away all of the debris that was deposited in the main channel by the flash floods. (A flash flood is a very rapid rise in the level of the river caused by extreme weather conditions.) The process of moving the rocks and sediment down the river to the Pacific Ocean has scoured the bed of the river with all of this fast moving material. This has slowly eaten away at the banks and bed of the river. As a result the river widened and cut down deeper into the lower rock layers, making the one mile deep trench it flows through today.

Figure 1 The Grand Canyon in Arizona, USA

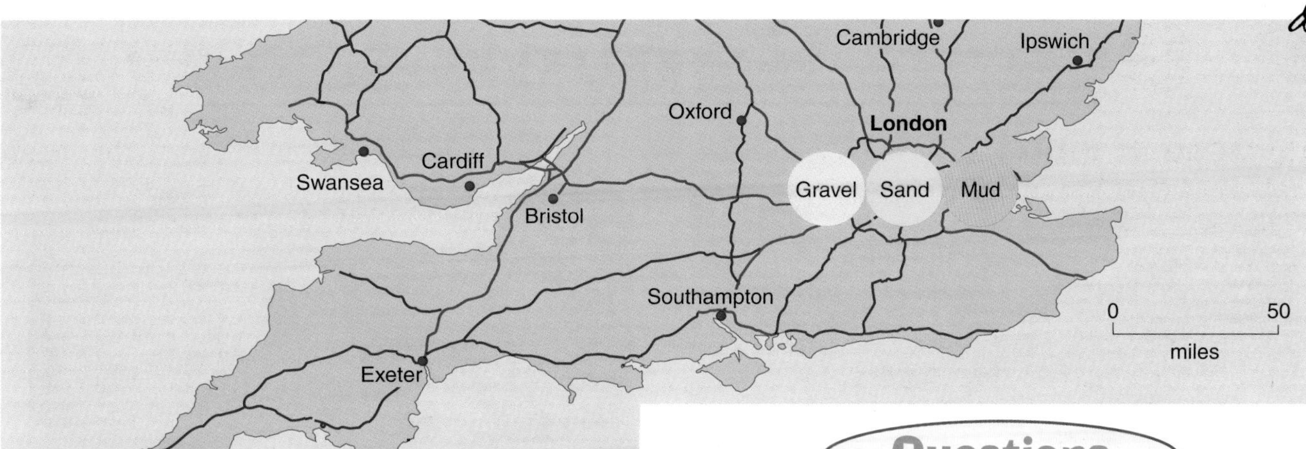

Figure 2 The London Basin

Gravel and mud flats

In contrast with the spectacular scenery of the Grand Canyon, the River Thames has a shallow, wide valley. But similar principles apply.

All along the river valley material has been transported by the running water. This material has been sorted by size, according to how fast the river was flowing. The fast flowing Colorado River can move rocks the size of cars, but because the Thames moves much more slowly, it has sorted much smaller pieces of rock.

Upstream from London there are huge deposits of gravel – small stones with diameters ranging from 5 millimetres to a few centimetres. In ancient times these settled out as the Thames slowed on its way to the sea. Often this gravel has been dug out leaving big holes which fill with water. Thorpe Park, an amusement park in Surrey, near London, is built on one such gravel pit. Smaller sandy particles (between 1 and 5 millimetres in diameter) got carried further. They settled out in what is now the London area so the ground there is very sandy. Tiny particles got carried furthest, but even these settled out when the river widened and reached the North Sea. They have made the mud flats of the Thames Estuary.

Weathering **mixes up** the minerals in rock, then flowing water carries them away and **sorts** them out by size.

Questions

1 Where is the Grand Canyon?

2 Into which ocean does the Colorado River flow?

3 Why does the soil get washed away so easily in this area?

4 How much water flows down the Colorado River?

5 What do you think a 'flash flood' is?

6 Why is spring the worst season for erosion in the Colorado River?

7 How big are the rocks that get carried along by the river's flow?

8 Why are there gravel deposits to the west of London?

9 Why are sandy beaches found near river mouths?

10 When any area gets flooded, the rivers widen and slow down. Explain how people's houses and gardens get mud in them when flooding takes place. Draw pictures to illustrate this.

Remember

Draw a cross-section along a river bed. Draw it from mountains to the sea. Show these sections:

Fast flowing – picks up material
Fast flowing – material gets broken up
Medium flow – large particles settle out
Slow flow – small particles settle out
Stopped at the sea – mud settles out

Closer

Worth a visit!

Amazing rock formations; Slickrock in Arizona (USA) and Giants Causeway, Northern Ireland

Natural rock formations are often beautiful or amazing. They bring tourists to gaze. It is the effects of the Sun, wind and water, over many millions of years, that make this scenery.

Questions

1 Make a thinklinks chart for these words: **weathering frost rain expansion contraction crack scree plant roots acid rain exhaust gases moving water rounded grains heating cooling mud**

2

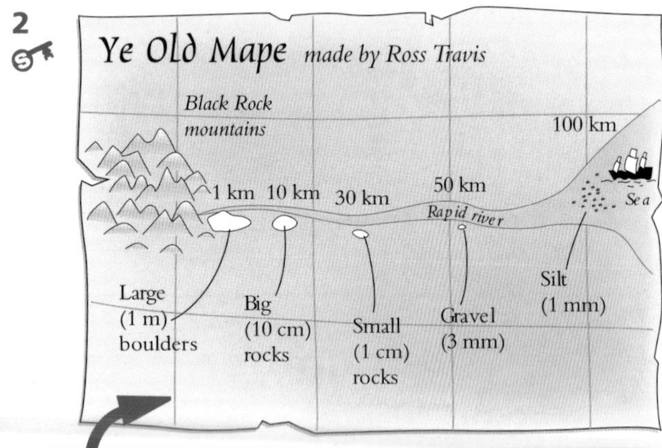

Ross Travis' map

Ross Travis explored an uninhabited land and made a map of his survey results.

He was interested in how far the rock particles from the Black Rock Mountains were carried by Rapid River.

a) Turn his results into a table of size of rock and distance moved.

b) Use the table to make a graph or chart that shows how far the different sized particles got carried.

c) Prospectors know that gold is often found mixed with 5 mm sized particles of rock. Use your chart to estimate where the prospectors should start to search for gold.

3 Copy and complete the equations for the reaction of rainwater and limestone. Use the words and symbols below:

acid hydrogen $Ca(HCO_3)_2$ rainwater carbonate calcium $CaCO_3$

Limestone	+	________	→	Hard water
________ carbonate	+	Carbonic ________	→	Calcium ________ ________ (solution)
________	+	H_2CO_3	→	________

Light

Opener
Alien senses

We don't know whether there are living things – 'aliens' – on other planets. If there are, then they might not be much like us. We can only guess what they might be like.

Our bodies can't sense radio waves. We need special equipment for that. Perhaps some aliens' bodies can sense radio waves. Maybe they can 'see' X-rays with special **detectors** on their bodies. But they might not be able to see the kind of light that we can see. And they might not be able to hear sounds.

We can see because light that travels from light sources like the Sun or light bulbs enters our eyes. Our eyes detect light.

We can detect **vibrations** around us. Vibrations can travel through materials as sound waves. When they reach our ears, we 'hear' the 'sound'.

Questions

1 What do you call your light detectors?

2 What do you call your sound wave detectors?

3 These are some animals from planet Earth. Sort them into two lists:

- animals with special skills at detecting light;
- animals with special skills at detecting sound waves.

Some of the animals might be in both of your lists.

4 Suppose that the aliens can't see the light that we can see. Suppose they can't hear the sounds that we can hear. How do you think they could communicate with each other?

9.1 Sources of light

Light spreads out from sources. Other objects reflect or scatter the light from sources. The Sun is a source of light, and so are light bulbs, candles and camera flashguns. Light travels very quickly to reach our eyes.

Figure 1 How not to take a picture! There is only a weak **source of light**. The light doesn't have much effect on the **film** inside the camera.

Figure 3 A quick burst of light from a flashgun spreads all around and gets into your eyes. Movie stars have to get used to bright lights.

Figure 2 The Sun is a really strong source of light. It can provide enough light for a good photograph.

Figure 4 The Sun is our natural source of light. When the Sun sets it goes dark. After sunset we have to use artificial lighting if we want to see anything.

Light shines into a camera through the **lens** at the front. It shines onto the film or CCD in a digital camera. The film or CCD changes. Where the light is brightest, it changes the most. The pattern on the film or CCD matches the light that shines on to it. We call the pattern a **photograph**.

The front of your eye is **transparent** so light can shine in. Your eyeball is shaped like a ball. Light shines into the ball and onto a surface at the back. The light produces changes in the surface. The changes cause the start of impulses in the nerves that are connected to your brain, and that's how you see.

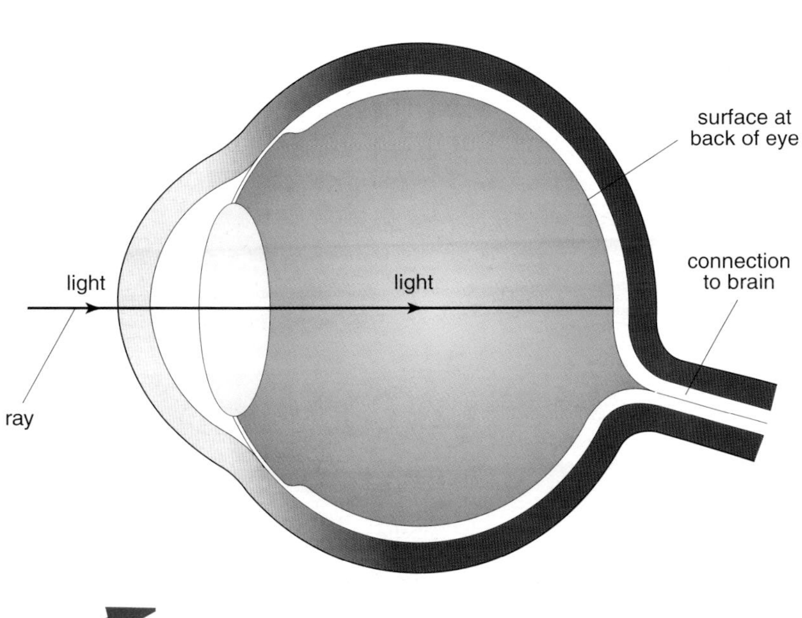

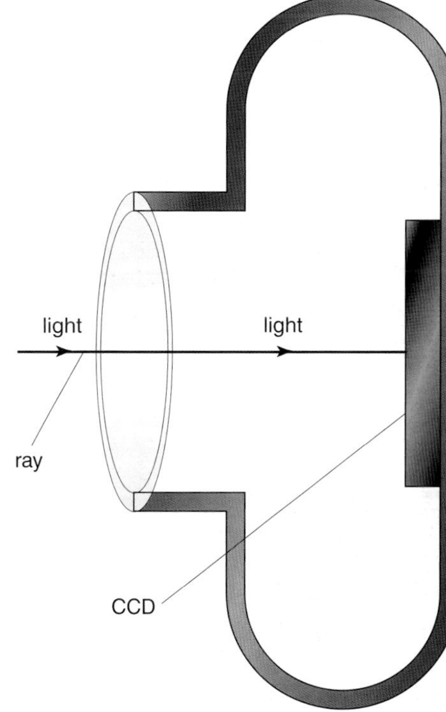

Figure 5 In an eye and a camera, light travels through a lens to a surface at the back. We draw rays to show pathways of light.

Questions

1 **a)** Is the room you are in lit by sunlight or by artificial light or both?

b) Make a list of different sources of artificial light.

2 Imagine that you are talking to someone two years younger than you. You are trying to explain how light makes a photograph. Write down what you would say.

3 Look on this spread to find evidence that:

a) a candle is a weaker source of light than a camera flashgun;

b) light travels very fast.

Write down the evidence you can find.

Remember

Use the following words to complete the paragraph below.

film Sun transparent photograph sources of light candles speed

Light must enter our eyes so that we can see. The light comes from _____1_____ such as the ____2____, light bulbs, ____3____ and camera flashes. It travels at very high ____4____. Light can shine through ____5____ materials such as the fronts of our eyes or the lens on the front of a camera. The light that reaches the ____6____ in a camera makes a ____7____. The light that reaches the back of our eyes lets us see.

Reflections

Surfaces reflect light that travels from sources. Different surfaces reflect light in different ways.

We know that mirrors reflect light. You can also see your 'reflection' when you look into a still pool of water. Mirrors and water have very smooth surfaces. They give us very clear reflections. But other surfaces also reflect light.

Figure 1 Cave painting from Lascaux in France

Figure 1 shows a cave painting in Lascaux in France. It was painted 17 000 years ago. It shows the animals that the people hunted.

For thousands of years the painting was surrounded by nothing but darkness. Nobody knew it was there. Then, about a hundred years ago, some people went into the cave with lamps. They were amazed by what they saw.

The light spread out from their lamps. It reached the surfaces all around. The surfaces **reflected** the light. Some of the reflected light reached the eyes of the people.

Figure 2 The surface of the rock has different textures – there are very rough areas and smoother areas. There are also different colours. Different parts of the surface reflect light in different ways.

Different surfaces reflect the light in different ways. There are shiny pools of water on the floor. The water surfaces are smooth, like mirrors. There are the rough surfaces of the rock. The **texture** of a surface – whether it is rough or smooth – affects how it looks to us.

The light from most sources of light is white, or nearly white. White surfaces reflect a lot of light. Black surfaces reflect very little light. Coloured surfaces are choosy. They only reflect some kinds of light.

Figure 3 Different textures, different colours. Surfaces reflect light in different ways.

Questions

1 a) Where is the light coming from for you to see this book?

b) Would you be able to see the book if there were no sources of light shining on to it (such as in a cave)?

c) What does the surface of the book do to the light?

2 Run your fingers across this page and the cover of the book. Describe all the differences you can feel and see between the two surfaces.

3 Mirrors are very good reflectors of light. What is special about the surfaces of mirrors?

4 Which is better at reflecting light, a white surface or a black surface?

Remember

Fill in the spaces in the passage below using the following words.

white sources reflect colour texture

We see surfaces because light from ___1___ spreads out and the surfaces ___2___ it. The ___3___ of a surface makes a difference to how it looks to us. We can't see clear reflections from rough surfaces. Surfaces also affect the ___4___ of the light that reaches our eyes. Light from most light sources is ___5___ or nearly white.

Seeing ourselves

We can use ray drawings to help us to think about reflections from mirrors.

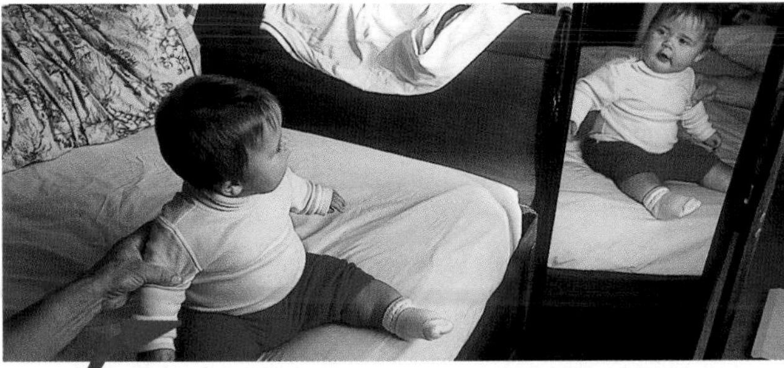

Figure 1 This baby is looking at its image in a mirror.

When you look in a mirror light from all parts of your face is reflected to your eyes. To make it easier to think about reflection we can imagine **rays** of light.

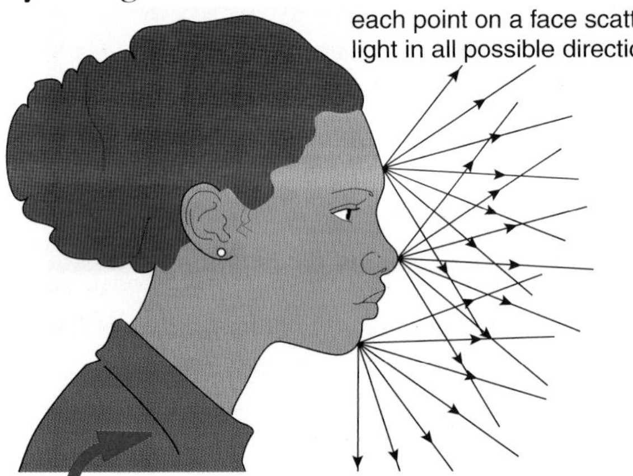

Figure 2 We could draw rays to show how the light spreads outwards from every point on a face. But trying to imagine all of those rays doesn't help very much. It's too complicated.

Figure 3 A ray is the pathway of a very narrow beam of light. It is much easier to think about how light is reflected if we think about just a single ray at a time.

With a single ray we can make measurements. First we can draw a **normal** line. That's an imaginary line that sticks straight out at 90° to the surface of the mirror. We draw it at the point where the ray of light is reflected. Then we can measure the angles that the ray makes before and after it is reflected. These are the **angle of incidence** and the **angle of reflection**.

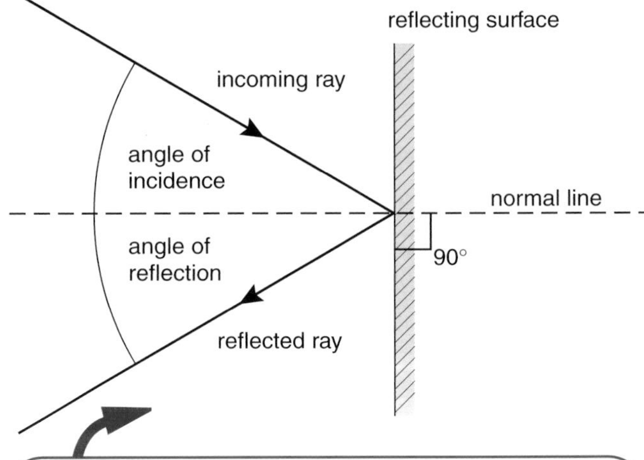

Figure 4 The reflection of a single ray by a mirror

The angle of incidence and the angle of reflection are **variables**. We can do an experiment to look for a **relationship** between the two variables. The angle of incidence is the **input variable**. We control the size of the angle of incidence and take measurements at different sizes. Every time we measure the angle of incidence, we then also measure the angle of reflection. The angle of reflection is the **output variable**. We record the results in a table to help us to look for a relationship.

Angle of incidence	Angle of reflection
14°	14°
26°	25°
38°	39°

Table 1 Some results you might find when you measure angles of incidence and reflection. The first column in the table shows the input variable which is the angle of incidence. The second column shows the output variable, angle of reflection.

There is a simple relationship between the two variables. The angle of incidence and the angle of reflection are always the same. This discovery is called the **law of reflection**.

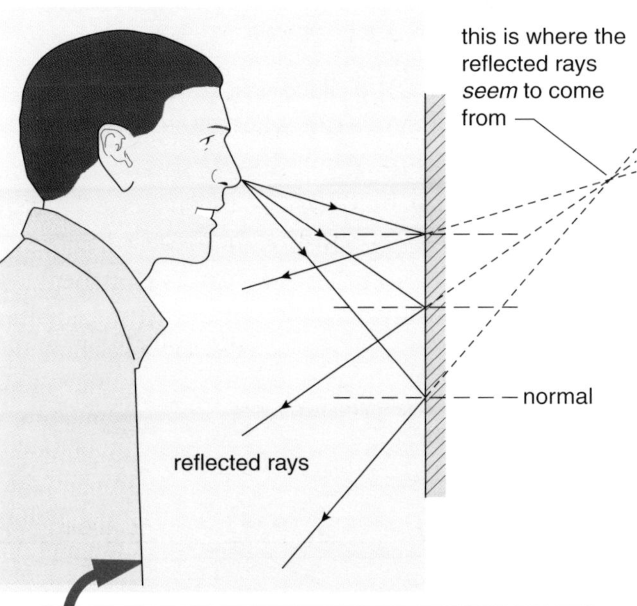

Figure 5 We can draw just a few rays spreading from a point on a face. The rays all obey the law of reflection. The rays seem to be coming from somewhere inside the mirror – that's where we see the image.

Questions

1 a) Which of these are correct drawings of reflection and which are wrong?

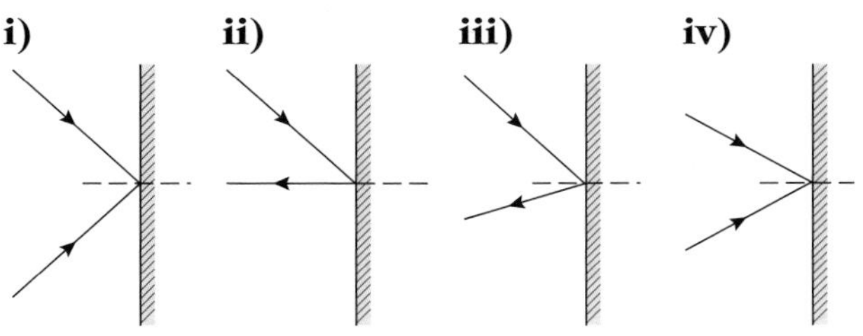

b) Use a protractor to measure each of the angles.

c) What is the name of the law that rays obey when they are reflected?

d) Write down the law.

2 The law of reflection tells us that angle of incidence and angle of reflection are the same. Why aren't they **exactly** the same in the measurements in Table 1?

Reflection and rough surfaces

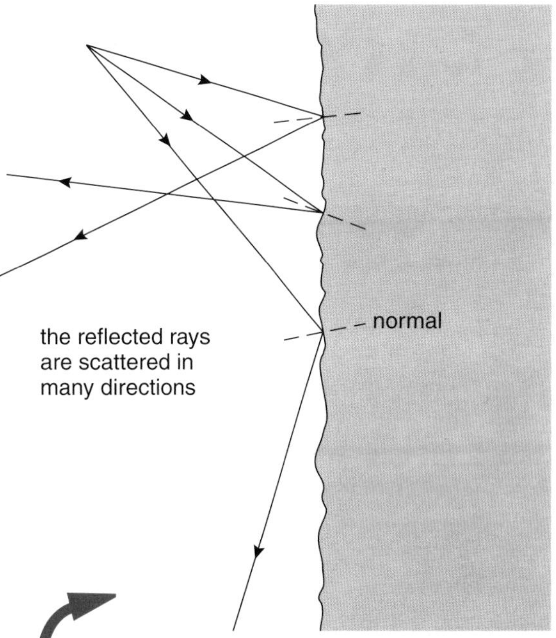

Figure 6 Normals point in different directions on rough surfaces so light is scattered in many directions.

Mirrors have very smooth surfaces. Rough surfaces can also reflect light but they don't produce clear images. The bumps on the surface reflect the light in different directions. Reflection like this is called **scattering** of the light.

Remember

Use the following words to complete the passage below.

law ray images scatter angle reflection output variable

When a ____1____ of light is reflected by a mirror, the ____2____ of incidence is always equal to the angle of ____3____. This is called the ____4____ of reflection. In an experiment on reflection, the angle of incidence is the input ____5____ and the angle of reflection is the ____6____ variable. Rough surfaces do not produce clear ____7____ but ____8____ the light.

9.4 Light changing direction

At a surface between materials, light can change direction.

Figure 1 Sharks at the Sydney Aquarium, Australia

The nearest most of us ever get to a dangerous shark is at a 'deep sea centre'. The sharks and the people are safely on opposite sides of a thick glass wall, or the people are high up above the water.

When you're above the water, it would take a shark with special skills to take a bite out of you. The shark would need more than just jumping skills. It would need to know about **refraction**. Refraction happens at surfaces (such as water and glass surfaces) and can change the direction of the light. When the shark looks up at you it can see you, but not in the right place. We have to draw rays to see why refraction causes this.

Figure 2 How to confuse a shark!

To the shark's eye, the place where the light seems to come from is not where it actually comes from. The shark sees you in the wrong place.

It's not just sharks who can be fooled. When you look through a water surface at a shark, the place the rays seem to come from is not the same as where they actually come from.

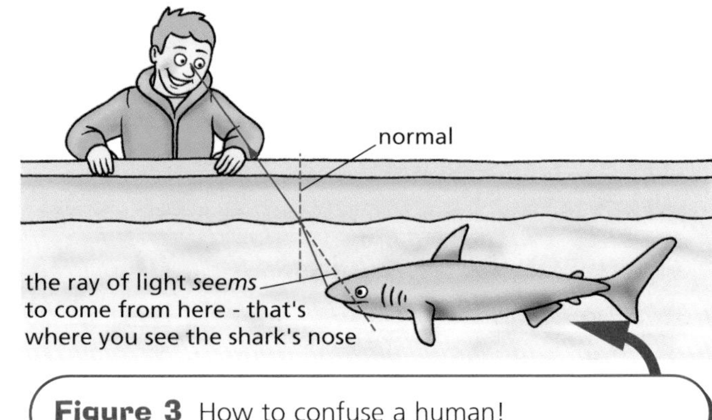

Figure 3 How to confuse a human!

Figure 4 Refraction of light at surfaces distorts what we see.

Using rays to study refraction

Figure 5 Refraction of light through a glass block

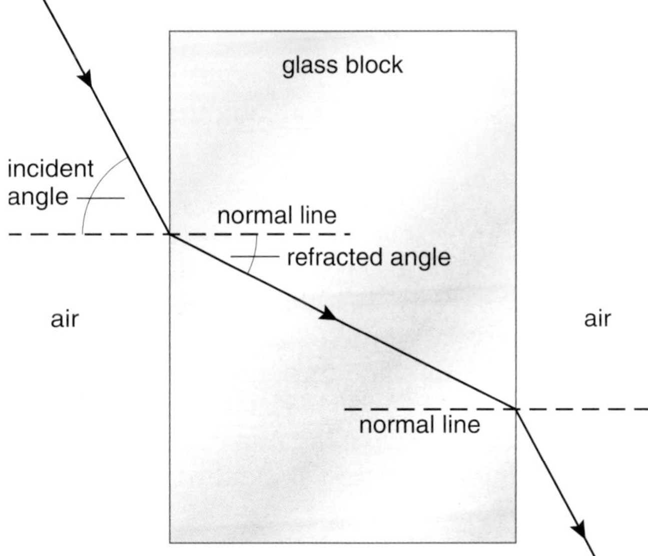

Figure 6 Glass surfaces refract light. To see just how much a ray is bent we can draw a normal line, and then measure the incident angle and the refracted angle. Notice that whether the light is going into the glass or coming out, the angle in the air is always the bigger one.

Questions

1 Which diagrams show refraction correctly?

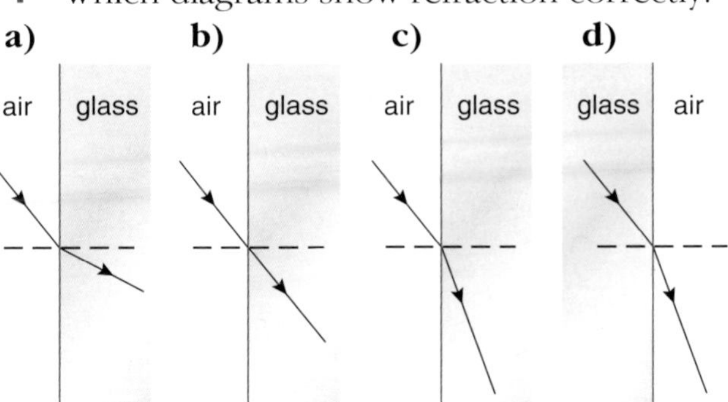

2 a) Which position, x or y, shows where the person sees the shark's nose?

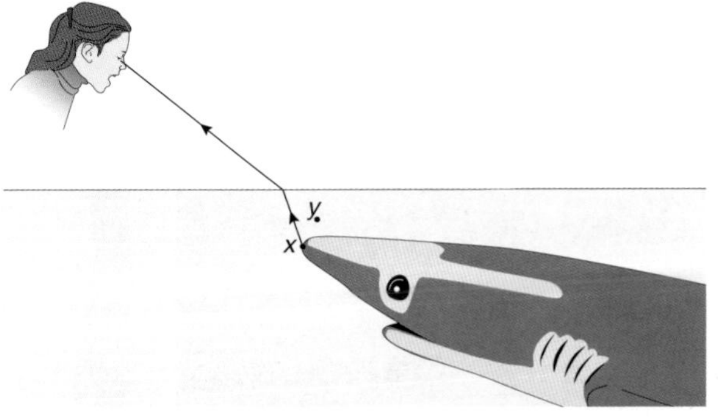

b) Write a sentence or two to explain why you think this.

3 Use your knowledge of refraction to explain why the world looks distorted when you look through a glass of water. You could use drawings to help your explanation.

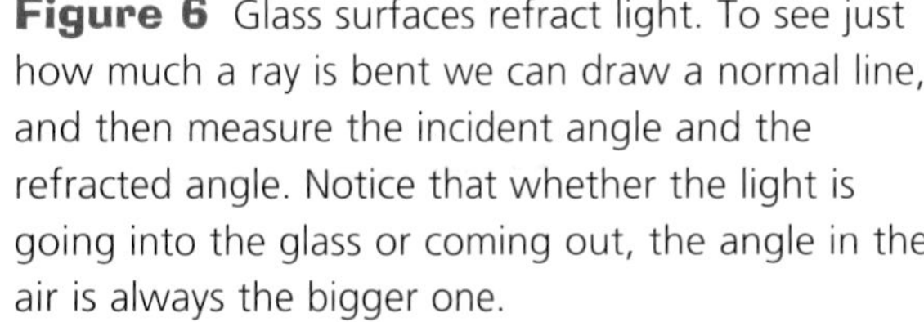

Remember

Unscramble the nonsense words to fill the gaps in the passage.

When light passes through a surface then <u>RICE NOT FAR</u> takes place. The pathway of the light can be bent. To someone watching from one side of the surface, the place where the <u>SAY R</u> of light seem to come from is not where they actually come from. To compare the sizes of the angle of <u>NICE D NICE</u> and the angle of refraction we draw a <u>LORMAN</u> line through the surface. Whichever way the light is travelling, the angle in the air is always <u>BIG REG</u> than the angle in water or glass.

9.5 Colour movies

White light is a mixture of all colours. Filters stop some of the light.

Old films are in black and white. Each frame of the film produces shadows on the screen. Black areas of the frame **absorb** the light and make dark shadows. We say that they are opaque. But **transparent** areas of the frame let the light from the projector shine through to the screen. Then we see the bright light that's scattered off the screen. Grey areas of the frame absorb some of the light and let the rest shine through to the screen.

Figure 1 Frames of film flicker in front of a projector lamp. The light shines through the film, and we see the light that's scattered from the screen.

Now when we go to the cinema we usually expect to see colour on the screen. Each frame of the film has areas of colour to absorb some of the light from the projector. A red area of the frame lets red light shine through. The screen scatters the red light to our eyes. A blue area of the film only lets blue light shine through. Then on the screen we see blue. The red and blue areas of the frame are acting as **filters**. They absorb some kinds of light but let other kinds travel on through.

From the white light of the projector it is possible to create any colour on the screen. White light seems to be a mixture of all colours. We can try out this idea by shining a thin beam of light through a **prism**. What we see is a rainbow of colour called a **spectrum**. We can see that the prism has separated the light into its different colours. We say that the prism has **dispersed** the light.

Figure 3 Dispersion by a prism shows that white light is a mixture of all the colours.

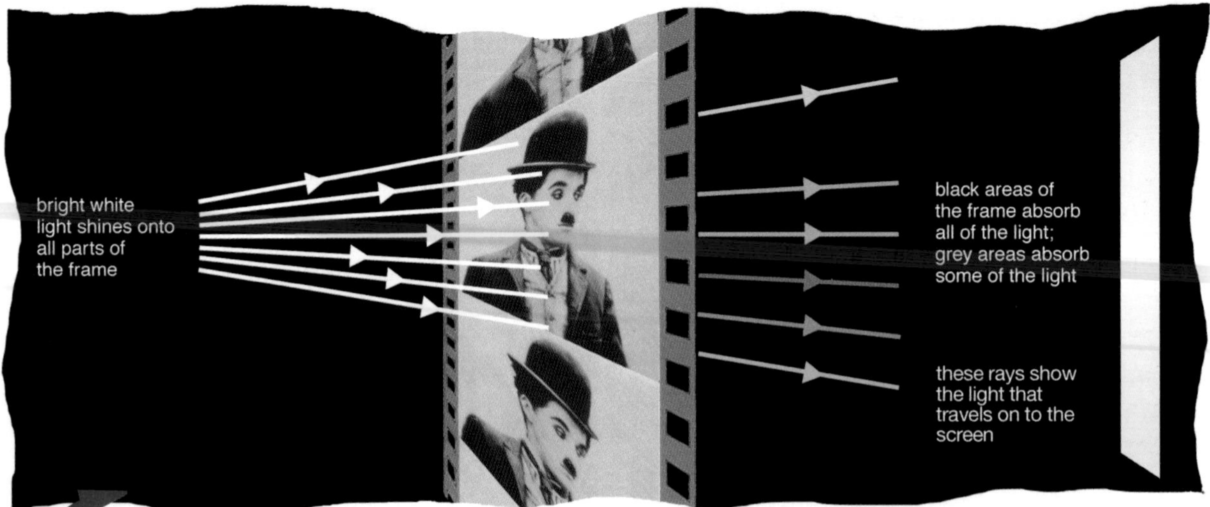

Figure 2 Grey areas of a film absorb some light and make shadows in shades of grey on the screen.

Figure 4 With colour film, different colours of light reach different parts of the screen.

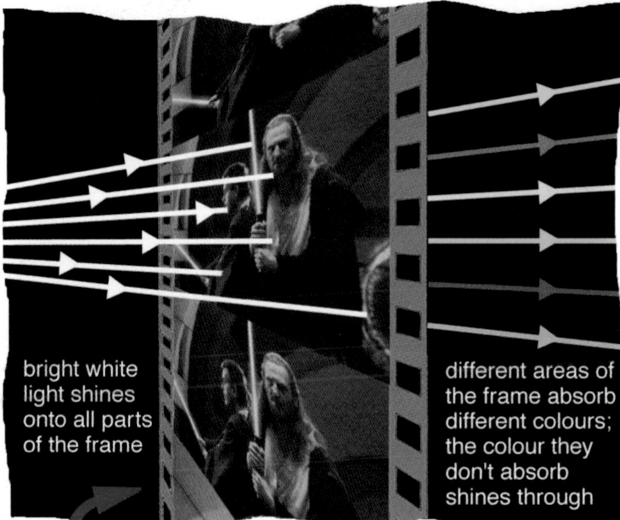

Figure 5 Coloured areas of film act as filters – absorbing some colours of the light but letting others shine through to the screen.

Questions

1 White light from a projector shines onto a frame of film. Describe the light that shines through areas of the film that are:

- **a)** completely clear or transparent;
- **b)** solid black;
- **c)** grey;
- **d)** red;
- **e)** blue;
- **f)** green.

2 A prism separates white light into colours.

- **a)** What is this process called?
- **b)** What kind of light would you see if you could mix the colours up again?

Green leaves and blue flowers

Figure 6 This plant has green leaves and blue flowers.

An object looks coloured because it reflects certain colours of light more strongly than others. For example, a blue flower reflects blue light strongly. If white light falls on the flower, the red and green are mostly absorbed. Blue light gets reflected to your eye so the flower appears blue. Similarly, the leaves look green because they absorb red and blue light, and reflect green coloured light.

Remember

Match the words below to the passage.

green pass spectrum absorb filters disperse white

Coloured areas of film ___1___ some colours but let other colours pass through. They act as colour ___2___. A green area of film, for example, lets green light ___3___ through. Then the screen scatters ___4___ light to our eyes.

A prism can ___5___ white light into a ___6___ of colours. This shows that ___7___ light is a mixture of coloured light.

Closer

The story of light

The story of light is a story of mystery. It is a story of how people have wondered about what our eyes are and what they do. It is a story that keeps on getting more and more interesting.

Today, scientists can make images to show the parts of the brain that are working hardest when we see. We can see that there are some parts that work hardest when we see something we like, and other parts are more active when we see something disgusting.

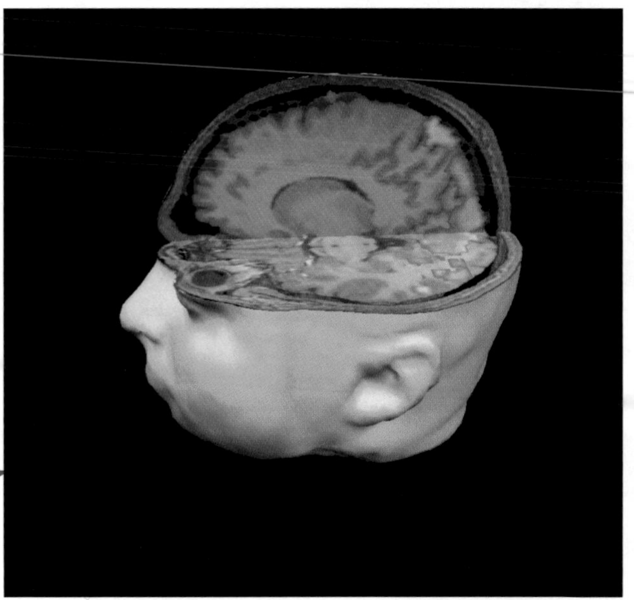

An artist's reconstruction based on brain scans.

Questions

1 The story of light is a story with a lot of people in it. These are some of the people:

- Ptolemy
- Al Hazen
- Isaac Newton
- James Clerk Maxwell
- Albert Einstein
- Hermann von Helmholtz
- Richard Gregory

Choose two of the names. Do internet searches to find out more. Choose your sources of information carefully. If you cannot understand what you see then find a website that makes more sense to you.

Make a short list with the following information:

- What did your two people say about light?
- When did they say it?
- Are the ideas of the two people the same or different?

For each of your two people choose an image and print it out. Write a paragraph or a caption to explain what you have found out. Compare your discoveries with what other people have found.

2 What is a ray? How do ideas about rays help us to think about:

- how rough surfaces reflect and scatter light?
- how smooth surfaces reflect light to make images?
- how cameras work?
- how our eyes work?
- how a glass of water distorts what we see when we look through it?
- how a frame of movie film makes patterns on a cinema screen?

Ecological relationships

Opener
Was *T. rex* a predator or a scavenger?

Tyrannosaurus rex

When *T. rex* fossils were first described, the huge teeth and jaws and its enormous size made people think that it was the king of the dinosaurs and capable of killing any other animal.

Now some scientists think we might have got it wrong. They think that *T. rex* was mostly a scavenger that lived off the carcasses of animals hunted by other things.

Look at the evidence and decide if you think the *T. rex* was a scavenger or a predator.

Evidence 1
If it fell down it wouldn't be able to get up easily or quickly because of its short arms.

Evidence 2
The teeth are long, smooth and if you cut them across they are circular. Most predators have teeth that have saw-like edges and are oval when cut across.

Evidence 3
Other fossil dinosaurs have been found with bite marks that match the teeth of a *T. rex*. Some of the bites are on the underside of the animal so it was probably dead before *T. rex* tried to eat it.

Evidence 4
Predators need to be fast, some scientists think that *T. rex* could not run very fast. It weighed about 7 tons.

Evidence 5
Scavengers often have a very good sense of smell so that they can find dead animals to feed off. Scientists think that *T. rex* had a good sense of smell.

Evidence 6
Predators need good eyesight to see their prey. Some scientists think that *T. rex* could only see moving things and didn't see still animals very well.

Discuss what you think with a partner.

Questions

1. Can you think of any very large animals that move very quickly?
2. Could the senses of smell and sight be helpful to a predator as well as a scavenger?
3. Could the *T. rex* have been a predator *and* a scavenger? Discuss these questions with your group. It's more about what you think than getting a right or wrong answer.

10.1 How many people are there in the world today?

The world's population is growing rapidly. The 6 billionth person in the world was born in 1999.

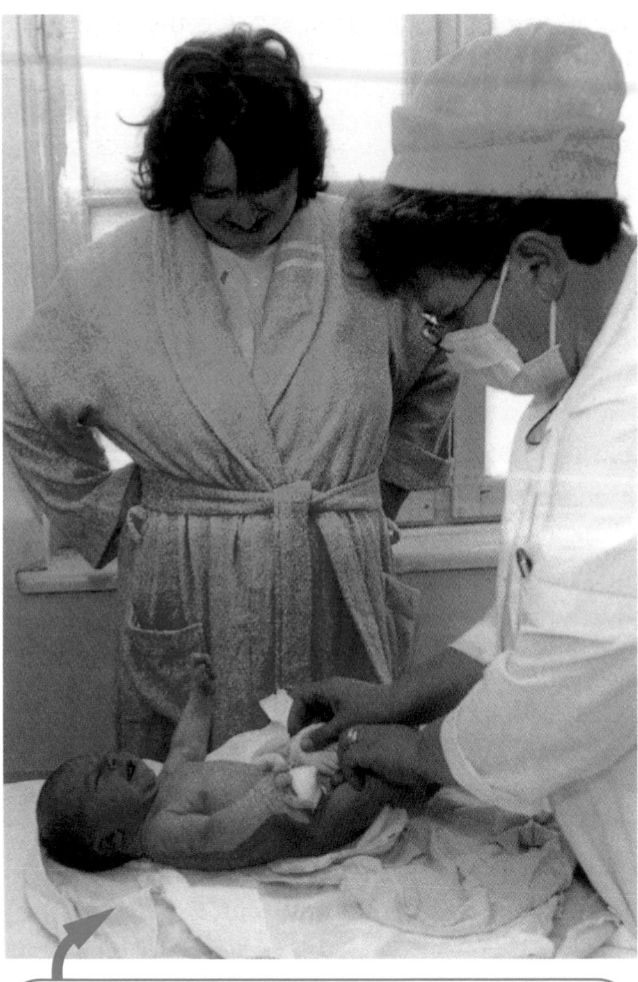

Figure 1 The 6 billionth person

Just how many people are there in the world today? It is impossible to know exactly how many people there are, but the United States Census Bureau estimates how many people are living on the Earth at any one time.

Table 1 gives the Bureau's estimates for the size of the population from July 1999 to July 2000. They estimated that the 6 billionth baby would be born on 19 July 1999 at about 12:24:02 am.

Date	World population estimate
1 July 1999	5,996,215,340
1 August 1999	6,002,727,327
1 September 1999	6,009,239,314
1 October 1999	6,015,541,237
1 November 1999	6,022,053,224
1 December 1999	6,028,355,147
1 January 2000	6,034,867,134
1 February 2000	6,041,379,121
1 March 2000	6,047,470,980
1 April 2000	6,053,982,967
1 May 2000	6,060,284,890
1 June 2000	6,066,796,877
1 July 2000	6,073,098,801

Table 1 Population estimates

The United Nations, however, say that the 6 billionth baby was a baby boy born in the Bosnian capital, Sarajevo, at 2 minutes past midnight local time on Tuesday 12 October 1999. The UN chose this as 'D6B', the Day of the 6 Billionth person.

The graph below shows how the world population has grown in the past and how we think it will continue to grow into the next millennium.

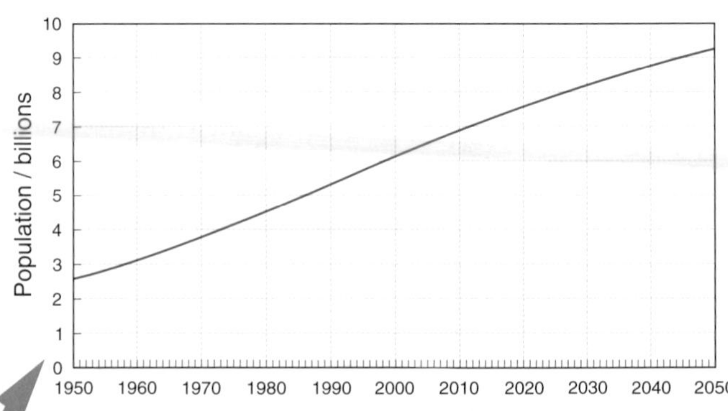

Figure 2 World population figures from 1950 to 2050 (Source: US Bureau of the Census)

If these estimates are correct, what problems could people living 100 years from now have? What do you think the population could be in the year 2100?

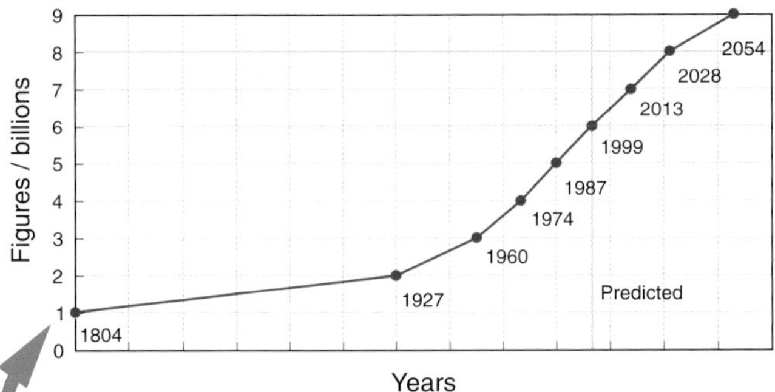

Figure 3 World population figures from 1804 to 2054

Year	Lower estimate (millions)	Higher estimate (millions)
10 000 BC	1	10
5000 BC	5	20
4000 BC	7	7
3000 BC	14	14
2000 BC	2	27
1000 BC	50	50
500 BC	100	100
400 BC	162	162
200 BC	150	231
200	190	256
400	190	206
600	200	206
800	220	224
1000	254	345
1200	360	450
1300	360	432
1400	350	374
1600	545	579
1800	813	1125
1900	1550	1762
1920	1860	1860
1940	2300	2300
1950	2400	2556

Table 2 World population growth

Figure 3 shows how the population will have changed from 1804 to 2054. The population growth was not as fast as it is today.

In Table 2 you can see how the population of the world has grown. Because we cannot be exactly sure of how many people there are at any one time, scientists give a lower estimate and an upper estimate.

It is not possible for population growth to continue for long at these levels. The current size of the human population, and the additions made to it each year, are bigger than at any other time in history.

In 1974 it was estimated that in 700 years only one square foot of land would be available for each human being. Population growth rates have slowed since 1974, but growth rates similar to those of today cannot continue indefinitely.

Questions

1 Produce a graph to show how the world population has grown since year 10 000 BC. So that the numbers don't get too big, change the millions into billions, so 170 million would be 0.1 (ignore the last two numbers), 200 million would be 0.2 and 1 billion would 1.0.

a) When did the population increase fastest?

b) During which times was the population growing at its slowest?

2 Humans don't usually have to worry about being eaten by a predator. What kinds of factors could stop the population from growing?

Remember

If you have access to the Internet, look at the Population Action International website at http://www.populationaction.org.

10.2 Predator vs prey

A **predator** is an animal that hunts, catches and eats other animals for food. The animals being hunted are called **prey**. Predators help to keep the numbers of prey down in an area and, in turn, the number of prey in an area will limit the numbers of predators that can live there.

If the two species have lived in the same area for a long time, the prey learn to deal with the predator, and try not to be caught and eaten. Therefore, the predator kills only the weakest prey. Animals are not necessarily always predators or always prey. For example, a stickleback fish may hunt and eat tadpoles, but it may also be hunted and eaten itself by a roach. Any animal that is prey must somehow try to survive. In other words it must try to **adapt**. Some adaptations give the prey an advantage over the predator, some are designed to fool the predator and others hide the prey from the predator.

Imagine you are a rabbit and you have just noticed a fox preparing to attack. What would you do? You'd run! Animals can use speed as a very effective means of escaping predators. The fastest prey escape and survive while the slowest get caught. Remember, you can't eat what you can't catch!

False features that appear to be enormous eyes or appendages can fool potential predators, as can making yourself look bigger than you are.

Pretending to be an animal that is dangerous to a predator is also a means of avoiding being eaten. Some animals' physical features make them a very undesirable meal. Hedgehogs, for example, are very difficult for predators to eat because of their extremely sharp spines.

Chemical features can be just as effective. The poison arrow frog (see Figure 2) also uses chemicals (poisons secreted from its skin) to deter attackers. Any animals that eat these small frogs are likely to get very sick or die.

Figure 1 The puffer fish inflates its body to make it difficult to eat and to make it appear larger than it really is.

Figure 2 The colour of the frog and its markings warn any predators that it should not be eaten.

Some animals blend into the background as their colour and the patterns on their skin or coats hide them from potential danger. This type of **camouflage** allows them to blend into the background, making them difficult to see. Humans have used this technique as well. Soldiers wear camouflage clothing to hide from their enemy. Can you see the soldier in Figure 4?

Predators, on the other hand, also adapt. They develop ways of searching out their prey. Those with the best eyesight, keenest hearing and/or greatest sense of smell will have more success in finding food than predators with poor senses.

Figure 3 The hedgehog's spines make it a difficult meal to eat.

Figure 4 Where is the soldier in this photo?

Questions

1 What particular features do these animals have to help them catch prey?
   a) eagle
   b) tiger
   c) anteater
   d) fox
   e) house spider

2 What features do these animals have that allow them to escape being another animal's meal?
   a) puffer fish
   b) hedgehog
   c) hare
   d) stick insect
   e) wood louse

3 Draw pictures of what an animal would need to look like to hide in these places:
   a) a pebbly sea bottom;
   b) a sandy desert;
   c) a snowy area in the Antarctic;
   d) tall grass and bright sun;
   e) a leafy woodland.

Remember

The predator–prey relationship is important in maintaining balance among different animal species in a habitat or ecosystem. Adaptations that are useful to the prey help to ensure the survival of species. Predators may also undergo changes that make finding and capturing prey easier.

10.3 Feeding habits

The barn owl is a predator. It is also a protected species, so it is an offence to disturb the birds in their nest or while they are breeding. Owls used to be a common sight in Great Britain but their numbers are dwindling. They live inside buildings (for example barns on farms, hence their name), inside large cavities in trees, and inside rock cavities in cliffs and rock faces. Figure 1 shows where barn owls can be found in this country.

Feeding habits

Barn owls eat a variety of prey. Most of their food is provided by hunting voles, but they will also eat shrews, mice and other small birds. Barn owls hunt mainly in long grassy meadows where the voles live. The barn owl breeding season begins in late February. During the season, the male will hunt to provide food for its mate. The female will lay between 4 and 6 eggs in late April or May. About 30 days later the eggs will hatch and the young are fed and looked after by the parents for between 60 and 90 days. During this time there must be a good supply of food, otherwise the chicks may not survive.

Figure 1 Barn owls can be found all over the British Isles.

Figure 2 shows you what might happen to the numbers of owls and voles as the owls hunt them in order to feed their mate and their chicks.

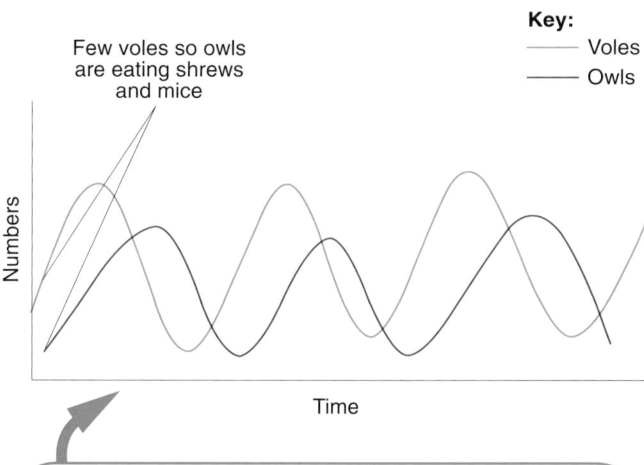

Figure 2 Graph showing the feeding relationship between the barn owl and the vole

Copy the graph into your exercise book, then read the following account of owls and their feeding habits. Mark on the graph when you think different things are happening. The first point is marked for you.

The vole is the commonest prey for barn owls. The field vole lives in long grassland fields and water voles nest along the edges of rivers. During the owl's breeding season the voles are hunted so their numbers go down. Over half of the food that an owl might catch and eat during breeding is made up of the field vole and the water vole (if there are rivers near the owl's nesting site). When there are plenty of voles, the numbers of owls increase as the young chicks are well fed and survive. If there are not enough field voles then the owls will hunt for field mice and shrews. These are not as easy to catch, so the amount of food for the owls goes down. This means that the number of owls may also go down as some of the chicks in the owls' second brood will be starved of food and die. Fewer owls means that the voles have a chance to recover and their numbers increase, providing more food for the owls that are left. More food means that more owl chicks will survive.

Figure 3 A barn owl with a mouse

Questions

1. Barn owls are not found in the Highlands of Scotland. What might prevent them nesting and living there?
2. Over 50% of a barn owl's food is provided by voles living in grassland. Other prey that owls eat may live in hedgerows. Why are fewer of these animals caught by the barn owl?
3. Barn owls hunt at night. What features of the barn owl make it a suitable night hunter? (*Hint*: look at the photo of the barn owl.)
4. Barn owl chicks need to be looked after for between 60 and 90 days. What effect does this have on the parents and what they have to do for the chicks?
5. Only about 5% of a barn owl's food comes from catching other small birds. Why is this?
6. Field voles are much larger than shrews and field mice. (They are about the same size as a rat.) Why might barn owls prefer to feed on voles rather than mice or shrews?

Remember

Although barn owls can feed on more than one type of prey, they mostly feed on voles. When there are plenty of voles around, the owls are more successful at breeding. This means that the population of owls goes up and there are more of them preying on the voles. The number of voles therefore goes down, providing less food for the owls.

10.4 Looking at pyramids

When we look at **food chains** and **food webs** we are seeing how energy is being transferred from plants to animals and on to other animals in the chain or web. We can also look at how energy is transferred by looking at pyramids of numbers and pyramids of biomass.

Ecologists use pyramids of biomass to show what happens in food chains and webs. Pyramids of numbers are also used but are not as helpful when looking at how energy is transferred.

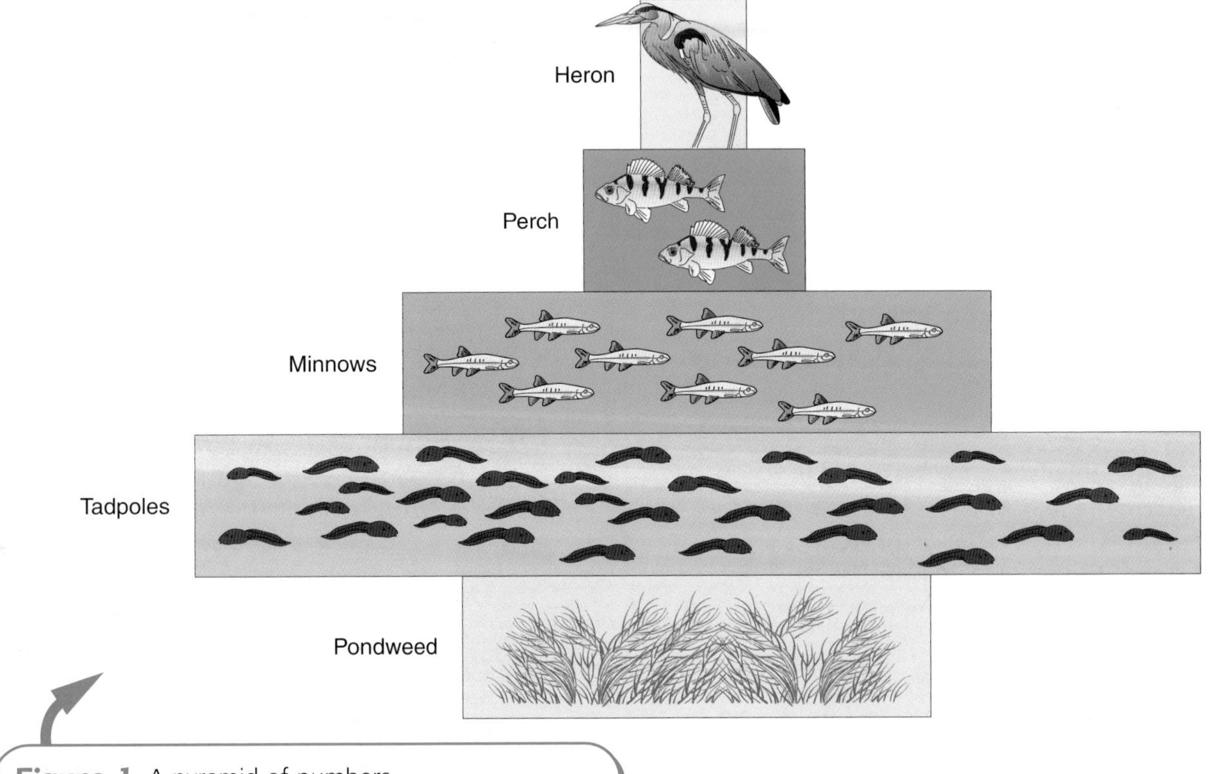

Figure 1 A pyramid of numbers

Pyramids of numbers

If you look at a simple food chain in a pond, you will see that one piece of pondweed can feed a lot of tadpoles. Also, one minnow might eat a lot of tadpoles, one perch might eat a lot of minnows, and one heron might eat a lot of perch. Trying to make a **pyramid of numbers** is not easy! It might look something like Figure 1. A pyramid of numbers is not always very helpful. It doesn't tell us, for example, how the energy is transferred and wasted as we move up the pyramid or chain. Instead ecologists use a **pyramid of biomass**. This tells us much more about the transfer of energy.

Pyramids of biomass

If we took a complete pond and removed all of the pondweed and weighed it, we could find out its biomass. (Biomass is simply a fancy way of saying how much of a living thing there is – its mass. Remember in science we measure mass in kilograms!) We do the same for the tadpoles, the minnows, the perch and the herons. If we did this, we would get a pyramid that looks like the one in Figure 2. There is less energy as we move up the pyramid, so at each step we are wasting some of the energy (remember also that we cannot create or destroy energy, we can only transfer it!).

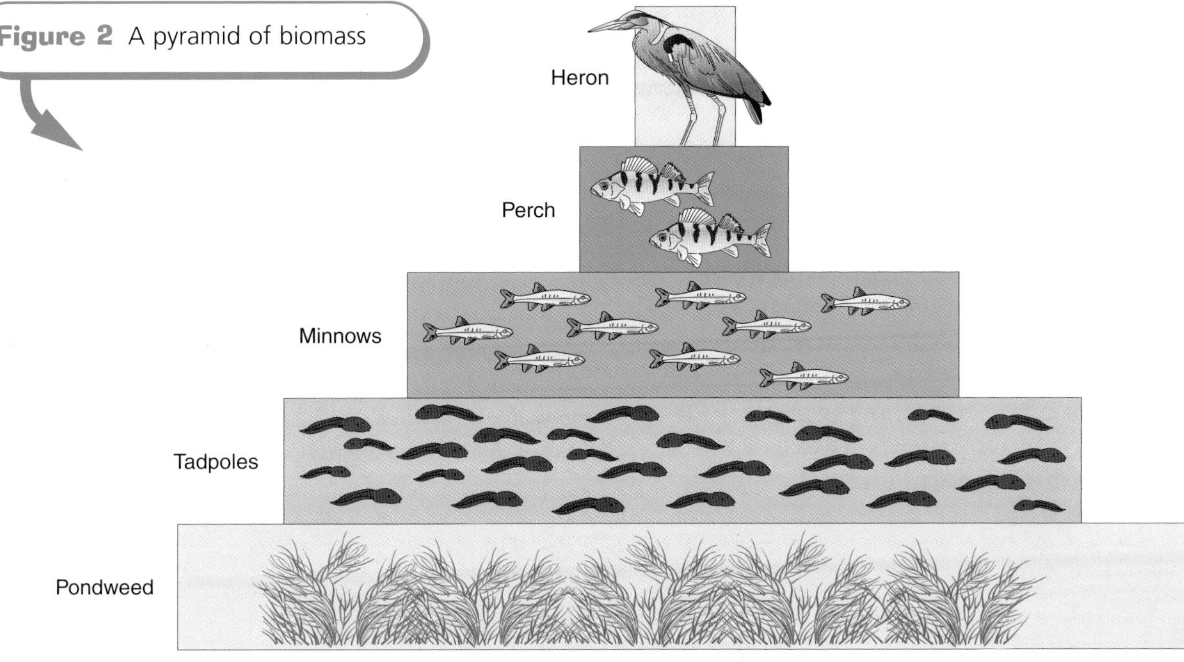

Figure 2 A pyramid of biomass

Stop and think!

How do you think that energy is being wasted as animals eat plants and other animals?

Nearly all of our energy comes from the Sun. Only about 10% of the Sun's energy is actually used by plants. What do you think happens to the rest?

Questions

1. How would a pyramid of numbers look for the following food chain?

   Rosebush (1) → Aphids (200) → Ladybirds (5) → Blackbird (2) → Cat (1)

2. What might a pyramid of biomass look like for the food chain in Question 1?
3. How can a single rosebush provide enough food for so many aphids (sometimes called greenfly)?
4. Ecologists often call the pyramid you drew in Question 1 an *inverted* pyramid. What does the word inverted mean?
5. Look back at the Stop and Think box.

Draw an energy transfer diagram using the information below.

10 000 joules of energy are transferred to a patch of grass by the Sun.
9000 joules of this are reflected back, 1000 joules are stored by the grass as carbohydrate.
100 joules are stored as food by rabbits that eat the grass. 900 joules are transferred to the environment by the rabbits as waste and heat.
10 joules are stored as food by the fox that eats the rabbit. 90 joules are transferred to the environment as waste and heat by the fox.

Remember

Match the following terms with their definition.

Pyramid of numbers: shows how energy is transferred from one living thing to another.
Food chain: shows us how many individuals there are in a food chain or a food web.
Food web: shows us how much the individuals in a food chain or web would weigh.
Pyramid of biomass: is made up of many food chains and shows who eats what or whom.

The killing chain

Food chains show us how energy is transferred from plants to animals and on to other animals. It isn't just energy that can be transferred, pesticides sprayed on plants or put into streams and rivers to control insects and other pests can also be transferred. In the 1960s and 1970s one particular pesticide, DDT, caused a lot of damage as it was transferred through the food chain.

Figure 1 DDT builds up in the food chain: zooplankton → small fish → large fish → heron. ppm means parts per million.

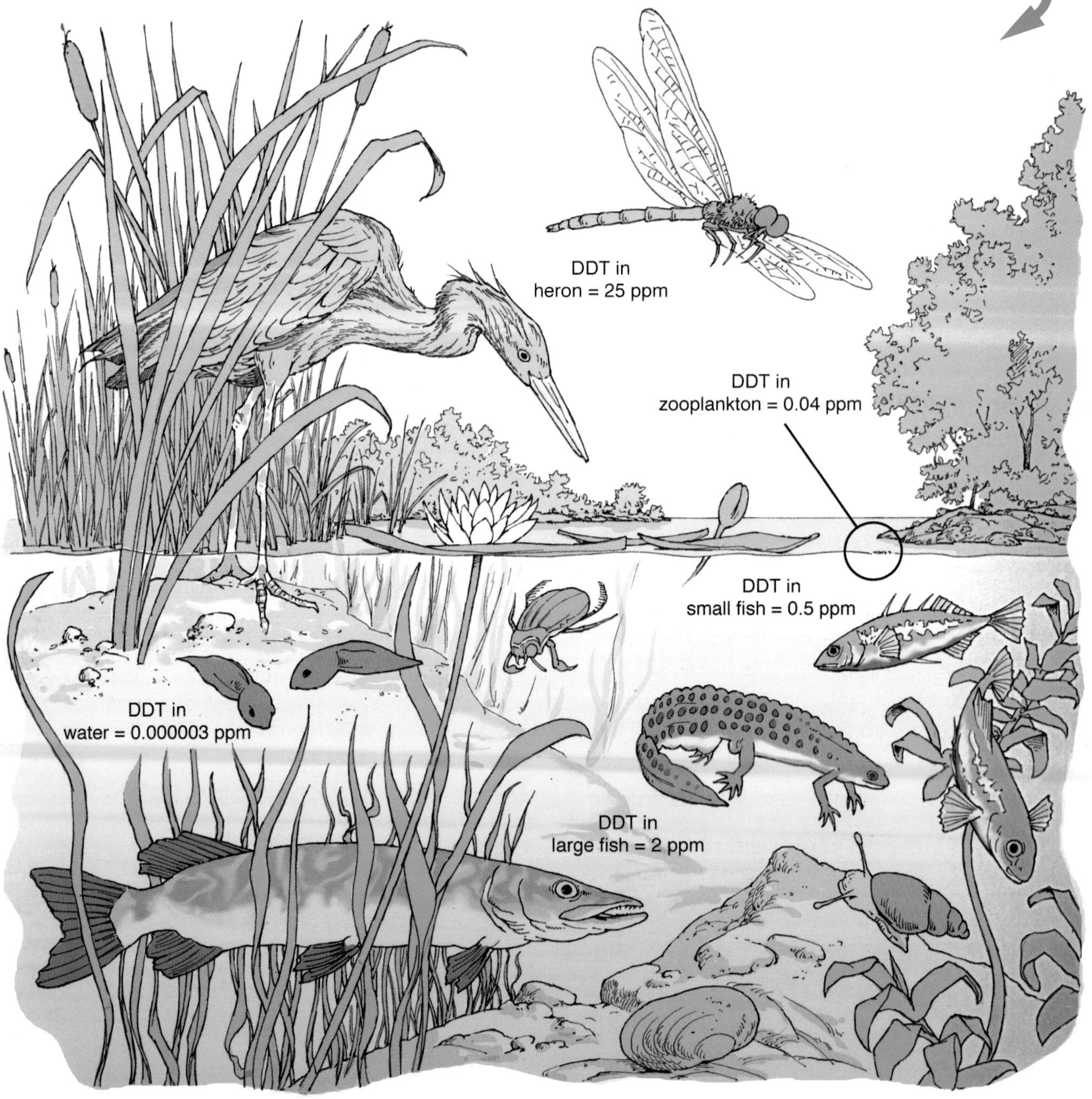

Read through the following information carefully, look at Figure 1 and then answer the questions.

DDT was first made in 1874, but it wasn't until 1939 that Paul Muller, a Swiss chemist, found that it could be a very effective insecticide. After the Second World War, it was widely used to kill off harmful insects which were destroying crops. It was later found that DDT could be harmful to more than just the insects. A lot of DDT was found in many animal species including fish, birds and mammals, as well as some plant species. DDT accumulated in the fat cells of organisms.

In the United States of America, it was found that birds such as the Californian Condor, which were being poisoned by DDT, began producing weak egg shells, which were crushed when the females sat on them to incubate them. The result was a decline in the bird population. These problems in the 1960s eventually led to its ban by the Environmental Protection Agency in the United States in 1972.

The proper chemical name for DDT is **D**ichloro**D**iphenyl**T**richloroethane, not an easy name to remember, which is why scientists prefer to call it DDT!

DDT was also a problem in this country. It was used to control pests, but ecologists noticed that the numbers of large fish-eating birds were reducing. Figure 1 shows how DDT travelled along the food chain. DDT entered the rivers after being sprayed on crops. It then entered zooplankton – microscopic one-celled animals – that were eaten by small fish. The small fish were eaten by larger fish which were, in turn, eaten by the fish-eating birds such as herons.

Questions

1 As well as using pesticides, we also have insecticides and herbicides to kill off pests. What do these chemicals kill off?

2 The DDT didn't actually kill the large fish-eating birds directly. Why did the numbers of these birds go down in this country?

3 If the DDT was sprayed onto the crops in the fields, how did the chemical end up in the rivers?

4 Pesticides kill off the pests that can ruin crops. Third World countries are still using DDT. Now that we know how harmful it can be, why are they still using DDT on their crops?

'Minamata Disease'

From 1932 to 1968 a company located in Kumamoto, Japan, dumped an estimated 27 tons of mercury compounds into Minamata Bay. Kumamoto is a small town about 570 miles southwest of Tokyo. The town consists of mostly farmers and fishermen. When this massive amount of mercury was put into the bay, thousands of people whose normal diet included fish, unexpectedly developed symptoms of mercury poisoning. The illness became known as the 'Minamata Disease'.

Over 3000 victims have been recognised as having 'Minamata Disease'. Many people have lost their lives. Others have suffered from physical deformities, or have had to live with the physical and emotional pain of the disease.

Not until the mid-1950s did people begin to notice this strange disease. Victims were diagnosed as having damaged nervous systems. Numbness occurred in their limbs and lips. Their speech became slurred and their vision constricted. Some people had serious brain damage, while others lapsed into unconsciousness or suffered from involuntary movements. Furthermore, some victims were thought to be crazy when they began to shout uncontrollably. These inexplicable occurrences brought panic to Minamata. However researchers from Tokyo traced the disease to poisons in the food chain.

Remember

Plants and animals lower in the food chain get eaten. The poisons they contain accumulate in the animals that eat them. The higher up the food chain an animal is, the more poisons get into its system. Pesticides intended for small animals can end up killing large animals as well.

Closer

Disappearing rainforests

Brazil has 30% of the world's tropical forests. Some estimates show that by the year 2020 up to 90% of these forests will have been destroyed by humans cutting them down to make farmland.

Tropical rainforest in Brazil

In a 11 km^2 square of Brazilian tropical forest there are over 750 species of trees, 125 species of mammals, 400 species of birds and 100 species of reptiles. Most of these species are found nowhere else in the world.

Ecologists estimate that up to 50 000 species are driven to extinction every year. Many of these species have yet to be studied and catalogued. This means that in the time taken for your science lesson, up to six species will have become extinct.

The Amazonian rainforest in Brazil is sometimes known as 'the lungs of the Earth', because it recycles carbon dioxide into oxygen. Over 20% of the oxygen present in the atmosphere is produced in the Amazon rainforest.

Many of our everyday foods originally came from the tropical rainforests. The table below lists some of the more common ones:

Fruits	Vegetables	Spices	Nuts	Commodities
Avocados	Corn	Black pepper	Brazil nuts	Chocolate
	Potatoes	Cayenne pepper	Cashews (this is also a fruit, we eat the hard centre of the fruit)	Cane sugar
Figs	Rice	Cinnamon	Coconuts (the bit we eat is the stone at the centre of the fruit)	Coffee
Oranges	Squash	Cloves		
Lemons	Yams	Ginger		
Bananas		Vanilla		
Guavas		Turmeric		
Pineapples				
Mangoes				
Tomatoes				

Questions

1. If six species become extinct every hour, how many will become extinct in:
   - a day?
   - a week?
   - a month?
2. What is the name of the process that plants use to convert carbon dioxide to oxygen?
3. What might happen to the level of carbon dioxide in the atmosphere if the tropical forests are destroyed?
4. What effect could increased carbon dioxide levels in the atmosphere have on the climate?
5. Which of the everyday foods in the table are least likely to be grown in the UK?

Driving the rock cycle

Opener
Rock cycle starts in a tropical island

Montserrat eruption

Montserrat's volcano sat silent for 400 years, until 1995. Then magma pushed up into the crater, creating a bulging dome of jagged grey rock. When the sides of the growing dome became too steep, rock avalanched away. Then deadly, huge, hot clouds of rock, ash and hot gas raced down the sides of the mountain.

This exposed the fresh, underlying magma. In a flash, gases in the magma expanded like the bubbles in a bottle of uncorked champagne and the volcano exploded, hurling stones and hot ash several miles into the air.

Most residents fled, many to Britain. They intend to return after the volcano calms down, but this could take years.

Questions

Ethan heated similar sized pieces of granite in a Bunsen flame for different lengths of time. Then he dropped the pieces in cold water. Some split up into fragments.

Heating period	Number of fragments 1st try	2nd try	3rd try	Ave.
0 min	1	1	1	
10 min	1	4	4	
20 min	6	7	5	
30 min	10	6	11	
40 min	8	12	10	
50 min	11	12	10	

Here are his results:

1 a) Write an account of what Ethan has done. Use the results table to help give you clues.

b) What were the main hazards in the experiment? How could Ethan reduce the risk of an accident?

c) Copy and complete the table for Ethan.

d) Plot a suitable graph or chart of Ethan's results.

e) Write a conclusion for Ethan's investigation.

Solids and liquids in the Earth

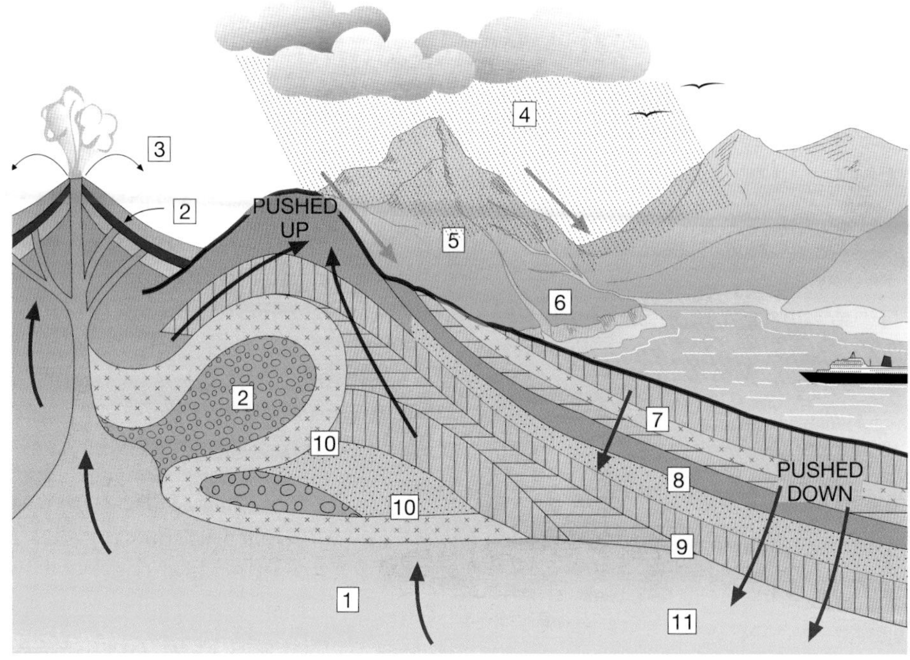

Figure 1 The rock cycle

Making rocks

Most of the evidence we have shows that the Earth is 4600 million years old. Its surface has changed a great deal in that time. We think of mountains, rivers and the sea as things that never change, but over millions of years there have been big changes.

The theory about continental drift says that mountain ranges rise up as one continent pushes against another. Sun, rain, freezing cold and wind gradually break up the mountains into smaller rocks. Running water in rivers carries away the rocks. As they move, they bang together and break up until they are sand or silt.

(**1**) This all happens because the centre of our Earth is very hot. Only the outer skin of the Earth is made of cool solid rock. This outer skin is very thin. If the Earth were the size of a football or netball then the crust would be the thickness of a stamp stuck on the surface. Below the crust is the **mantle**. The mantle contains very hot rock under very high pressure. Normally at such high temperatures the rock would be liquid but the high pressure keeps it like a plastic.

Igneous rock (2, 3)

Rock from the mantle can be squeezed into the crust. Because the pressure is less, the rock turns into a very hot liquid, called **magma**. This makes **igneous rock**. As the rock is pushed into the crust it cools down. If it is deep in the crust and cools slowly, large crystals can form. If it is pushed near to the surface it cools a lot faster and the crystals are a lot smaller. If the magma breaks through the crust it produces volcanoes and the liquid rock is called **lava**.

Washing down to the sea (4, 5, 6)

When rivers run fast they carry bits of rock of different sizes with them. As they slow down near the sea, the big bits settle to the bottom, but the sand is still carried along. At the sea the flow stops and the sand, silt and mud settle out.

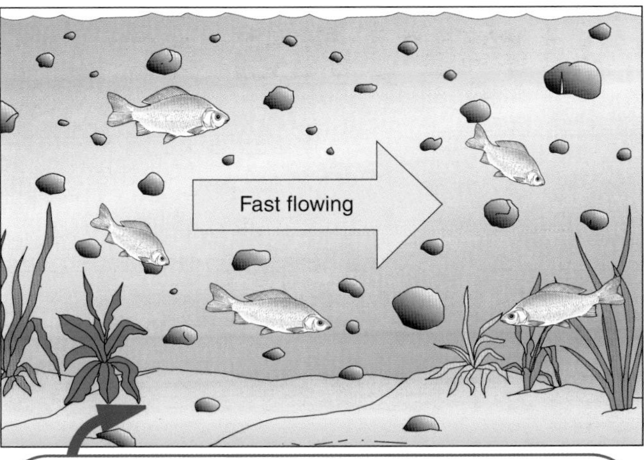

Figure 2 Fast-flowing water carries particles of all sizes.

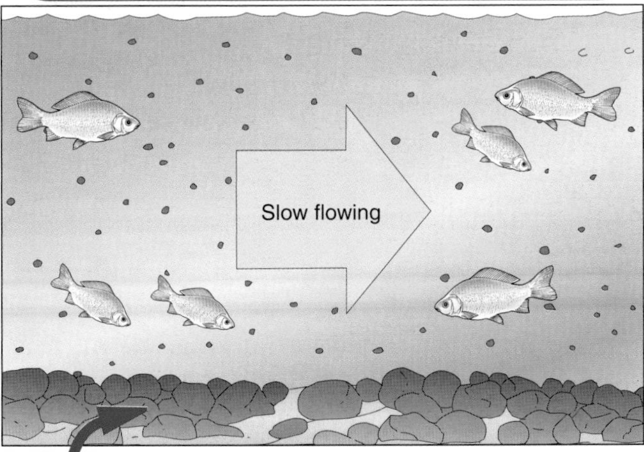

Figure 3 Slow-flowing water only carries small particles.

Sedimentary rock (7, 8, 9)

Over millions of years the layers of sand and mud get thicker and thicker. The layers deep down are squeezed so much that they turn into rock. This is called **sedimentary** rock. Some rock, like chalk, is made from the skeletons and shells of sea animals. Sedimentary rock is made of small grains cemented together by chemical salts.

Heat and pressure (10)

The layers of sedimentary rock get buried deeper and deeper. They get squeezed hard by layers of rock that get laid on top of them over millions of years. They are heated by the hot interior of the Earth. The squeezing and heating makes the sedimentary rocks change. They sometimes partially melt and the high pressure can make the crystals and grains line up. These are **metamorphic** rocks. This just means 'changes in shape'. You use a similar word when a caterpillar changes into a butterfly – metamorphosis. Igneous rocks can go through the same process and be changed into metamorphic rocks as well.

Mantle again (11)

The rocks get pushed down and down by rocks on top of them or by movements in the Earth's crust. They are heated, melted, then put under pressure until they become part of the plastic mantle again. The rock cycle has gone around once.

Questions

1 How old is the Earth?
2 What makes mountain ranges?
3 What wears down mountain ranges?
4 What is the centre of the Earth like?
5 How is igneous rock made?
6 What are the rocks made from layers of sand and mud called?
7 What is metamorphic rock?
8 What sort of rock gets turned into metamorphic rock?
9 What is another example of metamorphic change?
10 Deep down in the Earth, molten rock can gather in chambers that feed volcanoes. What is this molten rock called?

Remember

Use the words in the box to complete the sentences.

rivers	**sedimentary**	**metamorphic**	
magma	**buried**	**breaks**	**igneous**

In the rock cycle __________ rocks are formed when molten __________ cools. Weathering __________ these rocks up. The weathered rock is transported by __________ and the sea, and deposited to make layered __________ rock. This gets __________, heated and squashed to make __________ rock.

11.2 Making new rocks

Seventy percent of all rocks on the Earth's surface are sedimentary. These include limestone, sandstone, shale, salt deposits and coal.

Making new rock is a very wet process. First small fragments of sand and rock settle out from slow moving water. This happens where rivers flow into lakes and shallow seas. Gradually over millions of years the layers of sediment build up. During wetter times the rivers flow faster and bigger particles are carried by the water. When the times are colder and drier the slow rivers only carry fine silt. These different particles make distinct layers in the rock that is formed.

As the layers of silt and stones are compressed, they dry out. The water that dries out from them contains dissolved salts and minerals. These salts and minerals are left behind in the rock and they help to 'glue' the particles together into solid rock.

Different? Not really

There are many different sorts of cake, but they all have the same basic ingredients – flour, sugar and fat.

Figure 1 These are all different types of limestone.

Limestone is a type of rock, but like cake, not all limestone looks the same. It all depends what other materials got washed down the same river or what the under-sea conditions were like when the limestone formed.

Figure 2 Different types of cake mix

When cake is made, its texture and shape depend on what conditions and ingredients are used. But cake is still mainly flour, sugar and fat. Limestone is mainly calcium carbonate, but other materials change its colour and texture.

Lulworth Cove

Figure 3 The layers or strata are visible in the rock here at Lulworth Cove in Dorset.

In Jurassic times, 150 million years ago, Lulworth Cove was once the flat bottom of a quiet sea. The sea dried up and a forest grew on the sediments. Holes can be seen in the stone where the fossilised roots once were. Then the forest floor was folded by the same geological event that pushed up the Alps to form Europe's main mountain range. The result is this magnificent display of strata, now exposed to our view by weathering.

Fossils

Sedimentary rock is often created gently as slow deposits of silt are gradually compressed and solidified. It's an ideal environment to preserve a record of the past. Using the fossil record of the past to find out what happened leads to interesting questions.

Fossils are formed in the following way:

1 the animal or plant dies and its remains fall into the sediment;
2 soft parts decay, leaving just the harder material;
3 sediments form their layers round the harder material;
4 over a long period of time, the plant or animal remains are replaced by deposits of minerals in the rock;
5 the mineral deposits exactly match the shape of the plant and animal remains;
6 the sedimentary layers are exposed at the surface. The fossil record is used to discover what life was like long ago.

Questions

1 Where are sedimentary rocks made?
2 What are strata?
3 How do the rock particles stick together?
4 If you add an acid to a carbonate, what gas is given off?
5 How do you test for this gas?
6 How do geologists know that a forest used to grow at Lulworth Cove?
7 Fossils of dinosaurs are not the real bones. What are they?
8 How can we find the date when fossils were formed?

Fossils can be dated from the rock they are found in. The age of the rock can be estimated from the amount of radioactive material found in it.

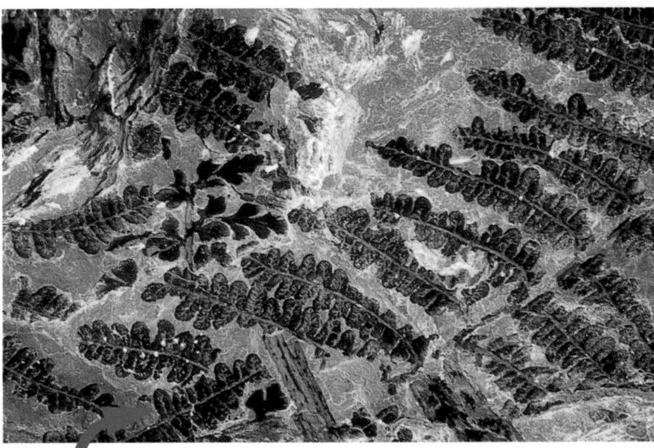

Figure 4 These tropical ferns were found in rocks in Germany. It shows that the climate must have changed dramatically.

Figure 5 These huge dinosaur skeletons have been pieced together from fossil evidence of what their bones must have looked like.

Remember

Draw diagrams for these captions.

- When running water slows, all the sand and grit being carried along settles out in layers.
- Over millions of years, more and more layers of wet sand and stones are dumped on top of it.
- The passing ages and huge pressure from above and below slowly dry out the rock.
- The substances dissolved in the seawater cement the grains of rock together.

Cooking stressed rock

Other types of rock can be changed by being heated and compressed. This process creates new metamorphic rocks.

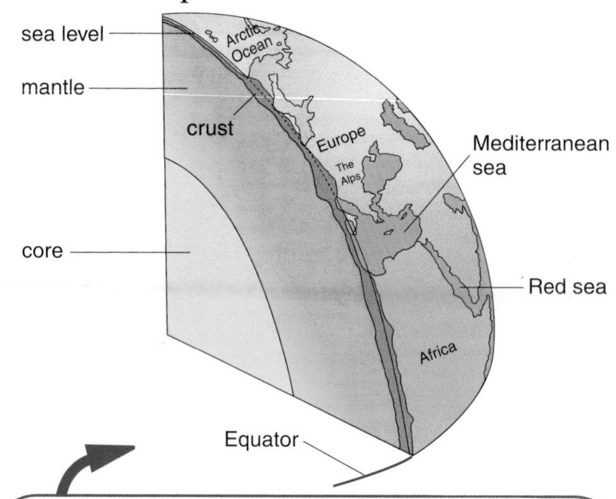

Figure 1 The Earth is not solid. It is like a ball of porridge with a thin crust.

Plate movements

The rock surface of the Earth is at most 10 kilometres thick. This is a planet that is nearly 1200 kilometres in diameter so less than one hundredth of the thickness of the globe is solid **crust**. Beneath the rocky surface is a hot liquid rock called **magma**. Its temperature is 1400°C.

In the vast volume of magma, **convection currents** move the rock about slowly like hot jam. These currents carry streams of rock around under the surface. The movement in the mantle pulls the surface crust with it.

The crust is not in one piece. It is formed of huge plates. Under the oceans there are **oceanic plates** made of very dense rock and under the continents there are **continental plates** made of a less dense rock. The movements under the crust drag the plates around the surface of the Earth. This movement of the plates is called **plate tectonics**. The movement at the edges of the plates causes many of the Earth's major geological disturbances such as earthquakes and volcanic eruptions. If you plot on a map where these major events take place, you can trace the edges of the plates.

Many years ago it was noticed that some parts of the world seemed to fit together although they were now many thousands of miles apart. If you look at a map of the world you will see that the eastern coastline of South America seems to fit into the western coastline of Africa. This is not a coincidence. 127 million years ago, during the reign of the dinosaurs, they were one landmass called **Gondwanaland**. Then they split apart, slowly moving to their present positions. In 1912 a geologist called Alfred Wegener noticed this fit and proposed a theory called **continental drift**. What Wegener didn't know was how these landmasses moved. About 50 years later geologists worked out that the crust was made of large plates and the theory of **plate tectonics** was put forward to explain how the world has changed.

New layers of sedimentary rock form continually on the surface. As millions of years go by the layers of rock get buried deeper and deeper.

Metamorphic rock is made when this buried rock gets heated and compressed. This happens so much that the rock re-crystallises into new material. The new material can be similar in colour to the old rock, but there are differences in texture and it is baked much harder. The rocks are compressed because of the pressure from the layers of rocks above the metamorphic rock.

The heating comes from the **mantle** below. Often magma will force its way up through a weakness in the strata. This creates an intrusion of igneous rock in the strata. As the liquid magma solidifies, it cooks the rock around it into a new type. If the magma makes a horizontal layer it is called a **sill**. If it forms a vertical (upright) piece of rock it is called a **dyke**.

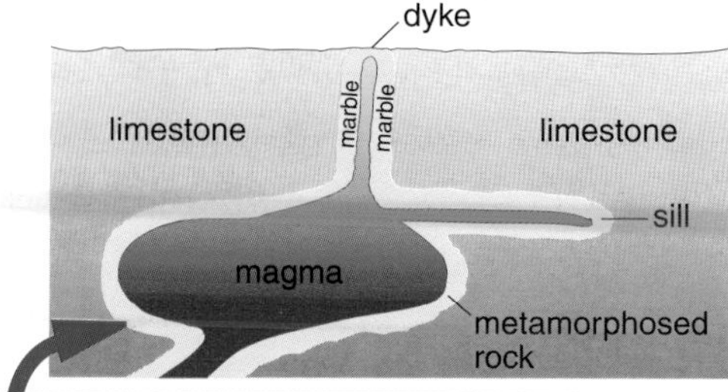

Figure 2 The magma pushes through the strata and makes an 'intrusion'. If there is a wide intrusion with lots of magma, a big volume of rock is changed into metamorphic rock.

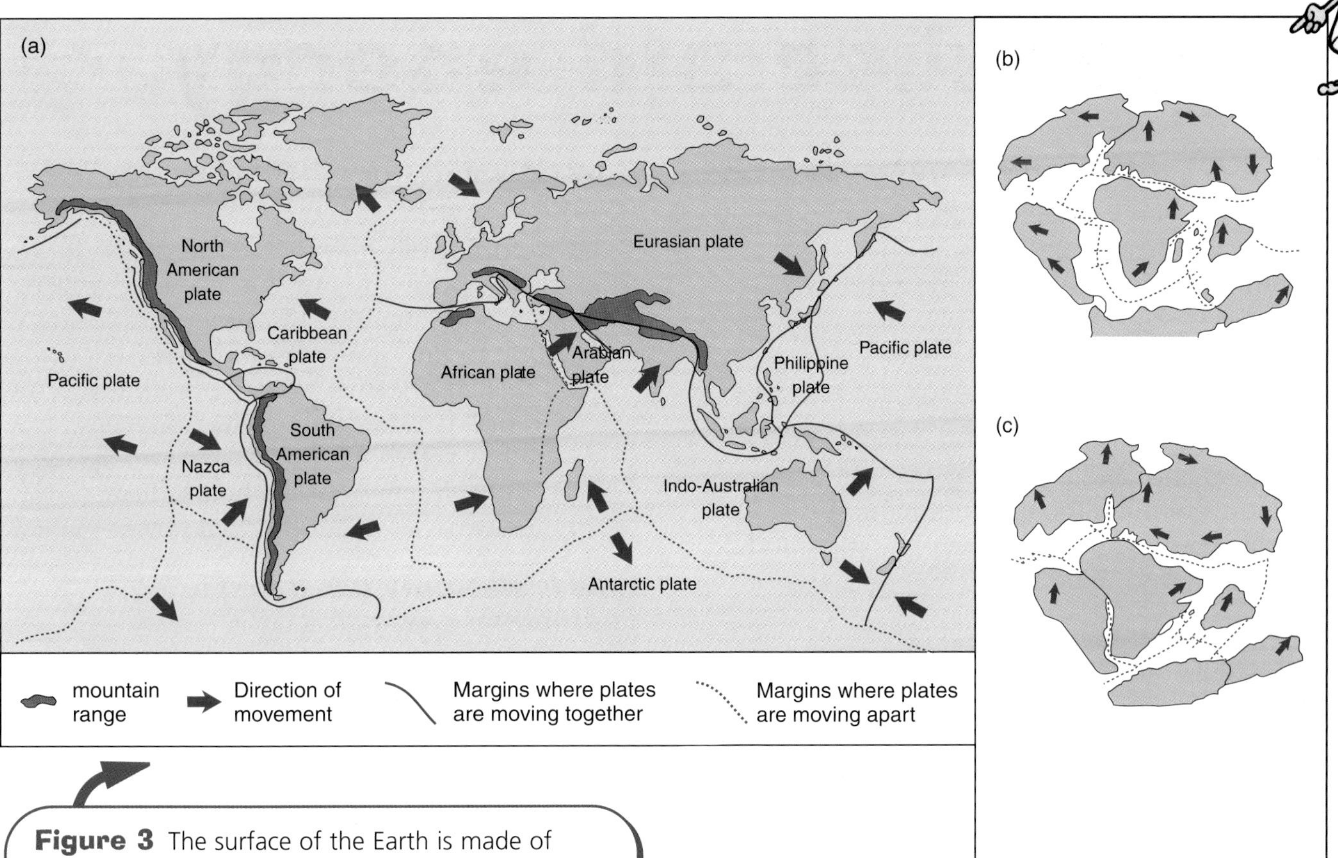

Figure 3 The surface of the Earth is made of plates that are slowly moving about. The movements cause volcanoes and earthquakes. (a) Distribution of the plates today. (b) The continents as they were 70 million years ago. (c) The continents 140 million years ago.

Questions

1 How thick is the Earth's solid crust?

2 What is the diameter of the Earth?

3 What is the temperature of the mantle?

4 What causes the movement of the molten rock in the mantle?

5 Explain what is meant by continental plates.

6 What happens when continental plates push against each other?

7 How do sedimentary rocks get buried?

8 What heats up the buried rock?

9 What is a sill?

10 Where would you look for the best quality marble?

Marble

Marble is a beautiful smooth stone. It is often used for sculpture and fine decoration. But it was once limestone.

Magma provided intense heat that baked the chalky limestone under pressure, turning it into marble. Marble is therefore a metamorphic rock.

The best quality marble is found next to igneous rocks pushed into the crust.

Remember

Draw pictures to illustrate these captions.

- Rocks gradually get buried as more layers are formed.
- Magma pushes up from underneath to make an intrusion.
- The rock on either side of the intrusion gets heated and compressed into new rock.
- Marble is metamorphic rock. It is very different in structure from chalk but they are made from the same chemical compound.

Geothermal energy

What is geothermal energy?

The word 'geothermal' comes from two Greek words, geo (earth) and therme (heat). So, geothermal means the heat from the Earth.

Some hot rocks are caused by radioactive materials in the crust, but near tectonic plate boundaries, our Earth's interior provides the heat energy. This heat – geothermal energy – yields warmth and power that we can use without polluting the environment. At the Earth's core – 4000 miles deep – temperatures may reach over 5000°C.

The Earth's core transfers energy by conduction to the surrounding layer of rock, the mantle. When temperatures and pressures become high enough, some mantle rock melts, becoming magma. Then, because it is lighter (less dense) than the surrounding rock, the magma rises by convection, moving slowly up toward the Earth's crust, carrying the heat from below. Sometimes the hot magma reaches all the way to the surface, where we know it as lava, but most often the magma remains below the Earth's crust.

How have people used geothermal energy in the past?

From earliest times, people have used the geothermal water that flowed freely from the Earth's surface as hot springs. The oldest and most common use was, of course, just relaxing in the comforting warm waters. But this 'magic water' was also used in other creative ways. The Romans used geothermal water to treat eye and skin diseases and, in the ancient city of Pompeii, to heat buildings. As early as 10 000 years ago, Native Americans used water from hot springs for cooking and medicine. For centuries, the Maoris of New Zealand have cooked 'geothermally' and, since the 1960s, France has been heating up to 200 000 homes using geothermal water. In Iceland, a whole tourist industry has grown up around bathing in hot lakes surrounded by snowfields. Most of Iceland's heating systems run on geothermal hot water.

How do we use geothermal energy today?

Today we drill wells into the geothermal reservoirs to bring the hot water to the surface. Geologists and engineers do a lot of exploring and testing to find underground areas that contain this geothermal water, so we know where to drill geothermal production wells. Once the hot water and/or steam travel up the wells to the surface, they can be used to generate electricity in geothermal power plants.

How is electricity generated using geothermal energy?

In geothermal power plants, the steam and hot water from geothermal reservoirs provides the force that spins the turbine generators to produce electricity. The water is then returned down into the Earth through a well to be reheated. There are three kinds of geothermal power plant. The temperatures and pressures of a reservoir determine which kind will be built.

1. A 'dry' steam reservoir produces steam but very little water. The steam is piped directly into a 'dry' steam power plant to provide the force to spin the turbine generator.
2. A geothermal reservoir that produces mostly hot water is called a 'hot water reservoir' and is used in a 'flash' power plant. Water ranging in temperature from 200 to 500°C is brought up to the surface through the well where, on being released from the pressure of the deep reservoir, some of the water flashes into steam in a 'separator'. The steam then powers the turbines.
3. A reservoir with temperatures ranging from 100°C to 200°C is not hot enough to be used in a flash power plant, but can still be used to produce electricity in a 'binary' power plant. In a binary system, the geothermal water is passed through a heat exchanger, where its heat is transferred into a second liquid that boils at a lower temperature than water. When heated, this liquid flashes to vapour, which, like steam, expands and spins the turbine blades. None of the organic solvent is allowed to escape and pollute the air.

What are some of the advantages of using geothermal energy to generate electricity?

- *It's clean*. Geothermal power plants, like wind and solar power plants, do not have to burn fuels to manufacture steam to turn the turbines. Generating electricity with geothermal energy helps to conserve non-renewable fossil fuels, and by decreasing the use of these fuels, we reduce emissions that harm our atmosphere. There is no smoky air around geothermal power plants – in fact some are built in the middle of farm crops. Geothermal installations don't require damming of rivers or harvesting of forests, and there are no mine shafts, tunnels, open pits, waste heaps or oil spills.
- *It's reliable*. Geothermal power plants are designed to run 24 hours a day, all year round. There are no interruptions due to weather, natural disasters or political rifts that can interrupt transportation of fuels.
- *It's cheap*. Money does not have to be used to buy fuel for geothermal power plants. Geothermal 'fuel' – like the Sun and the wind – is always where the power plant is.

What are some more uses of geothermal energy?

Geothermal waters can be used directly from the Earth to soothe people's aching muscles in hot springs and health spas. They are also used to heat greenhouses in which flowers, vegetables and other crops are grown.

Geothermal district heating systems pump geothermal water through a heat exchanger, where it transfers its heat to clean city water that is piped to buildings in the district.

Rock oil pioneers

From the Greek 'petra', meaning rock, and the Latin 'oleum', meaning oil, the word petroleum translates as 'rock oil'. The first discoveries of oil were natural seeps along fault lines and cracks in rocks.

Pits were dug to extract petroleum from the ground – the oil was sometimes found by accident when digging wells for water.

Then in 1859, near Oil Creek, Pennsylvania, USA, **Edwin Drake** drilled the first well in the United States specifically in search of oil. This was not the first oil well in the world. **F. N. Semyenov**, a Russian engineer, drilled the first ten years earlier, but neither knew of each other's work. Since then the world has been oil mad, and many scientists work in the oil industry.

Questions

1. What does geothermal mean?
2. How are the reservoirs of hot water formed?
3. How hot is the Earth's core?
4. What is molten rock inside the Earth called?
5. How have the New Zealand Maoris used geothermal energy?
6. What are the advantages of using geothermal energy for making electricity?
7. Produce a poster on one of these three themes

   Either 'Where geothermal heat comes from' or 'How we use geothermal heat – past, present and future' or 'Three ways of turning geothermal energy into electricity'.

11.4 Solid rock

Pure substances melt and boil at fixed temperatures. Adding impurities changes the melting and boiling point of a substance.

Particles in solids

Solids have shape. Each particle in the solid has a fixed place. It always has the same particles around it. But these particles are not standing still. All of the particles are moving all the time. They move backwards and forwards, up and down, left and right. Imagine yourself sitting on a chair in a packed classroom. You can still move about a bit, sit forward, stretch up to see across the room, reach down and scratch your ankle, lean to the left to see past people. Imagine everyone in the crowded room doing this. The movements will be exactly like those of the particles in a solid. Scientists use the word **vibrations** to describe these movements.

Substances melt when the rapid vibrations of their particles have enough energy to break the forces holding them together. These vibrations get quicker as the temperature gets hotter.

Shut your eyes and imagine a line of dancers in a disco all arm in arm. The music gets faster; they move quicker as they become excited. Eventually they dance so fast that they cannot hold on and they break free of each other. That's like melting.

When liquid materials cool down they form solids. The particles move slower and slower until they link together in regular patterns.

When a large amount of a molten substance is cooling, the solid state forms at many places throughout it. If it is cooling slowly, the solid 'pieces' form slowly and are widely spaced. If it is cooling quickly, lots of much smaller solid 'pieces' form as they start much closer together.

Each solid 'piece' that forms from the liquid is a **crystal**. The process is called **crystallisation**.

This effect is seen very clearly in rocks that have been formed from molten magma or lava such as granite and basalt.

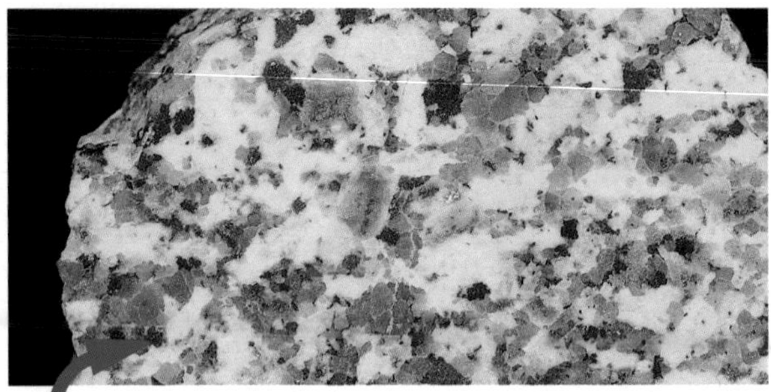

Figure 1 Granite rock is formed deep under the surface. Magma cools slowly to produce large crystals.

Figure 2 Basalt is a volcanic rock. The lava flows and cools very rapidly. This makes small, tightly-packed crystals.

Questions

1 Use the 'dancers at a disco' model to show crystallisation.

a) Draw a picture to show a slow end to the music. The dancers link together in large groups like large crystals.

b) Draw a picture to illustrate a sudden end to the music. The dancers could form lots of very small groups.

2 What is the correct scientific word for 'energy transferred as movement'?

3 How can a geologist decide whether a rock was formed underground or on the surface?

Solid shapes

Making candles

Sahera decided to try making candles. She mixed 250 g of paraffin wax and 50 g of stearic acid (another wax) in a glass bowl and melted them over a pan of boiling water. She poured this into the candle mould and left it to cool. The wax shrank as it solidified. When the wax was nearly solid, she topped up the level in the mould with more molten wax.

Figure 3 Burning candles

Melting mixtures

While she was making candles, Sahera investigated the melting point of stearic acid and paraffin wax. Here are her results.

Time (mins)	Cooling stearic acid	Cooling paraffin wax
0	90	90
1	84	83
2	79	77
3	75	72
4	69	66
5	69	61
6	69	60
7	69	59
8	69	58
9	65	57
10	63	56
11	60	52
12	58	49

Table 1 Sahera's results

Pure substances, such as stearic acid, melt at one specific temperature, but mixtures of substances, such as paraffin wax, melt over a range of temperatures.

When the particles have enough energy due to heating, they can break away from each other and form a jumble of particles rather than a regular arrangement.

The melting point is linked to the **hardness** of the substance. Both melting point and hardness depend on the forces between the particles in the solid.

Solid mixtures have many different forces holding the particles together, so they soften and melt gradually. Mixtures therefore melt over a range of temperatures. Think of chocolate, that's a good example.

Questions

4 Plot graphs for Sahera's investigation. These graphs are called **cooling curves**.

5 Explain why she decided that paraffin wax was a mixture and stearic acid was not.

6 What was the melting point of stearic acid?

7 Explain the link between melting point and hardness. Give some examples to help.

Remember

Use the words to work out the missing terms from the passage below.

temperature bonds hardness mixtures solids different particles

Particles in ____1____ wiggle about. The solid melts at one ____2____. This is when the particles vibrate so much they break the ____3____ holding them in place.

There are lots of ____4____ melting points depending on the solid. Melting and ____5____ are linked. They both depend on forces between solid ____6____. ____7____ soften and then melt at a range of temperatures.

11.5

Brave new island

As the Earth's surface moves, some molten magma gets to the surface through cracks in the rocks. This effect produces volcanoes. They make new igneous rocks.

In November 1963, fishermen working off Iceland's south central coast noticed a black column of smoke rising high above the ocean surface. They radioed the shore, and a plane was sent to investigate the cause of the spectacle. After flying over the area a few times, the pilot confirmed that a fresh volcano had broken through the waves, creating what was then the world's youngest island, **Surtsey**.

When the eruption first occurred, columns of ash were sent almost 10 000 m into the air. The birth of Surtsey took almost four years as eruption followed eruption until 1967. Because of pounding seas, there was a considerable amount of early erosion and two smaller islands disappeared. But the core of Surtsey quickly solidified as rock and is now holding its own. The new island is one square mile (2.6 square kilometres) in area and rises more than 170 metres above sea level; a total of 290 metres from the ocean floor.

Surtsey is not only the world's newest island, but also the most filmed and researched. Its progress has been carefully watched, giving scientists information about how a new island develops, how plants and animals get there and so on. Because of this, very few people are allowed to visit the island and special permits are only granted for **scientific research**.

Iceland is part of the **Mid-Atlantic Ridge**, a chain of mostly underwater mountains that runs down the centre of the Atlantic Ocean and marks the place where the North American plate is pulling apart from the European and African plates. Near the capital of Iceland, there are deep cracks in the surface of the Earth. One of the volcanoes there called Hekla has erupted violently 17 times since records began. It was thought in the Middle Ages to be the mouth to hell.

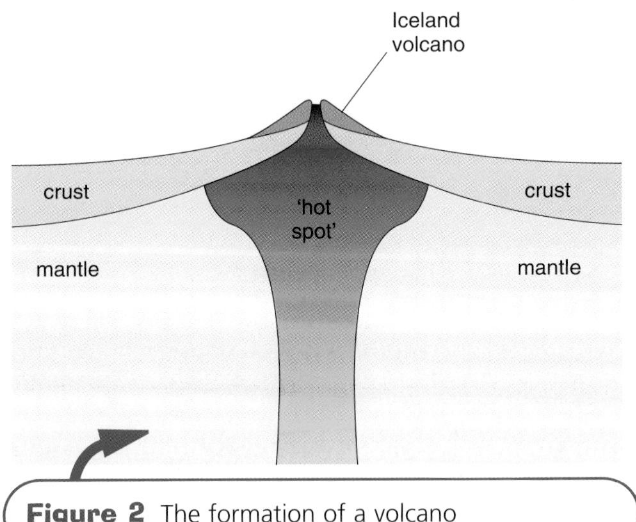

Figure 2 The formation of a volcano

Figure 1 An aerial view of Surtsey

These volcanoes are caused by 'ocean floor spreading', where a seam in the Earth's crust splits. This is very rarely visible. It is only visible above the surface of the waves in Iceland because there is a **'hot spot'** there. This means that very large amounts of magma well up to the surface in Iceland, causing eruptions and increasing the size of the island itself.

Another volcanic island is Hawaii. Hawaii is very much bigger than Surtsey. The piles of lava that form Hawaii rise as high as 32 000 feet (9750 metres) from the ocean floor. They have been built up by many eruptions to form the cone-shaped island. This has taken many years. Hawaii has very fertile soil and beautiful beaches.

Figure 4 An aerial shot of Hawaii, another volcanic island

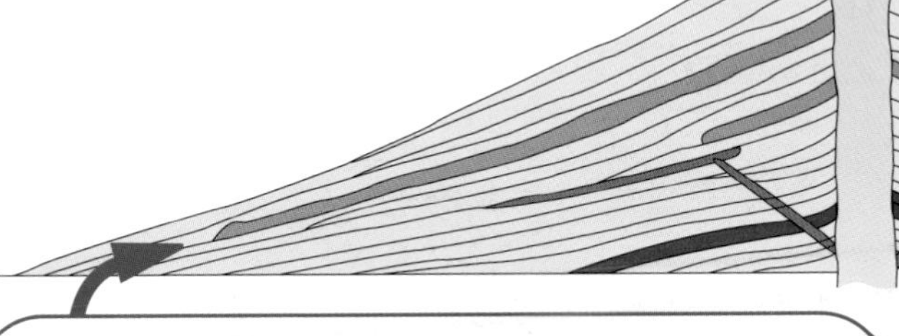

Figure 3 Volcanic islands like Hawaii and Surtsey are built up. Each eruption forms a new layer of rock until a cone-shaped mountain is made.

Questions

1 When did Surtsey first appear?
2 What had created the new island?
3 What has happened to the two other islands created at the same time?
4 How big is Surtsey? (Get a copy of a map of your school area and draw Surtsey's size on it.)
5 Why are tourists not allowed to visit Surtsey?
6 What is the 'Mid-Atlantic Ridge'? Explain why it has formed.
7 How are the volcanoes in Iceland formed?
8 Draw a cartoon strip to show how volcano eruptions form a cone-shaped mountain.

Remember

Complete the passage below using the following words.

surface molten Europe Surtsey lava volcanoes

___1___ are formed when molten rock comes out from a crack in the Earth's ___2___. The molten rock is called ___3___ and it cools to make new rock.

Rocks produced from ___4___ material are called igneous rocks.

The crack that produced ___5___ island was caused by ___6___ and North America moving apart.

Closer

Rock and choc

You can use chocolate bars to make a thinking model of how rock forms.

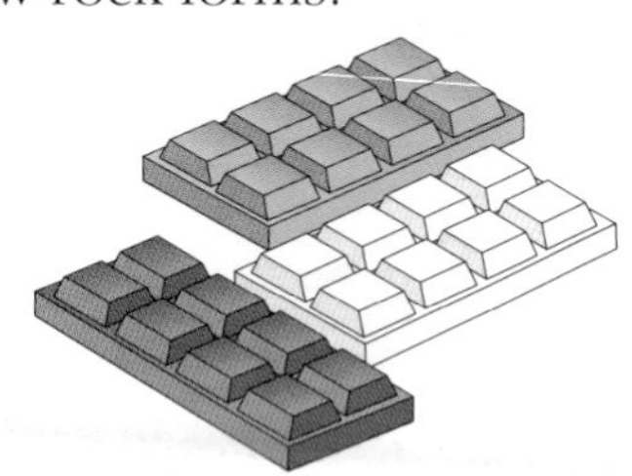

Igneous rocks

These chocolate bars were made from molten material. Molten rock cools as it gets near the surface of the Earth, and you get a smooth igneous rock with no layers. If the rock cools slowly you get big crystals forming. This rock has cooled very quickly so the texture is smooth. Different mixtures give different rocks like granite, gabbro or obsidian.

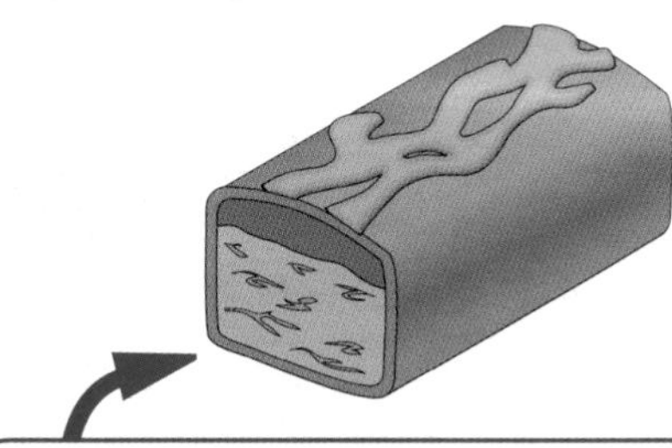

Sedimentary rocks

Sedimentary rocks are laid down in layers. At different times there are different materials settling out in the sea. You can see the layers in the rock that were formed at different times.

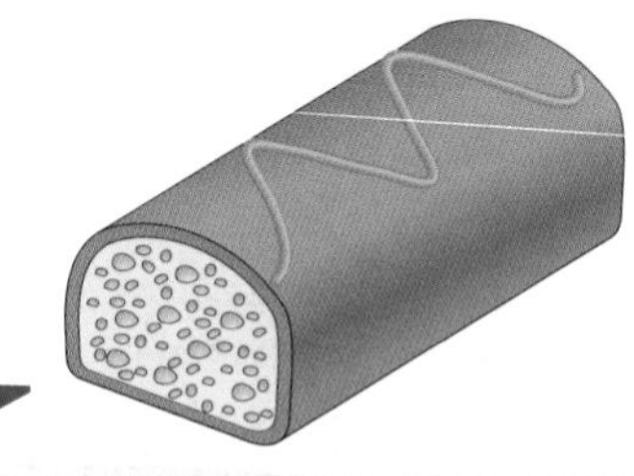

Metamorphic rocks

Metamorphic rock is formed by heat and pressure on the rock. This changes the hardness of the rock and its texture. If you take a cake bar, squash it and heat it, it goes flat and biscuity.

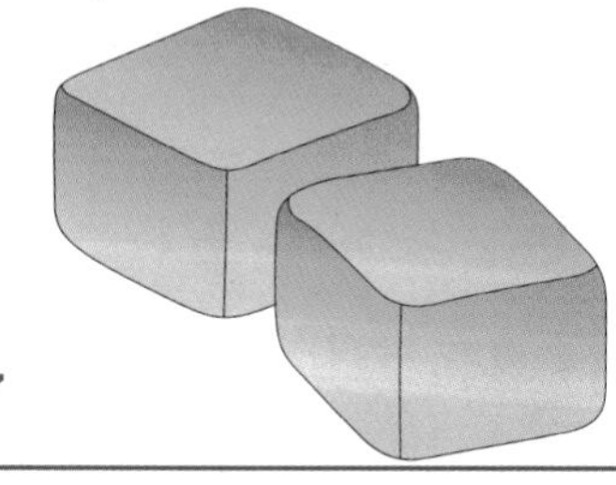

Magma – a very thick liquid

Magma is the molten rock under the surface of the Earth. Even though we think of it as runny, it is only as runny as toffee.

Questions

1 Habib tested clay samples. He wanted to find out if they got harder the longer he baked them. He used something to make a dent in the clay and then measured the width of the dent to find out how hard the clay was.

a) Design the sort of apparatus Habib could use to make a dent in the clay.

b) How could Habib get valid data from his investigation?

c) Plot a line graph for the data in the table.

d) Explain what the shape of the graph tells about the hardness of the clay.

Baking time (hours)	Width of dent (mm)
0	210
4	100
8	55
12	30
16	15
20	10
24	10
28	10

Sound and music

Opener
Good sounds, bad sounds

Sounds of the city

Questions

1 What sounds good and what sounds bad? Sort the items in the picture into good sounds and bad sounds. Does your sorting agree with what other people think?

2 Write a list of the sounds you see and then use three colours or some other method to highlight the sounds that:

- everybody thinks are good;
- everybody thinks are bad;
- people disagree about.

3 What kinds of patterns are there in the different sounds? For example, do some vary a lot in loudness? Do others have a steady loudness? Are some of them always high notes? Are they low notes, or a mixture of high and low?

Travelling vibrations

Sounds spread out from vibrating objects. The sounds can travel through different materials. When the sounds reach our ears they make our eardrums vibrate. If the vibrations are too strong they can damage our ears.

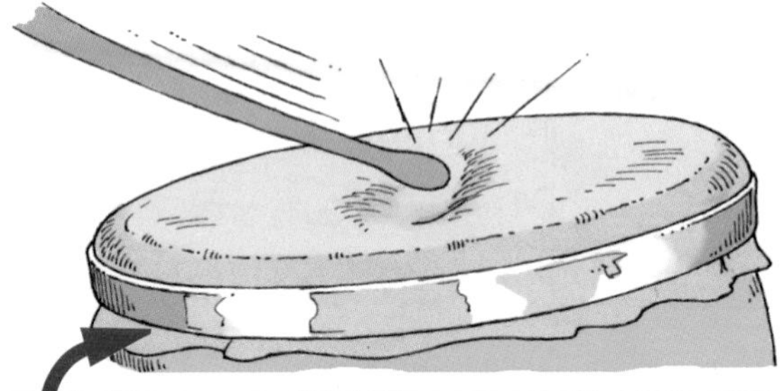

Figure 1 The crash of a drumstick makes the drumskin vibrate. You can't see the drumskin vibrate, but if you touched it you might feel the vibrations.

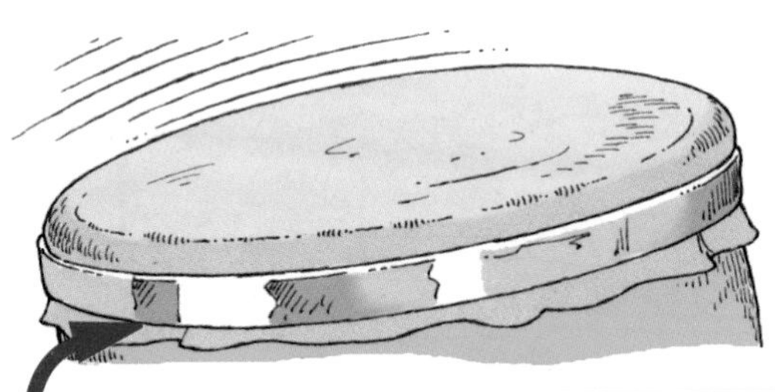

Figure 2 The drumskin makes the air around it vibrate. The vibration spreads through the air.

Figure 3 The vibrations have to travel through the air. They travel quickly – about one kilometre every three seconds.

Figure 4 Vibrations can travel through all kinds of materials. The vibrations travel through solid materials even more quickly than they travel through air.

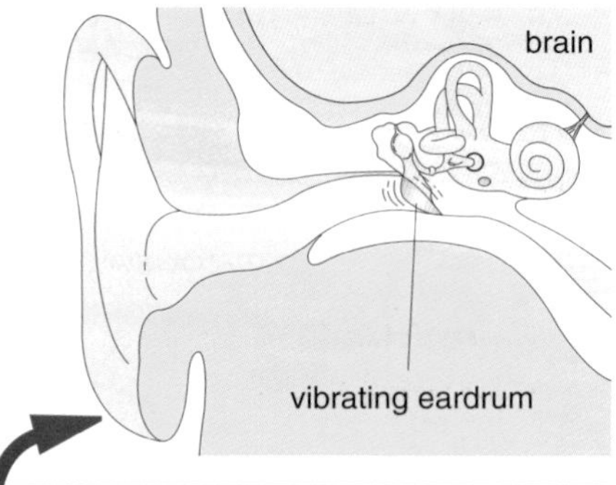

Figure 5 The vibrations can travel through the air to a small sheet of skin in your ear called your eardrum. The air makes it vibrate.

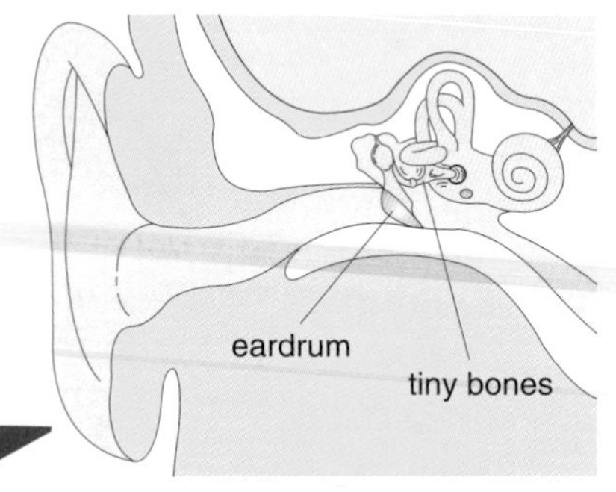

Figure 6 Your eardrum makes some tiny bones in your ear vibrate. They pass the vibrations deeper inside.

The bones pass the vibrations on to a liquid deeper in your ears. There are tiny hairs in the liquid. They vibrate too. The hairs make tiny electric bursts in your nerves. Your brain can understand these electric bursts. Your brain doesn't call them 'vibrations'. It calls them sound.

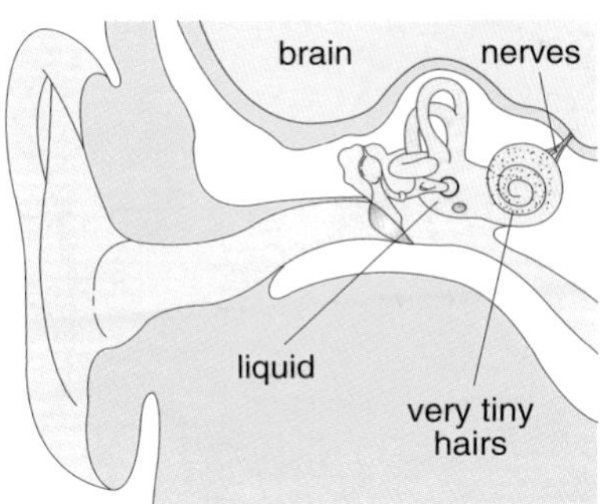

Figure 7 Journey's end – tiny hairs vibrate to make tiny electrical bursts that travel along nerves and into your brain.

Questions

1 **a)** What does a drumskin do when you hit it?

b) What does a guitar string do when you pluck it?

2 **a)** How long does it take for sound to travel one kilometre through the air?

b) How long does it take to travel two kilometres?

3 In what ways is your ear like a drum?

4 Why can it be harmful to listen to very loud music?

Too loud!

Loud noises like explosions or very loud music can make the tiny hairs vibrate too much. If this happens they can be damaged. Then they can't make those little electric bursts in your nerves. Your hearing will be damaged for the rest of your life.

Remember

Complete the passage below using the following words.

eardrums loud ears vibrating deaf air hairs brains

Sound that we hear starts out as a ____**1**____ object. The object makes the ____**2**____ around it vibrate. The vibrations travel through the air. Our ____**3**____ let us detect vibrations in the air. The vibrations reach our ____**4**____. Tiny ____**5**____ deep inside our ears vibrate. The tiny hairs are connected to our ____**6**____ by nerves. That is how we hear sound. If the sound is very ____**7**____ it means that the vibrations are very strong. The strong vibrations can damage the tiny hairs. That means that loud sounds can make us ____**8**____.

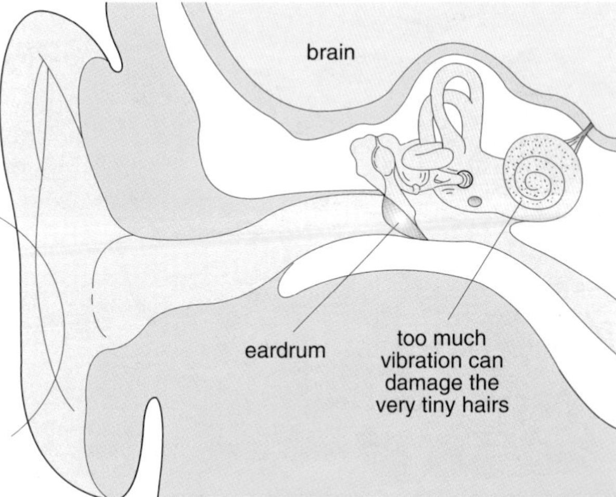

Figure 8 Be careful! Loud sounds do damage.

Different sounds

We can hear different types of sounds. Different vibrations of objects make different sounds.

The sound of words

You use the voicebox in your throat to speak. When you want to say a word, you make your voicebox vibrate. You can make it vibrate in different ways, so that you can make different sounds.

Your mouth is also important. When you whisper, you make the sounds of words without using your voicebox. Then you blow air through your mouth and make different patterns of vibrations.

Stop and think!

- Can you feel your tongue move when you speak?
- Can you make loud sounds of some letters just by whispering?
- Try to talk without moving your tongue. Try to talk without moving your tongue or your lips.
- Try to talk without using your tongue, your lips, or your voicebox!

Figure 1 a) Quiet sound – you don't need to use your voicebox to whisper.

b) Gentle talk – lungs, voicebox, tongue and lips are all busy. They make louder and quieter sounds. They make high and low notes.

c) Singing out loud – now your voicebox is really working hard. With the help of your brain it carefully makes high notes and low notes. We say the notes have different **pitch**. They can also have different **loudness**. The voicebox needs to put more energy into vibrations to make loud sound.

Some words of sound

One of the amazing things about people is that we have made so many different instruments for making different sounds. There are hundreds of different kinds of drums alone.

There are also very many kinds of string instruments. They all work by making some kind of string vibrate. It usually takes a lot of practice to be able to make music with strings. You have to be in control of the vibrations.

The **amplitude** of a vibration is the distance the string moves away from its resting position. When the amplitude of vibration increases, the loudness of the sound also increases.

The **frequency** is the number of vibrations the string makes in every second. Strings usually vibrate with high frequency, hundreds of times each second. All you can see is a blur. High frequency vibrations make high pitch notes.

Figure 2 In control of the amplitude and frequency of vibrations

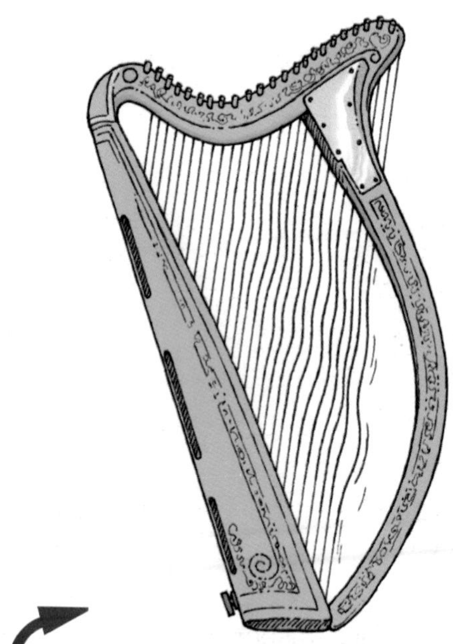

Figure 3 Harp strings can vibrate with different amplitudes and frequencies.

Questions

1 What parts of your body do you use to talk?

2 Which parts have to work extra hard when you sing loudly?

3 The sound made by the string of an electric guitar isn't very loud. What does that tell you about the amplitude of its vibrations?

4 What does a guitar player have to do to make sounds of different pitch – high notes and low notes?

5 Unscramble these letters to find a pair of words that go together.

I'D EAT LUMP   SEND SOUL

Remember

Use the words below to complete the passage.

frequency loudness pitch amplitude vibrates

Vibrations of objects make sounds. The amplitude of the vibrations affects the ___**1**___ of the sound. The frequency of the vibration affects the ___**2**___ of the sound. When you talk, your voicebox ___**3**___. You can change the sound of your voice by changing the ___**4**___ and the ___**5**___ of the vibrations.

12.3 Different notes

Every sound wave carries a pattern. The loudness of a sound depends on the amplitude of the vibration that causes it. The pitch of a sound depends on the frequency of the vibration.

Figure 1 Making the music sound good

Figure 2 Making the music sound better

Singing into the microphone

All sound starts off with a vibrating object. The vibrations spread out into the surrounding air a bit like the ripples spreading on a pool of water. The travelling vibrations are called **waves**.

A microphone is sensitive to sound waves. The sound waves cause vibration in the microphone. The microphone then converts the vibrations into a matching pattern of electric current.

Working on the notes

Every single piece of music is full of variety. There are the bass notes which have low pitch. They are produced by big bass drums or the long strings of a bass guitar. There are the higher notes of the female singer, each note carefully controlled in **pitch** and **loudness**.

In the recording studio, the producer can work on each individual note. That might involve changing not just the loudness, but also how long it lasts and even its pitch. To do all of that requires a knowledge of sound waves.

Seeing the sounds

We can connect a microphone to an **oscilloscope**. That's a machine like a TV that produces a single moving dot on a screen. It turns the electric current from the microphone into patterns we can see. This makes it easier to compare different sounds. It also makes it easier to work out how **frequency** and **amplitude** affect how the sound feels to us.

- The frequency of a sound is a measure of the number of vibrations in every second. It affects the pitch of the note we hear. We measure frequency in **hertz**, or Hz for short. 1 Hz is one vibration per second.
- The amplitude of a sound is a measure of the size of each vibration. It affects the loudness of the note. In a recording studio, the producer knows how to change and blend the frequency and amplitude to get the best sound.

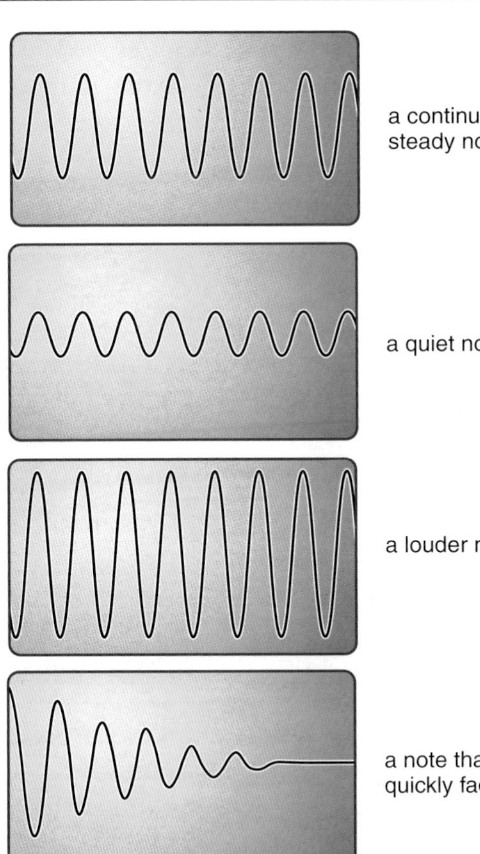

Figure 3 Sound shapes as they appear on the screen of an oscilloscope

Remember

Unscramble the anagrams to complete the passage.

A song is a mixture of STONE with varying loudnesses and pitch. All the sounds are made by RAVING BIT sources such as guitar strings, drumskins and people's voice boxes. The travelling vibrations that spread out are called SAVE W . Objects which vibrate with large I DATE LUMP make loud sounds. Female vocalists usually sing notes with higher pitch or CRY QUEEN F than male vocalists.

Questions

1 Which of these notes seen on an oscilloscope:

a) is the loudest to start with, **b)** is the highest, **c)** dies away most quickly, **d)** lasts for a long time?

i)

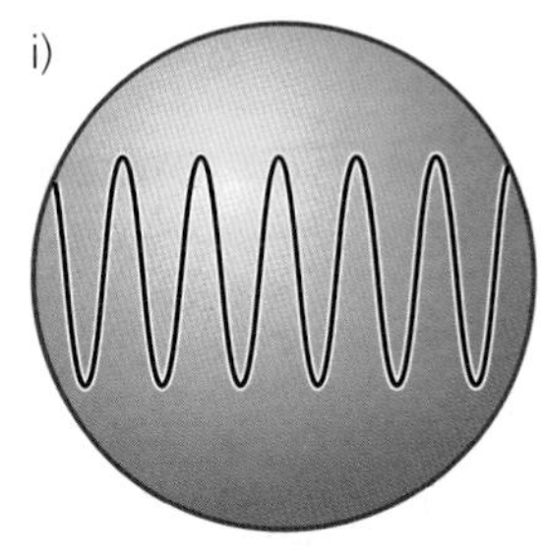

ii)

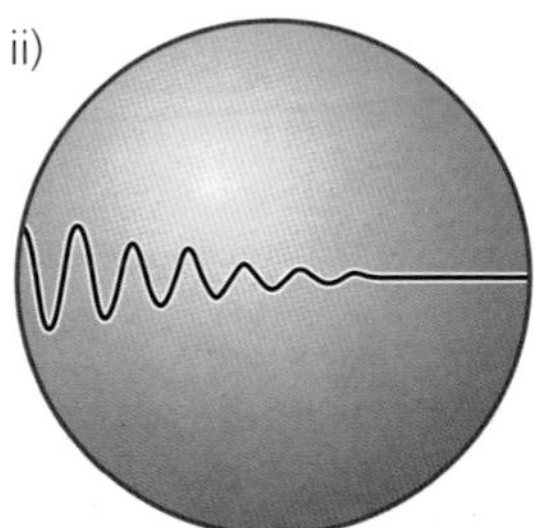

iii)

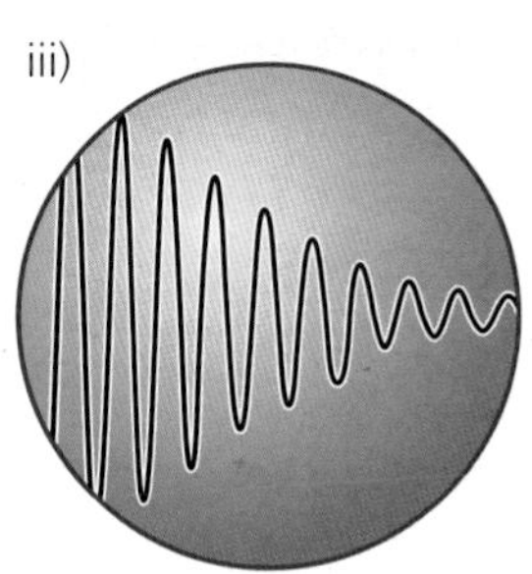

2 Describe the difference you'll hear between these two notes.

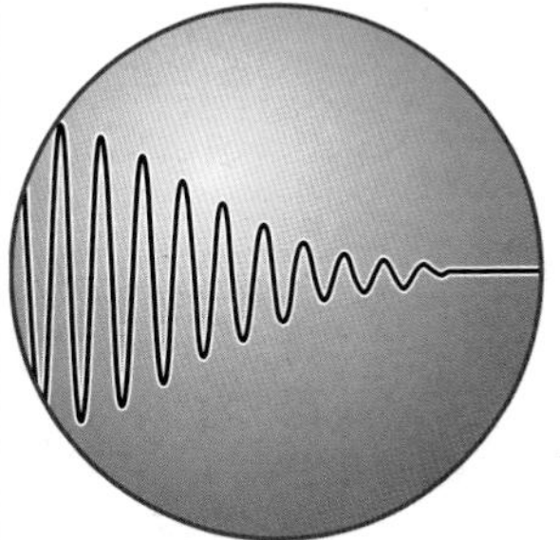

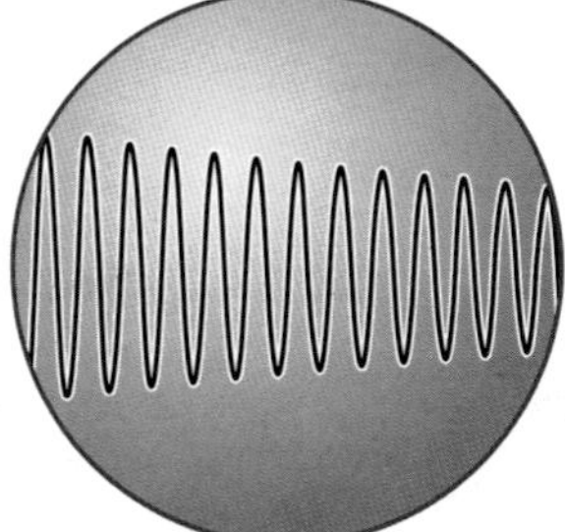

3 Put these words into pairs that go together:

microphone amplitude pitch frequency oscilloscope loudness

4 a) What difference can you hear between the sounds of a pencil tapping a cup and a drumstick hitting a bass drum?

b) What are the differences in the way the objects vibrate to make the sounds?

Reflections of light and sound

Sound and light spread out from sources and reflect from surfaces. There are various similarities and differences between light and sound.

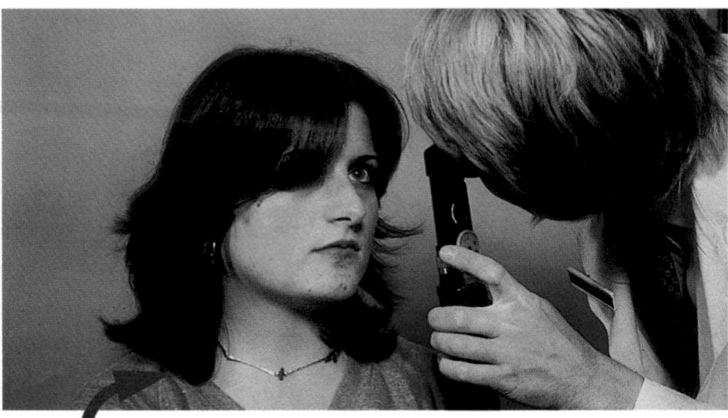

Figure 1 An optician at work

If you have an eye test, the optician might shine a thin beam of light into your eyes as in Figure 1. He is looking straight through the eyeball to the surface at the back – the **retina**. That's where your eyes detect the light and use it to create electrical impulses that travel to your brain. The optician's bright beam of light reflects off the retina. The optician sees the **reflected** light.

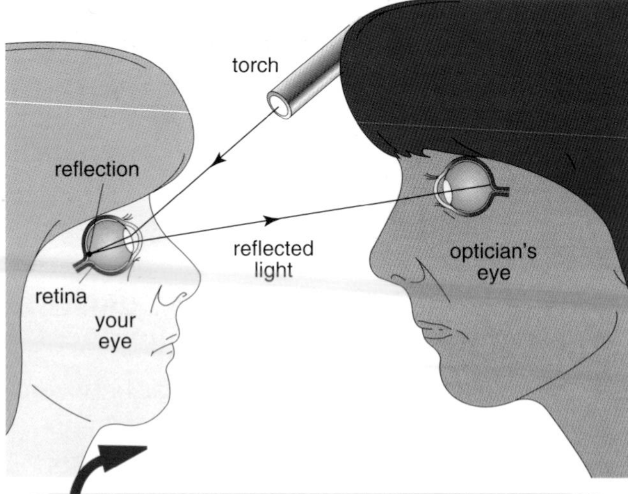

Figure 2 Light from a source travels so people can see it. Here, the optician sees the light after it has been reflected by the patient's eye.

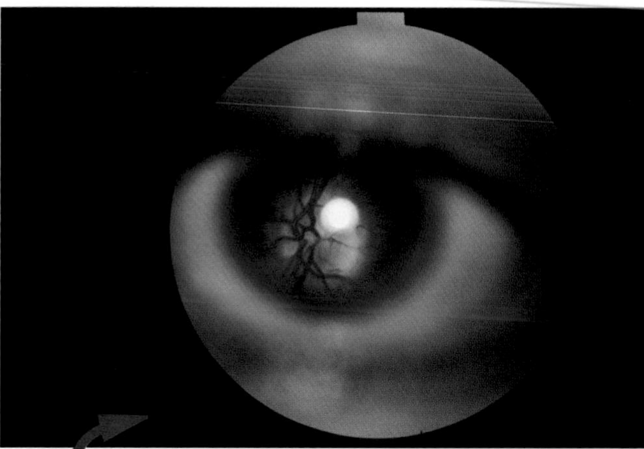

Figure 3 What your retina looks like to an optician

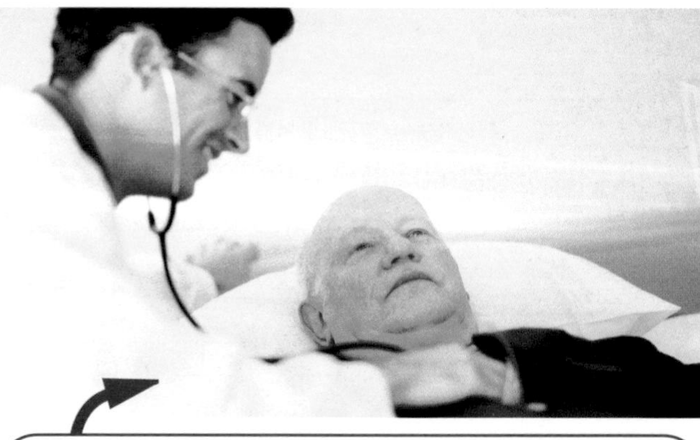

Figure 4 A doctor can listen to your body's sounds.

Light and sound

Sound travels much more slowly than light – almost a million times more slowly in air. The speed of sound in air is about 330 metres per second. But sound can travel through materials that light cannot penetrate. In fact sounds travel more easily, and faster, in solids and liquids than they do in gases like air. Sound can travel through you – as you can tell every time your stomach rumbles.

Sound needs a substance to travel through. It cannot travel through a vacuum. Both light and sound reflect off surfaces. The optician's beam of light reflects off your retina. A beam of sound reflects off the layers of your body.

Ultrasound reflections from inside a human body can be used to produce images of unborn babies. It is likely that your mother had an ultrasound scan before you were born. Ultrasound is very high frequency sound – too high for any human to hear. For scanning, the frequency could be as high as 3.5 **megahertz**. (1 megahertz is a million hertz, or a million vibrations in every second.)

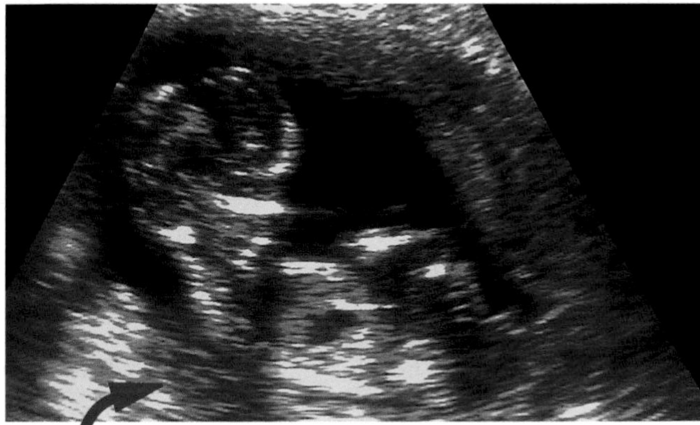

Figure 5 An ultrasound scan of a baby in its mother's womb

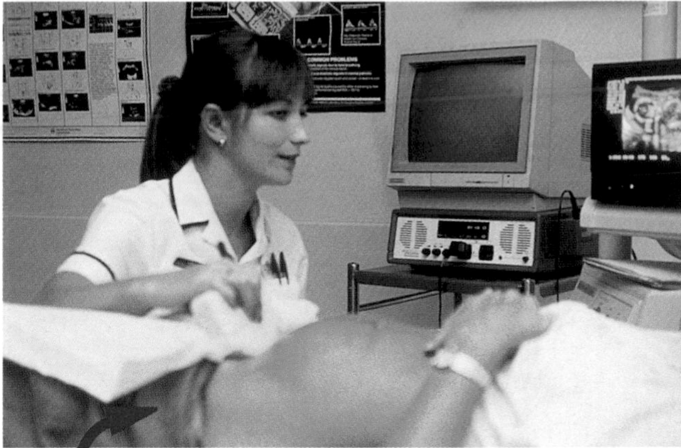

Figure 6 Having an ultrasound scan

The hospital radiographer will have run an ultrasound probe across your mother's abdomen (Figure 6). The probe vibrated in short bursts. Each burst of vibration produced a burst of ultrasound. At the various surfaces inside, including the surfaces of your developing body, the ultrasound was reflected. The vibrations travelled back to the surface and were detected by the probe. This information was fed into a computer and displayed on a screen. It's usually a special occasion for a mother to see a tiny new life growing inside her. It also provides a way of checking that the baby is growing as it should.

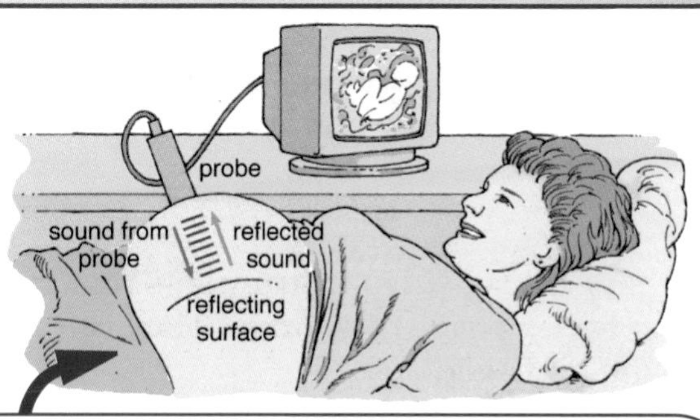

Figure 7 The probe vibrates at very high frequency to make ultrasound. Then it detects the reflected ultrasound to make a picture of hidden surfaces.

Questions

1 a) Make a list of things that are similar about light and sound.
b) Make a list of things that are different about light and sound.

2 What evidence is there that:
a) light can travel through a vacuum?
b) sound can travel through solids and liquids?

3 a) What do we measure in hertz, kilohertz and megahertz?
b) Copy and complete:

3.5 megahertz = __________ hertz

Remember

Use the following words to complete the sentences below.

ultrasound units high million vacuum metres faster

In a vacuum and in air light travels at 300 000 000 ____**1**____ per second. That's almost a million times ____**2**____ than sound.

Sound cannot travel through a ____**3**____ but can travel well through solids and liquids.

An ____**4**____ probe vibrates and produces sound with frequency that is too ____**5**____ to hear. One megahertz is a ____**6**____ hertz. Megahertz and hertz are both ____**7**____ of frequency.

12.5 Testing hearing

Our ears are sensitive instruments that can detect wide ranges of sounds. They can become damaged.

A small baby can't explain whether or not it can hear. But a parent can be very worried if it seems that their baby doesn't respond to sounds. Fortunately, there are ways to find out whether the baby's ears are working properly. They involve measuring the brain activity that's caused by sound. If there is a response in the baby's brain, then signals must be getting through and so the ears are OK.

At a hospital, technicians can put electrodes onto the baby's head. Then an earphone is held next to one of the baby's ears. Vibrations of the earphone produce a clicking sound. The technician can control the loudness of the sound and set it, say, to 60 **decibels** (60 dB). Decibels are units for measuring the loudness of sounds. The electrodes detect electrical activity inside the brain. They are connected to a computer that displays the activity as a wavy line.

Figure 1 There is constant activity in a baby's brain, but each click of sound produces a small peak on the computer screen display.

Questions

1 a) What difference could you hear between a 60 dB sound and a 40 dB sound?

b) When monitoring the hearing of a baby what difference would there be in the way the earphones were vibrating for 60 dB sound and 40 dB sound?

Ears – what can go wrong

- A build-up of ear wax in the outer ear can cause temporary reduction in hearing sensitivity.
- Sound arriving at the **eardrum** makes it vibrate. The eardrum is a circle of stretched skin that can be burst by sudden loud noises such as explosions.
- The **small bones** transmit the vibrations from the eardrum towards the inner ear. They are very small and delicate.
- The **cochlea** is in the inner ear. It is a coiled tube filled with liquid. Small hairs on the cochlea move in time to incoming vibrations. They create electrical signals that travel into the brain. When our brain receives electrical signals from the hairs in the cochlea, we say that we are hearing sound. The hairs can be damaged by loud sounds, such as the sounds from high-power music speakers or industrial machinery. The damage is permanent. There is no way to repair the tiny hairs.

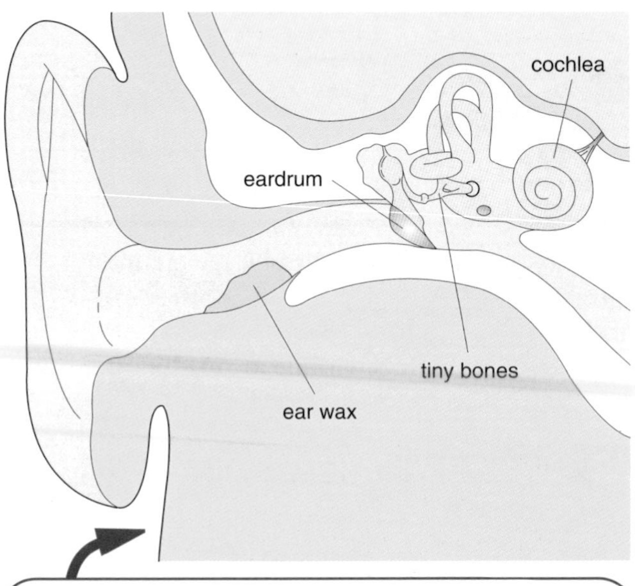

Figure 2 The internal structure of the ear

Amplitude graphs

Sound waves make eardrums vibrate. When your eardrums vibrate with high amplitude, you hear loud sound. We can use a graph like the ones in Figure 3 to show the vibrations. The graph can show how the position of the centre of the eardrum changes as time goes by.

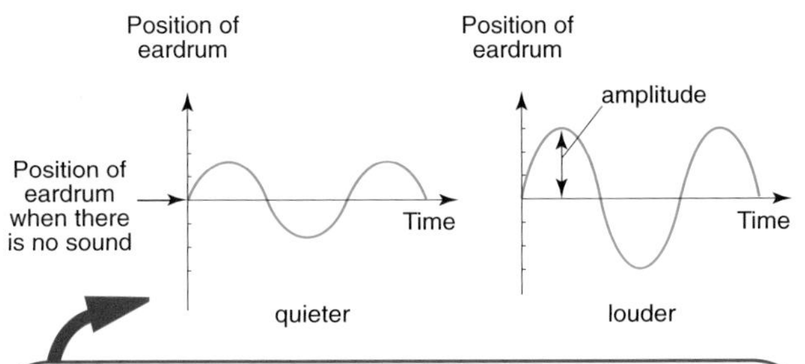

Figure 3 For quiet sounds, your eardrum vibrates with a low amplitude. The amplitude is bigger for louder sound.

Frequency

Frequency is a measurement of the number of vibrations per second. The unit for frequency is the **hertz**, **Hz**. Sound frequencies can be high – several thousand vibrations per second, or several thousand hertz. A thousand hertz is called a **kilohertz**. A million hertz is a **megahertz**.

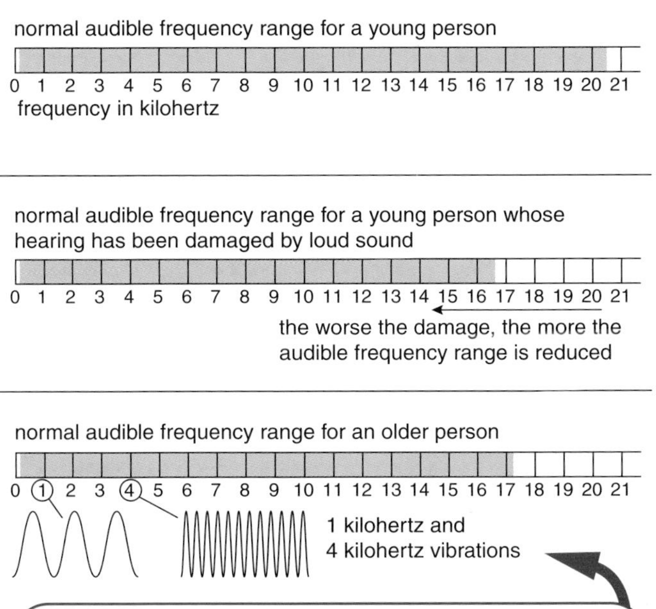

Figure 4 Some audible frequency ranges

Children have the biggest **audible frequency range**. As you get older you lose some of your ability to hear high frequencies. You might no longer be able to hear the constant squeak of a TV set, for example. If your hearing is damaged by loud sound then the reduction in your audible frequency range can be much worse.

Questions

2 Loud sounds are a health hazard.

a) What damage can they do?

b) In what situations are people exposed to loud sounds?

c) What safety precautions reduce the risk of damage?

3 What do each of these units measure:

a) hertz? **b)** kilohertz? **c)** decibel?

4 What happens to your audible frequency range as you grow up and get older?

Remember

Complete the sentences below using the following words.

amplitude kilohertz vibration decibels hertz

The loudness of a sound depends on the ___1___ of vibration of the source of the sound. It is measured in ___2___.

The frequency of a sound depends on the frequency of the ___3___ of the source of the sound. The standard unit for measuring frequency is the ___4___. Most people can hear sounds in the range of 20 hertz to 20 000 hertz. 20 000 hertz can be written as 20 ___5___.

Closer

Imagine what it's like ...

A bat catching an insect

Imagine what it's like to be a bat, finding your way round using your ears and not your eyes. Bats make very special patterns of squeaks. We can't hear most of their sounds, and we call it ultrasound. Then they listen for the echoes, or reflections, from the surfaces all around them. The echoes tell them where surfaces are. They tell them if the surfaces are hard like a brick wall or softer like the leaves of a tree. The echoes even allow a bat to detect the beat of an insects wing. At night there are lots of insects to eat, and nothing except bats to catch them.

Imagine what it's like to be an alien. If you come from a planet which doesn't have much atmosphere or water then you might need to have very sensitive ears to hear sound. Or it might be so hard for sound to travel on your planet that you don't have any sense of sound at all. You might rely on light. Or you might use radio waves. Perhaps you would use radar.

Imagine what it's like to be a dolphin. You can communicate with other dolphins using a lot of different sounds. You can hear sounds from a long way away. You have a special hearing system so that you are very good at telling what direction the sounds come from. A lot of your sounds have a frequency that is too high for humans to hear.

Questions

1 You can tell what direction a sound comes from, without seeing the source of sound. Get someone to make a gentle sound, like a quiet click of the fingers, somewhere behind you or with your eyes closed. Point to where you think the source of sound is. How good are you at that? (Put a finger over one ear and try it again. Are you just as good now? What does this tell you?)

2 What is special about how sound is used by:

- bats?
- dolphins?
- people?

Make a chart with pictures of bats, dolphins, people and aliens. Show the different ways in which they use sound.

3 Explain why frequency and amplitude of sounds matter to:

- bats
- dolphins
- people.

You could add this information to your chart.

4 Conduct a web search using one of these key words:

- radar
- sonar
- whale song
- dolphins
- bats
- ultrasound in hospitals.

Write a bullet point list about what you have found out about sound and communication. Print out pictures if you can.

Make a small poster that you can present to the rest of the class.

Periodic table of the elements

	1	2	Transition elements										3	4	5	6	7	Group 'O'
1	★ 1 H Hydrogen 1																	★ 2 He Helium 4
2	3 Li Lithium 7	4 Be Beryllium 9											5 B Boron 11	6 C Carbon 12	★ 7 N Nitrogen 14	★ 8 O Oxygen 16	★ 9 F Fluorine 19	★ 10 Ne Neon 20
3	11 Na Sodium 23	12 Mg Magnesium 24											13 Al Aluminium 27	14 Si Silicon 28	15 P Phosphorus 31	16 S Sulphur 32	★ 17 Cl Chlorine 35.5	★ 18 Ar Argon 40
4	19 K Potassium 39	20 Ca Calcium 40	21 Sc Scandium 45	22 Ti Titanium 48	23 V Vanadium 51	24 Cr Chromium 52	25 Mn Manganese 55	26 Fe Iron 56	27 Co Cobalt 59	28 Ni Nickel 59	29 Cu Copper 63.5	30 Zn Zinc 65.4	31 Ga Gallium 70	32 Ge Germanium 73	33 As Arsenic 75	34 Se Selenium 79	35 Br Bromine 80	★ 36 Kr Krypton 84
5	37 Rb Rubidium 85	38 Sr Strontium 88	39 Y Yttrium 89	40 Zr Zirconium 91	41 Nb Niobium 93	42 Mo Molybdenum 96	43 Tc Technetium	44 Ru Ruthenium 101	45 Rh Rhodium 103	46 Pd Palladium 106	47 Ag Silver 108	48 Cd Cadmium 112	49 In Indium 115	50 Sn Tin 119	51 Sb Antimony 122	52 Te Tellurium 128	53 I Iodine 127	★ 54 Xe Xenon 131
6	55 Cs Caesium 133	56 Ba Barium 137	57 ► La Lanthanum 139	72 Hf Hafnium 178	73 Ta Tantalum 181	74 W Tungsten 184	75 Re Rhenium 186	76 Os Osmium 190	77 Ir Iridium 192	78 Pt Platinum 195	79 Au Gold 197	80 Hg Mercury 201	81 Tl Thallium 204	82 Pb Lead 207	83 Bi Bismuth	84 Po Polonium	85 At Astatine	86 Rn Radon
7	87 Fr Francium 223	88 Ra Radium 226	89 ►► Ac Actinium 227	104 Rf Rutherfor-dium	105 Db Dubnium	106 Sg Seaborgium	107 Bh Bohrium	108 Hs Hassium	109 Mt Meitnerium	110 Uun Ununnilium	111 Uuu Unununium	112 Uub Ununbium						

Lanthanoid elements ►	58 Ce Cerium 140	59 Pr Praseo-dymium 141	60 Nd Neo-dymium 144	61 Pm Promethium	62 Sm Samarium 150	63 Eu Europium 152	64 Gd Gadolinium 157	65 Tb Terbium 159	66 Dy Dysprosium 163	67 Ho Holmium 165	68 Er Erbium 167	69 Tm Thulium 169	70 Yb Ytterbium 173	71 Lu Lutetium 175
Actinoid elements ►►	90 Th Thorium 232	91 PA Protactinium 231	92 U Uranium 238	93 Np Neptunium 237	94 Pu Plutonium	95 Am Americium	96 Cm Curium	97 Bk Berkelium	98 Cf Californium	99 Es Einstein-ium	100 Fm Fermium	101 Md Mendel-evium	102 No Nobelium	103 Lr Lawrencium

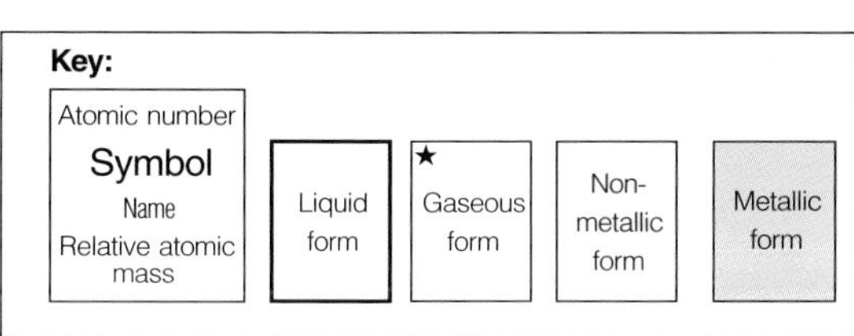

Confused words

Don't be caught out when these words are used. They have a special meaning in science.

Word	Common English meaning	Science meaning
Absorb	He used a cloth to absorb the water he'd spilt.	Most substances absorb light.
Acid	She has a very acid tongue.	Acids are corrosive substances that taste sour.
Antenna	Can you wiggle the antenna to pick up a better TV picture?	A structure found on the head of animals, usually to detect sound or smell.
Atmosphere	They didn't stay at the restaurant because it had no atmosphere.	Atmosphere is the layer of gas around a planet.
Boiling	Its boiling hot!	The boiling point of water is 100°C – it's never that hot.
Cell	He was locked away in a cell for five years.	A cell is an electrical energy store. A group of cells make a battery. OR The basic unit of which plants and animals are made up.
Concentration	Homework needs concentration.	Concentrated solutions have a lot of solid dissolved in them.
Condensing	I am condensing my argument into one sentence.	When a vapour turns into a liquid on a cold surface, it is condensing.
Conductor	The conductor was in charge of the orchestra.	An electrical conductor lets electric current flow through it and a thermal conductor lets energy flow through it.
Current	The current situation is difficult.	Current is an electrical flow.
Dense / density	He's really dense.	Density is heaviness for its size.
Drag	She had to drag the truth out of him.	Drag is a force that resists motion.
Elastic	You use elastic in clothes.	Elastic means a substance stretches but goes back to its original shape.
Element	I think the element in the kettle has burned out.	A substance that contains only one type of atom.
Energy	That boy has got too much energy!	Heating and cooling involve transfer of energy. When a force acts and something moves, that also involves transfer of energy.
Evaporate	She could feel her enthusiasm evaporate.	Particles of a liquid escape into the surroundings when it evaporates.
Force(s)	The police force	A force is a push or a pull.

Word	Common English meaning	Science meaning
Freezing	It's freezing cold.	The freezing point of water is 0°C – it can be that cold when it's frosty.
Gas	Light the gas (for a cooker).	A gas can be many substances e.g. oxygen.
Habitat	Shall we go to Habitat and buy some furniture?	The home for a group of organisms.
Hip	That's quite a hip outfit you're wearing!	A part of the skeleton that supports the legs.
Host	Will you be the host of the party on Saturday night?	The animal that a parasite lives inside.
Humerus	That comedian thinks she's humerous (note the different spelling).	The bone that connects the shoulder and elbow.
Impulse	I feel a little impulsive today, I might have an impulse buy in the shops!	The electric charge that travels along a nerve fibre.
Indicator	Indicators are orange winking lights on cars.	An indicator is a material that changes colour in solutions of different acidity.
Ions	Iron is a metal that can go rusty.	Ion sounds similar to iron, but it is a particle in a chemical change.
Irritant	That boy is an irritant!	An irritant is a chemical that affects the skin – it is a hazard.
Kingdom	As your sovereign I rule this kingdom!	All living things are divided into five kingdoms.
Lift	They took the lift to the fourth floor.	Lift is an upwards force on the wings of a bird or a plane.
Lime water	Lime is a green fruit like a lemon, and a white chalky powder.	Lime water is made with chalky powder not with fruit.
Liquid	I need a drink of liquid.	Liquids can be many different substances – not just water based.
Mass	She goes to Mass every Sunday.	Mass is a measure of the amount of material an object has.
Material	What colour material do you want for your new dress?	All the stuff things are made from
Matter	What's the matter?	Matter is the stuff we are made from.
Moment	Wait just a moment!	A moment is a turning effect of a force.
Negative	He felt very negative about going to school this morning.	A battery has a negative terminal.
Neutralise	A large police force will neutralise the threat of disorder.	Acids will neutralise alkalis in a chemical change.
Normal	Everything is normal here.	A normal is a line which is at 90° to a surface.
Organ	On Sundays I play the organ in church.	A group of tissues working together.

Confused words

Word	Common English meaning	Science meaning
Peat	Hi Pete, where are you going? (Note the spelling.)	Rotted vegetable matter formed thousands of years ago.
Pest	You are a pest during the summer holidays!	An animal, often an insect, that is a nuisance.
Plastic	A plastic washing up bowl.	Plastic means a substance stretches and stays in the new shape, like putty.
Positive	The results of the test were positive.	A battery has a positive terminal.
Power	We have the power to arrest you.	Power is a measure of how quickly energy is transferred, such as by a kettle or a lamp.
Pressure	I feel under pressure to pass exams.	Pressure is the force per unit of area.
Pure	Not harmful	Contains only one substance.
Range	The eggs are free range.	A range of values is the difference between the highest and the lowest.
Ray	You are my little ray of sunshine.	A ray is a very thin line that we draw to show a pathway of light.
Reflect	Reflect on your behaviour.	Surfaces can reflect light.
Renewable	His membership of the sports club is renewable every year.	A renewable energy resource is one that will not run out.
Salt(s)	Salt and vinegar on chips	Table salt is one kind of salt made in neutralisation reactions.
Saturated	I got caught in the rain and I'm saturated!	A saturated solution will not dissolve any more solute.
Scale	Fish have scales on their skin.	Measuring instruments have scales with marks and numbers.
School	Off you go to school today, no arguments please!	A group of animals that live in water, e.g. a school of dolphins.
Solution	Have you found the solution to the puzzle?	A solution is made by dissolving a solute in a solvent.
Thrust	She thrust her face into other people's business.	Thrust is a driving force.
Transfer	Blogtown United have put their goalkeeper on the transfer list.	Energy can transfer from place to place and from system to system.
Unbalanced	If I have to put up with much more of this my mind will become unbalanced.	Unbalanced force produces acceleration.
Unit	They've chosen some nice new kitchen units.	Degrees Celsius, newtons, metres and seconds are all examples of units of measurement.
Vacuum	He decided to vacuum the floor.	A vacuum is a space with no air or other material.
Variable	The weather was variable when I went on holiday.	A variable is a quantity that can change.
Work	I did eight hours hard work today.	Work is a kind of energy transfer that happens when force changes the motion of an object.

Glossary

Term	Definition	Page
Acid rain	Rain that has been made more acid by pollution	96–97
Adaptation	Characteristic that helps an organism survive	113, 117
Aerobic	Involving oxygen (for example, aerobic respiration)	48–49
Alloy	A mixture of two or more metals	52
Alternating current	A current which flows first in one direction and then in the opposite direction in a wire	68
Alveoli	Air sacs at the ends of the tubes in the lungs; where exchange of gases with the blood takes place	43, 46–47
Amino acids	The units which join together to form protein molecules	8
Amplifier	An electronic device used to increase the loudness of sound signals	72–73
Amplitude	The height of a wave	72, 74, 143, 144, 149
Anaerobic	Not involving oxygen (for example, anaerobic respiration)	48–49
Angle of incidence	The angle between the normal (line at 90° to surface) and the ray of light striking the surface	106–107
Angle of reflection	The angle between the normal (line at 90° to surface) and the ray of light being reflected from the surface	106–107
Antarctic	The region of the Earth near the South Pole	32
Antibodies	Chemicals in the blood that fight a particular disease	83
Anus	Place where solid waste passes out of the body	7
Artery	Blood vessel that carries blood away from the heart to all parts of the body	43, 44–45
Asthma	Breathing difficulty caused by a swelling of the mucus membrane in the trachea and bronchi	48
Atom	The smallest particle of material that can exist on its own	13, 14, 22, 23, 26, 58–59
Atomic number	The number of protons in an atom	16
Bacteria	Single-celled organism	75–77, 80–81
Bile	Substance which helps break down fats	7
Biomass	How much of a living thing there is	120, 121
Blood vessel	Tube which carries blood around the body	44–45
Boiling point	Temperature at which a liquid turns into a gas	
Bolus	Pellet of food and saliva travelling down the oesophagus	7
Bone marrow	Material inside the long bones of the body that produces blood cells	82
Brittle	Easily snapped	21
Bronchi	The two tubes that join the trachea to the right and left lung	46
Bronchioles	The smaller tubes that branch off from the bronchi	46
Calcium carbonate	The compound which is the major constituent of marble, chalk and limestone	93, 96
Camouflage	Colouring to blend into the background	116–117
Capillary	Tiny, thin-walled blood vessel that joins arteries to veins and carries blood into the tissues	43, 44–45
Carbohydrates	Food group which provides energy	2, 8
Cement	A material that holds the particles together in sedimentary rock	93
Cholesterol	Chemical carried by the blood that can block veins and arteries	4
Chyme	Liquid substance made up of partially-digested food	7
Cochlea	Organ inside the ear that is sensitive to vibrations	149

Combustion	Type of oxidation reaction in which fuels are burnt to transfer energy as heat and light. . . . 56
Compass	Small pivoted magnet that points to the North pole of the Earth 64
Compound	A pure substance made by two or more elements reacting together 14, 15, 22–23, 51, 60–61
Conduction (electrical)	The flow of electrons through a material 35
Conduction (thermal)	Transfer of energy through a solid material by colliding or interacting particles . . 35
Continental drift	The slow movement of large plates of rock on the Earth's surface 90, 130, 138
Continental plate	Tectonic plate found under a land mass; thicker than oceanic plates 130
Convection	Transfer of energy by the natural movement of a gas or a liquid 34, 130
Cooling curve	Shape of graph produced as a material cools down. . . . 135
Corrosion	Chemical attack on the surface of a metal e.g. rusting. . . . 19
Cowpox	Disease similar to smallpox 85
Cramp	Painful condition caused by the build up of lactic acid in the muscles during anaerobic respiration. . . . 49
DDT	Dichlorodiphenyltrichloroethane, a well-known pesticide; its use has now been restricted 122–123
Decibel	Unit for measuring the loudness of sound 148
Decomposer	Organism that breaks down dead material 113
Diamond	Very hard crystals of pure carbon. Another, softer form of pure carbon is graphite 58, 92
Diet	The balance of all nutrients taken in by a person. . . . 2–5
Diffuse	Mix randomly, spread out through a material 43, 44
Digestion	The process by which food is broken down into smaller molecules that will dissolve in the blood 1–12
Dispersed	Spread out 110
DNA	Deoxyribonucleic acid; genetic material inside cell 76
Ductile	A property of metals meaning that they can be pulled into wires 20
Dyke	Exposed vertical intrusion of igneous rock into softer rock 130
Eardrum	Membrane in the ear canal that is made to vibrate by sound 139, 140–141, 149
Earthquake	Violent shaking caused when two tectonic plates slip past each other 91, 138
Ecologist	Person who studies the inter-relations between organisms and their natural environment 123
Electromagnet	A magnet made by an electric current flowing in a coil of wire. . . . 66–67, 70–71, 74
Electromagnetic relay	An electrically-operated switch 71
Electron	A very small particle normally found orbiting the nucleus of an atom 16
Element	A substance made from only one type of atom 13, 14, 15, 51
Emphysema	Disease of the lungs which causes breathing difficulties 48
Enzymes	Complex substances that break down large molecules 7, 9
Erosion	Weathering and transport of sediments 89
Evaporation	Turning to gas from the surface of a liquid. . . . 34–35
Fats	Food group for energy storage and warmth 3, 8–9
Fatty acids	Small molecules which combine with glycerol to form fats 8–9
Fibre	Material that is essential for the healthy working of the large intestine 3
Field lines	Lines used to represent a magnetic field; also called lines of force 64–65
Filter	A material which absorbs certain colours and lets other colours through 110–111
Flash flood	A rapid flood caused by extreme weather conditions 98

Glossary

Term	Definition	Pages
Food chain	Feeding relationship between organisms showing transfer of energy	113, 120–121
Food web	A network of food chains	113, 120–121
Fossil	Imprint or remains of once-living creature	113, 125, 129
Frequency	Number of waves per second, e.g. of sound waves or radio waves; measured in hertz	74, 143, 144, 149
Fungus/fungi	Plant-like organisms. They have no chloroplasts so they are often parasites	78–79
Gabbro	A dark-coloured, igneous rock	93, 97
Gastric juice	Acidic liquid produced in the stomach that helps to digest food	7, 11
Glaciers	Large bodies of ice, usually formed in mountain valleys	95
Glucose	Type of sugar, carried by the blood. Used as the energy supply for respiration	8, 40–43
Glycerol	Molecule which combines with fatty acids to form fats	8–9
Granite	A light-coloured, highly-speckled igneous rock	89, 93, 97, 134
Gravel	Particles of stone between 2 cm and 2 mm in size	99
Gullet	Tube connecting throat to stomach (also called the oesophagus)	6–7
Habitat	Area where a plant or animal lives	113
Haemoglobin	The substance in red blood cells that carries oxygen	42
hertz	The unit of measurement for frequency	144, 149
Igneous	Type of rock formed from hot, liquid rock	93, 126, 131, 136, 138
Ileum	Lower part of the small intestine	7
Infection	When a micro-organism has entered your body and made you ill	80–81
Insulation	Slowing down the transfer of energy	32
Intrusion	When magma forces itself through existing rock and cools to leave igneous rock	130–131
Junk food	Food which is high in fat; not a balanced diet	1, 2
kilohertz	Unit of frequency (1 kilohertz = 1 thousand hertz)	149
Lactic acid	Substance produced in the muscles during anaerobic respiration which can build up and cause cramp	49
Lava	Liquid rock that has escaped onto the Earth's surface from a volcano	90, 126, 134
Lens	A shaped piece of glass used to change the direction of light rays; the structure in your eye that focuses light	102
Limestone	Hard sedimentary rock, formed from the shells of sea creatures; mainly calcium carbonate	93, 96, 97, 128
Loudness	A characteristic of sound dependent on the amplitute of a sound wave	143, 144
Lymph system	A series of tubes that carry a colourless fluid called lymph around the body; helps fight disease	82
Magma	Liquid rock inside the Earth	126, 130, 131, 132, 134, 136, 138
Magnetic field	The space around a magnet where its force can act	64, 74
Magnetic	Describes a material that is attracted by a magnet	20, 64–74
Malleable	A property of metals meaning that they can be hammered into shapes	20
Mantle	Part of the Earth below the crust which contains hot rock under very high pressure	126, 127, 130
Marble	A white, smooth, hard metamorphic rock	89, 92, 93, 94, 96, 131
Mass number	The number of protons and neutrons in an atom	16
Meander	Tight bends in a slow-moving river	91
megahertz	Unit of frequency (1 megahertz = 1 million hertz)	147

Melting point	Temperature at which a solid turns into a liquid . . . 21
Metamorphic	Type of rock that has been changed by the action of heat and pressure . . . 93, 127, 130, 131, 138
Micro-organism	An organism so small that it can only be seen with a microscope . . . 75–88
Microphone	Device to turn sound waves into electrical signals . . . 144, 145
Minerals	Small quantities of substances essential for a balanced diet (biology); grains of single substances found in rocks (geology) . . . 3, 9, 92–93
Molecule	A particle made from a small group of atoms joined together . . . 14, 22, 59
Mucus	Sticky substance that traps particles on the internal surfaces of the body . . . 48
Mudstone	A sedimentary rock formed from tiny silt particles . . . 93
Neutralisation	Reaction between an acid and an alkali to produce a salt and water . . . 57
Neutron	A particle with no charge found in the nucleus of an atom . . . 16
Normal	A line drawn at 90° to a surface . . . 106
Nucleus	The tiny, dense centre of an atom, made of protons and neutrons . . . 26
Obese/Obesity	Extremely overweight . . . 4–5
Obsidian	A very hard, black, glassy igneous rock . . . 92, 93
Ocean floor spreading	Process which occurs in the middle of some oceans where tectonic plates move apart and new rock is formed in the gap . . . 137
Oceanic plate	Tectonic plate found under the oceans; thinner than continental plates . . . 130
Oesophagus	Tube connecting throat to stomach (also called the gullet) . . . 6–7
Onion peel weathering	Type of weathering in which expansion and contraction of rock causes successive layers to peel off . . . 94
Oscilloscope	Machine which displays a signal such as that produced by sound waves . . . 144, 145
Oxidation	Reaction where oxygen combines with other material to make new substances called oxides . . . 56
Pancreas	Gland which produces several digestive enzymes . . . 7
Penicillin	A mould (fungus) that was found to have the ability to kill disease-causing bacteria . . . 78–79
Pepsin	Enzyme that breaks down proteins in the stomach . . . 7
Periodic Table	A list of all the known elements grouped together . . . 15, 16–17
Photosynthesis	Process by which plants produce sugars by taking in carbon dioxide, water and energy from the Sun. Oxygen is a waste product of this reaction . . . 113
Pitch	Frequency of a sound wave . . . 142, 144
Plasma	The pale yellow liquid part of the blood that carries the blood cells around the body . . . 42, 43
Plate tectonics	The study of the movement of interlocking areas of solid rock on the Earth's surface . . . 130
Platelets	Fragments of cells in the blood that cause it to clot when you get a cut . . . 82
Population	Number of organisms of a certain species living in an area . . . 114–115
Porous	Open in structure and letting water through easily . . . 24, 93, 132
Pothole	A deep cave formed by rainwater dissolving its way through limestone . . . 90
Precipitate	An insoluble solid produced when two solutions are mixed . . . 56
Predator	An animal that eats other animals . . . 116–117, 118
Prey	An animal that gets eaten . . . 116–117, 118, 119
Primary consumer	Organism that eats the producer . . . 113
Prism	A glass block which has the same cross-section all the way through . . . 110–111

Glossary

Term	Definition	Page(s)
Propanone	An organic solvent used for nail varnish	13
Proteins	Food group for growth and repair	2, 8
Proton	A positively-charged particle found in the nucleus of an atom	16
Pulse	Pumping action of the heart	44
Pumice	A very porous igneous rock, formed during volcanic eruptions	93, 125
Pure	Only containing one type of particle	52, 134
Radiation	The transfer of energy through space	35
Rectum	The final section of the large intestine	7
Red blood cells	The cells in the blood that carry oxygen	42
Refraction	The change in travel of light as it passes between different materials	108–109, 112
Renewable	An energy source that will never run out	37
Respiration	The process by which energy is released from food	40–50
Retina	Light-sensitive layer of cells at the back of the eye	146
Rock cycle	Natural process by which one type of rock gets turned into other types	93, 127
Roughage	Dietary fibre to keep the large intestine working properly	3
Sandstone	A sedimentary rock formed from compressed sand particles	89, 92, 93, 128
Secondary consumer	Organism that eats the primary consumer	113
Sedimentary	Type of rock formed by the deposit of water-borne particles	93, 127, 129, 138
Shadow	Dark area produced when a solid object blocks rays of light	110, 112
Shale	A layered, dark-coloured, hard, sedimentary rock	93, 128
Sill	Exposed horizontal intrusion of igneous rock into softer rock	130
Silt	Very fine grained, water-borne sediment	128, 129
Slate	A black, highly-layered metamorphic rock	89
Smallpox	Very contagious, deadly disease that has been around for over 2000 years; the World Health Organisation believes it has now been eradicated	84–85
Solute	Solid that gets dissolved	13
Solution	Liquid and dissolved solid mixed together	13
Solvent	Liquid that does the dissolving	13
Sores	Symptom of smallpox; pus-filled structures on the skin	85
Spectrum	Rainbow of colour produced when white light is split up into its component colours by refraction (dispersion)	110–111, 112
Starch	Carbohydrate found in many common foods such as rice, potatoes and pasta	7
Strata	Layers in rock formations	91, 128–129, 138
Tastebuds	Specialised cells on the tongue which allow you to taste food	12
Thermal decomposition	Process by which compounds fall apart when heated	56
Thymus gland	Gland which controls the immune responses of the body	82
Trachea	Pipe joining the throat to lungs; also called the windpipe	46
Transparent	Clear, see-through	102
Ultrasound	Sound signals beyond the range of human hearing (above 20 kHz)	147, 150
Valency	The combining power of an atom	59
Variolation	Method of vaccination using scabs from infected people	85
Vein	Blood vessel which returns blood to the heart	43, 44–45
Virus	A parasite which lives inside cells and causes diseases	76–77, 80–81
Vitamins	Small quantities of substances essential for health	3, 9
Volcano	Cone produced when liquid rock escapes onto the Earth's surface	125, 136–137, 138
Weathering	Breaking up of rock into smaller particles by natural forces	89–100, 129
White blood cells	The cells in the blood that resist infection and disease	82–83